FLAGS OF THE WORLD

1

2   3

4   5

6

Plate 1   Frontispiece

FLAGS OF THE UNITED STATES OF AMERICA

Plate 1

Frontispiece

FLAGS OF THE UNITED STATES OF AMERICA

FLAGS

OF THE

WORLD

EDITED BY

E. M. C. BARRACLOUGH

C.B.E., R.N.

WITH 370 FLAGS IN FULL COLOUR

AND OVER 375 TEXT DRAWINGS

FREDERICK WARNE & CO LTD: LONDON

FREDERICK WARNE & CO LTD: NEW YORK

Published by
Frederick Warne & Co Ltd
London, England

© *Revised edition Frederick Warne & Co Ltd 1969*

LIBRARY OF CONGRESS CATALOG CARD NO. 68–22445

7232 1101 9

Printed in Great Britain
Text printed by William Clowes & Sons Ltd, London & Beccles
Colour plates printed by Henry Stone & Son (Printers) Ltd, Banbury
938 . 569

CONTENTS

LIST OF PLATES

PREFACE

Flags of the World has been in existence for many years and there have been many editions, and although throughout its lifetime it has been kept up to date in its details, there has been little change in the basic arrangement of the work. For this new edition it seemed desirable, in view of the large number of changes which have taken place in the world during the last few years, to undertake a major re-arrangement. For instance, the independent countries of the British Commonwealth, although retaining ties with Britain, are now masters of their own destinies, so they have been grouped according to their geographical position.

In spite of these alterations I have endeavoured to retain the essential character of the book, which is a history of flags and not just a catalogue.

In this edition I have tried to give a little more information about the flags of the armies, and especially of the Colours borne by regiments, but these are so many and varied that they would need a large book of their own to do them justice, and I have been able only to include a few random examples.

I have had help from so many persons, diplomatic and consular representatives, the High Commissioners of the Commonwealth countries and many friends that it is impossible to mention them all, and it would be invidious to make a selection. However, I must mention Doctor Whitney Smith for the help that he has personally given to me, and for the assistance that I have received from the Flag Research Center which he founded (*see* page 19); and I must also include the staff of Frederick Warne & Co. Ltd for their assistance in preparing this edition, particularly Mr. A. F. Stuart for his work in connection with the illustrations. I hope that everybody to whom I am indebted will accept my grateful thanks for all they have done, and that as some slight recompense they will find something of interest in this work.

E.M.C.B.

Chapter One

INTRODUCTORY

Since time immemorial man has felt the need of some sign or symbol as a mark to distinguish himself, his family or country, and such symbols have taken many differing forms, of which one is the flag.

The word 'flag' seems to have come into use in the 16th century and soon became the general name for the many types of flag that existed under a multiplicity of titles, such as banners, ensigns, gonfanons, and so on. Although the majority of these names still exist they are used very loosely and mean different things to different writers. It is generally agreed that the word flag derived from the old Saxon or Germanic word *fflaken* or *ffleogan*, meaning to fly or float in the wind. Thus a flag is something that must be free to be agitated by the wind and can be defined as a device on a piece of pliable material which is fastened to a staff or mast along one of its edges, leaving the rest to fly or flap in the breeze. The name flag is now generally confined to the pattern which flies from a vertical staff, while the type that hangs from a horizontal bar is called a banner (but *see also* page 11).

One of the earliest references to flags or banners is that in the year 1122 B.C. it was recorded that the Emperor Chou, founder of the Chou Dynasty in China, had a white flag or banner carried before him. We have no record as to what this flag was like; however, a very early representation of a Chinese flag is on the tomb of Wou Leang T'Seu, of the Han Dynasty (200 B.C. to A.D. 200). A low relief on this tomb shows horsemen (illustrated), although one is riding a somewhat peculiar steed, the first bearing a flag and the other what appears to be a banner.

There is also mention about the end of the fifth century B.C. of a primitive form of flag known as a 'phoinikis', or 'purple garment', in use in the Athenian Navy. This may have inspired the legend that at the battle of Salamis (480 B.C.) Themistocles, the Greek Commander, ordered a red cloak to be affixed to an oar and hoisted aloft. At this signal the Greek fleet, although outnumbered four to

EARLY CHINESE FLAGS

one, bore down and routed the Persians under Xerxes. Apart from these isolated scraps of what might be called folk-lore there is no record of flags having been used in the western world until shortly before the time of Christ. We know that the ancient Egyptians marched to war beneath the sacred emblems of their gods and the fans of feathers of the Pharaohs, and that the insignia of the Assyrians were discs bearing devices which almost invariably included bulls in some form or other. As well as the phoinikis, the Greeks also used symbols of their deities, for example the owl of

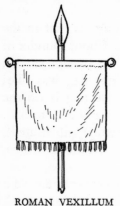

Athens or legendary animals such as the pegasus of Corinth, the minotaur of Crete, the bull of Boeotia, and the strangest of all, the tortoise of the Peloponnesus.

The first 'flag' in the western world of which there is historical evidence and of which illustrations exist was the Roman 'vexillum'. Although the exact date is unknown this appears to have come into use about the year 100 B.C.

It is perhaps not unreasonable to assume that flags, originating in China, travelled

ROMAN VEXILLUM

westwards until they arrived in the Middle East, and the Romans, finding them there, adopted them for their own use. The Romans appear to have used the vexillum as a tactical distinguishing mark to enable one legion to be recognised from another. This was a simple piece of material usually purple or red, but sometimes white or blue, generally quite plain, occasionally carrying some device, and often richly fringed. It was hung by its upper edge or two top corners from a cross-bar on a lance and carried in addition to the eagle, which was the 'standard' of the legion. Other simple flags were used in classical times, but these were of minor importance and so far as the western world was concerned the vexillum remained the only 'flag' until the 9th century A.D. In fact the Venerable Bede, writing of the conversion of King Edwin of Northumbria in 622, and of King Ethelbert's meeting with St. Augustine a few years earlier, speaks of vexilla being borne before them. Henry of Huntingdon mentions that in the Battle of Burford in 752 the Wessex standard was a golden dragon.

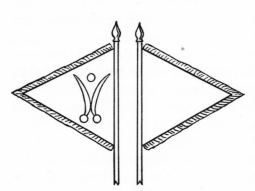

In the 9th century flags were used in western Asia, and there exists evidence of standards of the grandsons of the Prophet Mohammed; these were triangular fringed flags flown from a vertical flagstaff, one plain green and the other with the traditional double sword (or dagger) of the Mohammedans.

MOHAMMEDAN STANDARDS

In the year 878 the famous Raven Flag of the Vikings appeared on the scene. This flag was surrounded by stories of magical properties and mystery. It is reputed to have been the first flag to be flown in the continent of North America, taken there by Leif Ericsson on his famous voyage in about the year 1000. We do not have any actual illustrations or accurate descriptions of this flag; however there are in existence Northumbrian coins of the early part of the 9th century

RAVEN FLAG

which show a heavily fringed triangular flag flying from a vertical staff with the upper edge horizontal. This flag had a cross as a device, but other Northumbrian coins of this period show a stylised raven, and taking these fragments of evidence together with what is shown on the Bayeux Tapestry it seems probable that the flag was something like that illustrated here.

It has the distinction of probably being the first flag in the west to fly from a vertical staff. The Bayeux Tapestry, which actually is an embroidery, is thought to have been made between 1070 and 1080, although the exact date is uncertain. It can be seen at Bayeux in France. It tells in pictorial form, like a modern strip cartoon, the story of the invasion by William, Duke of Normandy, the Battle of Hastings and his conquest of England in the year 1066. To the student of flags it is of great interest, for it shows first and foremost that by the year 1066 flags were well established. The principal flags shown on the tapestry are gonfanons or war flags. These were square in shape with a number of tails, mostly three but in some cases four or five; the number of tails seems to have had no particular significance. One of the most ornate is that presumed to have been blessed by the Pope and given to Duke William. This is decorated with a cross and has three tails; the majority of the others have simple designs of roundels or stripes.

Depicted in the tapestry are three more flags which are of peculiar interest: the first, the dragon standard of the English King Harold; this is shown twice, once held by the standard bearer, and secondly in the scene of Harold's death where it is lying on the ground. How the dragon came to be used as a battle standard is one of those intriguing stories of which the answer will always be somewhat wrapped in mystery, but it is fascinating to speculate how the dragon came to be a symbol in the far west and also in China, the farthest east of the known world. Perhaps it was the serpent of the garden of Eden who was the ancestor of the dragon.

In the scene depicting the deaths of the brothers of Harold a flag

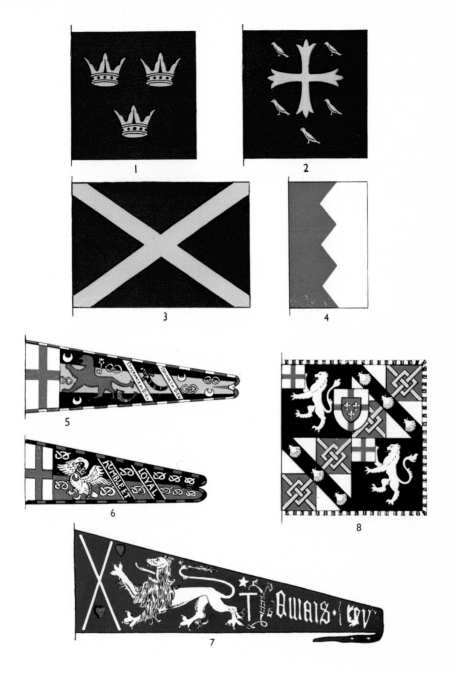

Plate 2

f.p. 4

BANNERS AND STANDARDS

is shown lying on the ground. This is triangular in shape and fringed, very similar to flags shown on the old Northumbrian coins of the 9th century which have been mentioned. Harold is reputed to have fought between two banners, one the 'dragon' and the other his personal banner which was said to be richly embroidered with precious stones. It is presumed that it is this latter which is shown lying on the ground, but this can only be speculation as there is no decoration or device shown on the flag.

FLAG FROM THE
BAYEUX TAPESTRY

Finally, there is shown a Norman flag, semi-circular in shape, fringed and charged with a bird. It has been suggested that this flag represents the mythical Raven Flag of the Vikings, the ancestors of the Normans; others reject this view, saying that the Raven of the Norsemen was never depicted in the tame position shown on the flag in the tapestry, and that this flag was that of the Celts of Brittany whose leader Alan commanded the third division of the Duke's army. Although the exact role of this flag must always be open to speculation, the opinion that it is the legendary Raven Flag is supported by the position that it occupies in the tapestry. For it is, together with a gonfanon, placed directly behind Duke William in the scene showing the Duke leading his knights into battle. It seems unlikely that the flag of one of the divisional commanders would have been shown in such a prominent place.

The next stage in the development of flags was the advent of heraldry. It is not easy to define heraldry as it is an art that has grown and developed over the centuries. Primarily it is a method of identification by means of devices placed on shields, and while the practice of decorating the shields of warriors was in vogue many years earlier, the art of heraldry dates from about the second quarter of the twelfth century. The need for some form of identification arose when the participants in the popular pastime of jousting, or the 'knightly tournament', took to wearing helmets with visors which covered their faces and thus rendered them unrecognisable;

and so the devices on their shields became the means by which they were identified. The knightly tournaments were organised by specialists who were called heralds, and as it was the heralds who designed and allocated the various devices to the contestants the art of designing these badges became heraldry. An alternative name for heraldry is armory. In the course of time the first simple designs on shields grew into complicated designs called Achievements of Arms. It soon became the custom to pass these insignia down from father to son, and so the arms became the badge of the family, and thus heraldry became closely linked with genealogy.

The College of Arms in London, the Court of the Lord Lyon in Edinburgh, and the Office of the Chief Herald of Ireland are the authorities who, under the Crown, control heraldry in England and Wales, Scotland and Ireland respectively.

Although the art of heraldry is principally European, and has grown and developed in Europe, it is not the prerogative of any one country, and Japan has a very similar science known as 'Mon'. This has developed quite independently of European heraldry, its roots reaching back to about A.D. 900.

It was not long before the heraldic badges came to be emblazoned on flags. The first such flags were simple extensions of the gonfanon, which has already been mentioned, and consisted of a flag on the lance, but the gonfanon soon became a banner, the flag of a king, lord or knight, on which his arms were displayed. The early banners were generally longer in their vertical dimension (breadth) than the horizontal (length), but very soon the great majority became more or less square in shape. Some of the banners were, and still are, extremely beautiful. Examples can be seen in St. George's Chapel, Windsor, where the richly decorated banners of the Knights of the Garter are hung above their stalls (Plate 2, 8).

About 1350, during the reign of Edward III of England, the term standard came to be used to describe the banner of an important noble, or member of a royal house. The origin of the word standard is obscure: originally a standard was an emblem that 'stood by itself', i.e. it was not carried by a bearer, although strangely enough the flag bearer came to be called a standard-bearer.

Plate 3

BRITISH NATIONAL FLAGS

Plate 3

BRITISH NATIONAL FLAGS

The earliest standards consisted of a device, often religious, and sometimes accompanied by a flag or flags, carried at the top of a tall pole or the mast of a ship, mounted on a waggon or some form of cart. A standard of this type, with a 'pyx' and three banners, was present at the battle of Northallerton in 1138, which in consequence has been called the Battle of the Standard.

The use of the title standard to describe this form of device was not confined to England but was general throughout Europe. In the course of time the standard came to be the name given to the personal banner of a king, or important nobles such as dukes, and in the 12th century the standard of a noble became a long slender flag—what we would now call a pennant (Plate 2, 5 and 6). On the Continent the designs varied, but in England the term came to be applied to any flag of noble size that had the Cross of St. George or St. Andrew next to the staff, with the rest of the field divided horizontally into two or more stripes, either the livery or the prevailing colours in the arms of the bearers, and it was decorated with the motto and badges of the owner. The flag was richly fringed or bordered. There is at the College of Arms a drawing of the Standard of Sir Henry de Stafford (Plate 2, 6), and one of the oldest flags in existence is the very Standard of the Douglas (Plate 2, 7) carried at the Battle of Otterburn (Chevy Chase) 1388. This is still in the possession of Douglas of Cavers at the family seat in Roxburghshire. The Douglas Standard is known as the Douglas Banner, which is not strictly according to English usage, but the titles banner, ensign and standard were often confused; generally the banner or ensign was the personal flag, and the standard the official flag.

Heraldic standards and ensigns are still in use in Scotland where at Highland gatherings the standard of the chief is set up before his tent as a rallying point for his clansmen, and the standard is often displayed on the pipes of the pipe major of the chieftain.

Thus it can be seen that originally flags were the banners or insignia of individuals. A nation or tribe or regiment used the flag of its king or leader. Gradually, however, the use of the personal flag of the king as the national flag of the country was abandoned and in its place the nations adopted flags of a design

2

which had some national significance—often the flag of the patron saint. The first of such national flags appeared in the Mediterranean when the city state of Genoa adopted the banner of the Cross of St. George as the flag of their state; this was in the 12th century. With the introduction of national flags the personal flag of the head of state became his standard, flown only when he was present.

In the course of time some, but by no means all, countries adopted the practice of having more than a single national flag. A few countries have a special ceremonial or state flag in addition to the 'everyday' national flag. The majority, although there are notable exceptions such as France and the United States of America, have special variations of their national flag as the flags or ensigns for their ships.

Not only are there national flags, but practically every province or county of a country and also each city or town of any importance have their own flags. Many of these provincial flags, especially the European ones, are of great interest and ancient design, for Europe was once divided into many small principalities which in the course of time have combined to make the nations we know today. In modern times the use of flags as a 'sign of distinction', to use an old

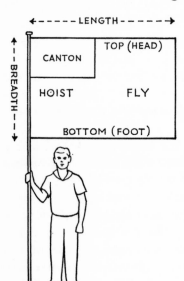

English expression, has grown so that there is scarcely a corporate body, be it a large commercial undertaking, a sports club, or an international organisation such as the United Nations, which does not have its own flag.

Finally, one of the most important functions of flags is that they provide a means of sending messages over a distance, i.e. for signalling, and for this role special flags and codes have been devised (*see* Chapter Twelve).

In heraldry certain rules and conventions have been adopted which greatly facilitate the description (or 'blazon') of a coat of arms and certain rules and conventions have also been adopted to assist in the description of flags. Both for flags and heraldry the description can be greatly assisted by a simple drawing (*see* page 8).

When describing the details of a flag it is assumed that the flag is flying from a staff held by the right hand of a bearer who is facing the observer, with the flag flying over the head of the bearer towards his left. That side of the flag which faces the observer is called the 'obverse' and the other side is called the 'reverse'. Generally these two sides are the same, but sometimes they differ; this usually occurs in complicated and intricate heraldic flags, or flags with inscriptions. When dealing with the flags of those Arabic nations and others who write from right to left and whose flags carry inscriptions, the flag staff must be held in the left hand of the bearer and fly from his left to his right. In describing a flag where the obverse and reverse differ, it is obvious that separate descriptions must be given for each side.

The description of flags is simplified if the various characteristics are described in the same sequence. Firstly the shape of the flag is given, i.e. square, rectangle, triangle, pennant-shaped (*see* page 10), with more than one tail or swallow-tailed etc. Then come the proportions or dimensions: the vertical dimension is known as the 'breadth' although some now call this the 'hoist', and the horizontal dimension is known as the 'length'. As flags come in varying sizes it is usual to describe their proportions as the ratio of the length to the breadth, i.e. a flag in which the length is twice the breadth is described as proportions two by one. Next is given a description of the field, the basic or background of the flag; to assist in doing this the field is roughly divided into two parts, the 'hoist' and the 'fly', the hoist being that portion next to the staff, and the remainder the fly; generally the hoist is taken to be one-third of the total area of the flag and the fly two-thirds, but these fractions are not rigid and can be varied to suit individual cases. Then the description should continue to give the salient features of the flag. A very common device is to have a special emblem or badge in the top corner of the flag next to the hoist; this is known as a 'canton'. To be more specific a canton is a rectangle placed in the corner of the flag next to the staff. Usually it is not larger than a quarter of the area of the field, although this is not vital. In describing the flag one can say that it has a plain field, or a vertically or horizontally striped field, or that the field is divided vertically or horizontally. If the flag consists of three stripes of three different colours it can be called a vertical or horizontal tricolour. There are some who say that the term 'tricolour' can be only used when the three stripes are of equal width, but this is not considered to be essential, for in very few cases are the stripes equal in width, as it

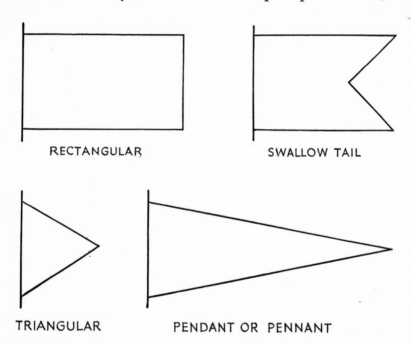

RECTANGULAR   SWALLOW TAIL

TRIANGULAR   PENDANT OR PENNANT

has been found that they must vary slightly in dimensions if they are to appear of equal width when the flag is flying (*see* French Flag, page 131). A simple flag like that of Malta (Plate 23, 4) would be described thus: 'A rectangular flag, proportions three by two, divided vertically into two equal parts, white to the hoist and red to the fly, with a white George Cross fimbriated in red in the top corner of the hoist.' It will be noted that the heraldic term 'fimbriated', meaning a narrow border, has been used; although as a general rule the heraldic method of describing the blazons is not generally used for

Plate 4　　　　　　　　　　　　　　　　　　　　　　f.p. 11

BRITISH ROYAL STANDARDS

Plate 4

BRITISH ROYAL STANDARDS

flags, the occasional use of the simple heraldic terms can sometimes be helpful. Fimbriated, as has been stated, is a narrow border; 'a saltire', a diagonal cross similar to that of St. Andrew. 'Charged with' means that a device or badge has been placed on the flag. Also there are many flags which are charged with a coat of arms or similar heraldic devices; in such cases it is easier to use the heraldic conventions to describe such a charge. Thus a student of flags should have a working knowledge of heraldry and the conventions used by heralds to describe heraldic devices. However, with flags it is usual to use the ordinary names for the colours instead of the heraldic rules where there are metals, tinctures, furs etc. The colours used for flags will be discussed more fully below in the section dealing with flag design.

In modern times the flags currently in use are in general confined to the following: banner, standard, ensign, jack, pennant, guidon and colours. The many old names such as pennons, pennoncelles, streamers and so on are not now employed and are only used in the historical sense. In order to clarify this matter the following are brief historical notes about each, together with the modern meaning of the title:

As explained in the section dealing with heraldry the 'banner' is the flag of a distinguished person, or it may be used to describe the flag of a body of persons. Thus a banner can be defined as an ornate flag with a heraldic type of design used for ceremonial purposes. The term banner is also often applied to the form of flag which is suspended from a horizontal bar similar to the old Roman vexillum, principally in use for ecclesiastical purposes. The device often seen in processions, consisting of a large piece of material supported by two poles and carried by two persons, is not in the strict sense of the word a banner; a banner is a form of flag and a flag must be free to flap in the wind (*see* page 1).

The history of the 'standard' has also been outlined on page 6, and although the title standard is used to describe the banners of certain notables and regimental flags, it is in general now given only to the banner of a head of state, e.g. the Royal Standard of Great Britain, or the Standard of the President of the United States of America.

The word 'ensign' is derived from the Greek *semeion*, and its Latin equivalents *insigne* and *signum*.   Originally a rather abstract word meaning a sign, or signal, it came to be the name given to a flag or banner used as a distinguishing flag.   It is not clear whether the Army or the Navy first used this term; probably it was the Navy for the first record of the word is dated 1574 and refers to ship ensigns.   There was a short period of time when the regimental flags of the Army were called ensigns, but this did not last long, and while the term ensign is still occasionally used in heraldry, for all practical purposes it can now be taken that it is the name given to the national flag of a ship.   In most countries, but not all, the ensign discharges a dual function: it not only shows the nationality of the ship wearing it (for ships 'wear' their ensigns), but also the function of the ship, whether it is for instance a warship, a merchant ship, a ship in government service such as customs, or yachts, etc. Thus most countries have two or more, very often three different ensigns—one for their warships, one for their merchant ships and one used by the ships in government service.   These ensigns are often further differentiated by carrying, or, as it is called, being 'defaced' by the badge of the particular government office to which the ship belongs, or, in the case of a yacht, the yacht club.   As has been said, the practice is not the same in all nations, for instance Great Britain has a great variety of ship ensigns, whereas France and the United States of America have very few.

The name 'Jack' when applied to flags is described in the Oxford Dictionary as a 'diminutive of the National Flag flown from the bows of a ship'. The term 'Jack' was first used in the British Navy to describe the Union Flag that was at that time flown at the main masthead.   Although this flag was not quite as large as the ensigns worn by ships at that time it was, nevertheless, a flag of fairly generous proportions.   As diminutives are often used as terms of affection and familiarity, it seems possible that the sailors of that time used the diminutive 'Jack' in that sense, i.e. as a nickname or affectionate way of speaking of this flag.   Whatever the origin, the term 'Jack' was firmly established towards the latter part of the 17th century.   A vote of the Houses of Parliament on May 1st 1660 referred to 'such standards, fflags and Jacke

Colours of the ffleete', and in 1666 a Warrant was issued by the Lord High Admiral 'for taking into custody such Masters of merchant ships as shall presume to wear the Kings Jack'. These are only two of many examples, and they make it clear that a Jack was a special distinguishing flag. This is further confirmed by the fact that the special flag (very similar to the Red Ensign) introduced as the distinguishing flag for privateers, and similar flags 'defaced' with a badge as the distinguishing flags for Government vessels which were not ships of war, were also called Jacks.

Although at first Jacks were flown from the masthead it soon became the practice to fly them from the 'sprit topmast' which was fixed to the bowsprit. This seems to have been quite unofficial and how the practice came about to fly it from the bow of the ship is obscure. Probably it was a matter of convenience. It would not have been easy to hoist a large flag to the masthead, and this difficulty would have increased as masts became taller and the rigging more complicated; conversely it would have been comparatively easy to hoist the flag at the sprit on the bowsprit, in which position it would be prominently displayed for all to see. When the practice of using the sprit topmast was first adopted square sails were used on this mast, but when these were replaced by 'fore and aft' sails it was difficult for the Jack to be flown while the ship was under way. Thus it was that the Jack came to be worn only when the ship was lying in harbour, a practice which has lasted to the present day—with the exception that it is kept flying when a ship that is 'dressed' to celebrate a special occasion is under way. When square sails were no longer hoisted on the fore sprit mast a special flag staff was placed there for the Jack, and this was called the 'jackstaff'. It has often been thought that the flag is called a Jack because it flies from the jackstaff, but as has been explained above the staff is called a jackstaff because the 'Jack Flag' flies from it. Whether it is proper to call the flag of Great Britain the Union Flag or Union Jack will be discussed in the next chapter.

The 'pennant' or as it was formerly spelt the 'pendant', is a long narrow flag which has apparently developed from the 'streamer'. These long flags, often of immense length, can be seen in many pictures of old ships from mediaeval days to well on in the

17th century. When describing a pennant it is necessary to differentiate between that and a triangular flag. The proportions of the latter are generally in the nature of one and a half by one: which means that the horizontal dimension is one and a half times as long as the vertical dimension, whereas in the case of a pennant the proportions are at least four by one. A pennant is an important part of the array of flags (or colours, *see* below) that are worn by warships; they also form an important part of the International Code of Signals.

'Guidon' is derived from the French *guide-homme* and is a military flag. The Regimental Colours of certain British cavalry regiments are called guidons; these are forty-one inches long and twenty-seven inches in depth, with a slit in the fly and the corners rounded off. The name guidon is also given in other armies, for instance that of the United States of America, to a 'marker flag'. This is a small flag which is used in parades to mark the place at which the different companies etc. are to form up.

The term 'colours' was originally applied to ships' ensigns. Captain Boteler in his *Six Dialogues*, dated 1633, has his Admiral say: 'Colours and Ensignes I take to be all one'. And in the British Merchant Shipping Act of 1894 it is laid down that 'the proper colours for any ship or boat owned by a British subject is the Red Ensign'. In the course of time, however, the term colours has come to be given to the whole array or suite of flags, e.g. the proper colours for a warship are the ensign, jack and pennant; for a regiment, in most countries, the national or sovereign's banner and the regimental banner; for a merchant ship its ensign and house flag.

Although the art of the heraldic artist and the designer of flags are very akin, they differ in certain important aspects. A heraldic flag of complicated design is a beautiful thing and very suitable for ceremonial occasions, processions and the like (Plate 2, 1–7), but the normal flag has to stand up to very strenuous conditions of wind and rain and all that the elements can bring. Ideally the different colours should consist of different pieces of cloth, or bunting as the flag cloth is called, sewn together to make the correct design. A painted design would last but a short time at the masthead of a ship. Furthermore the flag should be the same, or very nearly the same, on both sides so that it consists of but one thickness of material. A flag flying in an exposed position is more or less transparent, especially when the sun shines upon it, so unless the two sides 'match up' the flag will have to be made of two thicknesses, increasing its cost, and such a flag never flies as well as one of a single thickness. Then the designer must think of what colours to use, and if he is aiming at designing a flag that can be made as a 'sewn flag', he will be limited by the colours in which bunting is manufactured and will not be able to choose fancy or exotic colours. The British Admiralty, or as it now should be called, the Ministry of Defence, Navy Department, has certain standard colours of bunting, and most flags in Britain have their colours adapted to fit in with these. The standard colours with the British Colour Council numbers are given below:

Black	B.C.C.220
Azure (light blue)	B.C.C.131
Intermediate Blue	B.C.C.196
Royal Blue	B.C.C.218
Blue (Navy Blue)	B.C.C.219
Crimson	B.C.C.36
Green	B.C.C.100
Red	B.C.C.210
White	B.C.C.1
Yellow	B.C.C.113

The flag designer would be well advised to have regard to one of the basic rules of heraldry that 'Metal should not be laid on metal, and colour should not be laid on colour'. In other words, white (silver) should never be placed next to yellow (gold), and white or yellow should always be interposed between any of the other colours. The object of this simple rule is to make the various colours stand out distinctly from each other. It does not make the rule any less desirable because many well-known flags contravene it.

It has been mentioned that the material which flags are usually made from is called 'bunting'; silk is also used, but it is confined to special ceremonial flags. Many of the ships of the British Navy in the past used to own silk ensigns, often presented to the ship by the sponsor or person who had launched the ship. These ensigns were treasured and worn on special occasions and Sundays.   Synthetic man-made fibres have largely taken the place of silk.   Bunting is a hard and durable woollen fabric specially made for flags, and used to come in cloth nine inches wide.   The modern bunting is now almost invariably made of a mixture of wool and synthetic fibres; generally nylon or terylene in Great Britain.   This cloth is even harder and more durable than the old woollen bunting.

The majority of flags which exist follow well-established patterns. For instance, there are many flags which are striped, either vertical or horizontal, sometimes with only one, two or three stripes, sometimes with many stripes.   Then again it is very usual to have a simple flag with the more complicated national flag or some other device in the canton.   Again, although many authorities charge their flags with heraldic devices there are a great number of flags which are decorated with a cross: the Cross of St. George, with its horizontal and vertical arms; a diagonal cross or saltire, such as the Cross of St Andrew; or one of the many forms of heraldic crosses which exist, such as the Maltese Cross.

The cross in all its forms is, of course, the emblem of Christianity and has undoubtedly found its way into the European flags because so many of the national flags were in the beginning the emblem of the patron saint.   There are many legends about these crosses, perhaps one of the best known being the story of the Dannebrog, the flag of Denmark (*see* page 123).

The star and crescent is the emblem of many Mohammedan countries, but it was not always so.   The crescent is more a symbol of Constantinople than of Mohammed and dates from the days of Philip of Macedon, the father of Alexander the Great.   When, so the legend runs, that enterprising monarch beseiged Byzantium in 339 B.C. he met with repulse after repulse, and tried as a last resource to undermine the walls, but the crescent moon shone out so gloriously that the attempt was discovered and the city saved. Thereupon the Byzantines adopted the crescent as their badge, and Diana, whose emblem it was, as their patroness.   When the Roman Emperors came the crescent was not displaced and it continued to be the city badge under the Christian Emperors.   In 1453, when Mohammed II took Constantinople, it was still to the fore and as he wanted something to vary the monotony of the plain red flag under which he had led his men to victory, he, with great discrimination, availed himself of the old Byzantine badge, explaining that it meant Constantinople on a field of blood. That is story number one, but there is another.

Some 150 years before the city fell, the Sultan Othman, founder of the Ottoman dynasty, had a dream in which he saw a crescent moon growing bigger and bigger until it reached from the farthest east to the farthest west. This led him to adopt the crescent, which designated Constantinople, or Istanbul as it is now called.

Whichever story we accept, it is clear where the crescent came from. Even now in Moscow and other Russian cities the crescent and the cross may be seen combined on the churches, denoting the Byzantine origin of the eastern rite.

Where the star came from is not so clear. A star within a crescent was a badge of Richard I more than 250 years before Constantinople fell, which implies that the crescent was adopted by the Saracens if, as is alleged, the device was emblematic of the Crusades and the star stood for the Star of Bethlehem. In his badge Richard placed the crescent on its back and the star above it; but when Mohammedanism became triumphant the Turks placed the star beside the upright crescent where the dark area of the moon should be, from which on some flags it has emerged. Others tell us that it is the star of piercing brightness, the morning star, Al Tarek, the star that appeareth by night described in the eighty-sixth chapter of the Koran; but why is not stated and no dates are given.

Some nations have a carefully laid down code of flag etiquette which gives precise instructions as to how the flags can be used under all conditions. Such a country is the United States of America. Great Britain at the other extreme has no code at all and there are some people of other countries who are horrified at the familiar way with which the British treat their flags. The above generalisation does not apply to ships, because at sea there has grown up an etiquette of how the flags should be used and where they should be hoisted and the occasions when they are used. Throughout the world when the ship is in harbour the ensign is invariably hoisted at 8.00 a.m. local time and lowered at sunset (in arctic waters where the days are unusually long these times are sometimes modified). A ship salutes another ship by dipping its flag.

Half-masting a flag to indicate mourning is a curious custom, the origin of which has yet to be ascertained, but its observance appears to date back to about the 16th century as another of the customs of the sea which has spread to the land. Then there is the custom of dressing the ship overall, called by those who are not sailors 'rainbow fashion', which is used to decorate ships on special occasions. Theoretically a ship should only be dressed overall when at anchor or moored up in harbour. It would have been impractical for an old sailing-ship to get under way when dressed overall, but this custom is now more honoured in the breach than in the observance by most merchant ships, which can often be seen under way with their dressing flags still hoisted.

It is often puzzling to know whether one should say a ship is wearing a flag, or bearing a flag, or flying a flag. However, it is generally agreed that a ship is wearing its national ensign or national colours and that the other flags are flown. The only exception to this is that when a ship has a Royal Standard aloft it is said to be wearing the standard.

When a ship is in a foreign port it is the custom to fly in a prominent position the maritime ensign of the country in whose port the ship is lying. This is known as a Courtesy Ensign and it should be noted that where there is any choice, it should be the ordinary merchant ship ensign of the country being visited which is flown.

The red flag is now a flag which is associated with revolution, but it was originally called the flag of defiance and is so described by Bowles in *Naval Flags of All the Nations in the World*, published in May 1783.

The black flag with skull and cross bones is always supposed to be the pirate flag; however, there does not appear to be any historical evidence for this.

One often reads of the term 'flags of convenience'. This is a device whereby ships are registered (for convenience or economy) in, and wear the merchant flag of, Panama, Liberia, Honduras or

Plate 5

PERSONAL FLAGS OF HER MAJESTY
QUEEN ELIZABETH II

Plate 5

PERSONAL FLAGS OF
HER MAJESTY QUEEN ELIZABETH II

Costa Rica. They are sometimes called the 'panlibhonco' fleet. There is concern at the increasing use of this means to enable owners to escape obligations inherent in using the flag of their own country.

In subsequent chapters the many flags of different nations and other authorities will be described, but before proceeding it is gratifying for the student and lover of flags to note that there has been a great increase in the interest taken in flags; so much so that 'flag societies' have been formed in many countries, and a name vexillology has been coined to describe the study of flags, their history and modern development, and all 'to do with' flags. Although there are some reservations this name, vexillology, has been adopted by many, and no doubt will in the course of time become universal. The inventor of the title is Doctor Whitney Smith, the Director and one of the founders of the Flag Research Center of 17 Farmcrest Avenue, Lexington, Mass. 02173 U.S.A. This organisation publishes four times a year a journal called 'The Flag Bulletin'. This bulletin is of great interest to all who are interested in flags and wish to keep abreast of all the many changes that are continually taking place. In addition to the American organisation, similar flag societies are springing up in many countries, the Netherlands, Switzerland, France, to mention a few, and in Great Britain the Heraldry Society, whose address is 59 Gordon Square, London, W.C.1, has formed a 'Flag Section'. All who are interested in flags are advised to contact the Secretary of this society. There have been two international meetings of flag societies, and a third is to be held in September 1969, and as a result and to co-ordinate all the National bodies an international body, known as the International Federation of Vexillological Associations, has been created. As yet this is still in the formative stage, but it is hoped that its constitution will be finalised at the meeting to be held in 1969.

Chapter Two

GREAT BRITAIN

Great Britain differs from most other countries in that she has no official national flag. The Union Flag is a royal flag used by the sovereign and the services and representatives of the Sovereign. However, it has twice been stated in Parliament—once in the House of Lords by the Earl of Crewe in 1908, and once by the Home Secretary in 1933—that there is no objection to any British subject using the Union Flag ashore. The Merchant Shipping Act of 1894 forbids its use afloat. This Act states that the Red Ensign is the proper colour for any ship or boat owned by a British subject.

Although the evidence is somewhat sketchy it appears probable that St. George became the Patron Saint of England in the year 1277, and his cross was first used as the emblem of England during the Welsh wars of Edward I, when it was displayed on the bracers of the archers (that is to say, the protectors on their arms) and on the pennoncelles (small pennons) on the spears of the foot soldiers. In the Scottish wars of Richard II (in 1385) the Cross of St. George was placed on the surcoats of the soldiers, and about the same time the Scottish soldiers started wearing the Cross of St. Andrew.

Of all the saints, probably less is known about St. George than many others. He was a soldier who was martyred in the reign of Diocletian in A.D. 303. Why he became England's Patron Saint is one of the mysteries. Probably it was because as a soldier he was popular with the crusaders and so came to be chosen in place of Edward the Confessor who was a native British saint. Nevertheless, it cannot be denied that his red cross on a white field makes a fine and distinctive flag for England (Plate 3, 1).

The reason for the choice of St. Andrew for Scotland is also somewhat obscure—he was the apostle who in A.D. 69 was crucified on a diagonal cross (known as a saltire in heraldry), and was buried in Patras in Greece. In the year A.D. 370 a monk called Regulus, hearing that the saint's remains were to be removed to Constantinople, took an arm bone and other portions of the body of the saint and escaped with these to sea. After a stormy voyage he was wrecked on a rocky coast which turned out to be Scotland. It seems possible that King Angus (A.D. 736) of Scotland chose St. Andrew as Scotland's Patron Saint because had he chosen one of the several native saints this would have raised an outcry from the followers of the unchosen ones.

And thus the Cross of St. George became the flag of England and the white saltire cross on a blue ground the flag of Scotland (Plate 3, 1 and 2). It is worth remembering that these are still the flags of England and Scotland. When the thrones of England and Scotland were United under James I of England (James VI of Scotland) in 1603 it was necessary to have a flag representing the two countries, now Great Britain, and in the year 1606 a Royal Proclamation announced the introduction of the first Union Flag, which was described as 'the red cross, commonly called St.

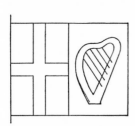

COMMONWEALTH
JACK

George's Cross, and a white cross commonly called St. Andrew's Cross, joined together' (Plate 3, 4). This flag remained in force until the execution of Charles I and the establishment of the Commonwealth, which led to the introduction of the special Commonwealth Jack, which consisted of St. George's Cross in the hoist and the gold harp in the fly; but with the Restoration and return from abroad of Charles II in 1660, the Union Flag of James I was reintroduced and remained as the flag of Great Britain until 1800 when Ireland was incorporated in the union of Great Britain and it became necessary to have a new Union Flag. This was brought into force by a Proclamation issued on January 1st 1801, and the flag which was established combines the three crosses of St. George, St. Andrew and St. Patrick— the flag of Great Britain until this day (Plate 3, 5).

The choice of St. George for England and St. Andrew for Scotland has already been remarked upon; the choice of the so-called

'Cross of St. Patrick' (Plate 3, 3) was also curious. St. Patrick was the Patron Saint of Ireland, but he was not a martyr and so was not entitled to a cross as his badge. The Irish have never used this cross as a national emblem. In reality it originated in the arms of the powerful family of the Geraldines, whose presence in Ireland as representatives of Henry II was due to the efforts of the English sovereign to subjugate the country. Ireland's traditional badge is either the shamrock or the golden harp. On becoming an independent country, Eire adopted quite a different flag (*see* page 126).

The design of the first or 1606 Union Flag was comparatively simple as it only required the combination of the two crosses of St. George and St. Andrew. Nevertheless, when first introduced it did run into difficulties as the Scottish mariners objected and said that the Cross of St. George was placed over and above that of St. Andrew. The design for the Union Flag of 1801 was more difficult because in this the three crosses had to be accommodated.

The new Union Flag which was established by a Proclamation dated January 1st 1801 was described heraldically as follows: 'the crosses Saltire of St. Andrew and St. Patrick Quarterly, per Saltire countercharged Argent and Gules; the latter fimbriated of the second, surmounted by the Cross of St. George of the third, fimbriated as the Saltire.' This description was accompanied by a drawing but the drawing and description could be interpreted differently, so much so that between 1801 and the present time there have been a dozen different versions of the Union Flag. The differences have only been in minor details. These varying patterns have now been reduced to two. The one which is adopted almost universally is the pattern used by the Royal Navy which is also the pattern flown on the Houses of Parliament and on government offices. In this the Irish (red) saltire is reduced in width by having its fimbriations taken from itself instead of from the blue ground (Plate 3, 5).

The other pattern, established in 1900 by the War Office, attempted to comply literally with the proclamation of January 1st 1801. In this pattern the two saltires are of equal breadth and the fimbriation of St. George's Cross has been reduced (Plates 7 and 8). It was, of course, in an endeavour to ensure that both the Cross of

Plate 6

PERSONAL AND SERVICE FLAGS

1 Broad Pennant of a Commodore, Royal Navy (p. 34)

2 Flag of a Vice-Admiral, Royal Navy (p. 33)

3 Broad Pennant of a Commodore in the Royal Fleet Auxiliaries (p. 35)

4 Flag of the Chief of Defence Staff (p. 30)

5 Flag of the Cinque Ports (p. 45)

6 Ensign, Ministry of Transport (p. 44)

7 The Civil Air Ensign (p. 43)

8 Flag of Lords Lieutenants of Counties (p. 44)

9 Trinity House, Ensign (p. 47)

10 Trinity House, Flag of the Master (p. 46)

11 Commissioners of Northern Lights, Ensign (p. 48)

12 Commissioners of Irish Lights, Ensign (p. 49)

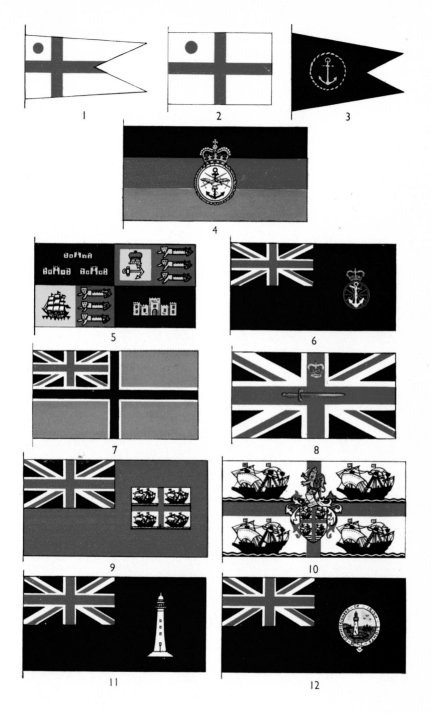

Plate 6

PERSONAL AND SERVICE FLAGS

St. Andrew and the Cross of St. Patrick were of equal size that they were, as the heralds described, countercharged. This requirement has not been met in the Navy pattern flag but the differences are so small as scarcely to be noticed and it must be agreed that the Union Flag with its colours fresh and new, flying in the breeze is an outstandingly beautiful flag.

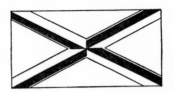

The original Union Flag was introduced in 1606 as a maritime flag, and in 1634 a Royal Proclamation laid down that the Union Flag was reserved for His Majesty's Ships of War and forbade merchant ships to wear it. It has been explained (*see* page 12) how this flag came to be called a 'Jack', and how the term Union Jack came into being. It is quite clear that the name Union Jack was the name given to the distinguishing flag of His Majesty's ships, and that it is proper to call this flag a Union Jack when flying in a ship, but this flag which was formerly purely maritime is now used as the National Flag of Britain and some consider that it is incorrect to call it a Union Jack when it is not flying in a ship and that when flying ashore it should be called the Union Flag. Strictly this view may be correct, and there would be no doubt as to its correctness if the flag used were the 1900 War Office pattern, but this is not so, and the flag that is seen in Britain flying from the Houses of Parliament and other public buildings is the pattern adopted by the Royal Navy (*see* above). Furthermore it has been called the Union Jack in modern times in Parliament, and so by common usage it is considered that it is correct to call this flag, which is to all intents the National Flag of Great Britain, the Union Jack. It would also appear that the 1900 War Office version should not be called the Union Jack; in fact it is generally known as the 'Great Union Flag'.

A flag which shares the position of 'National Flag' with the Union Flag is the Royal Standard of Great Britain. The first Royal Standard was that of King Richard I, which was flown in 1189, almost one hundred years before the Cross of St. George. This consisted of the three lions 'passant guardant' in gold on a red field. There seems to be some possibility that before the banner with

3

three lions came into being there were earlier ones with one or two lions. It is said that William the Conqueror bore two lions on his shield.

Although this flag is now universally known as a Royal Standard, properly it should be called the Royal Banner (*see* page 11).

During the course of its life the Royal Standard of Great Britain has undergone many changes. In 1339 it was for the first time divided into four quarters, the fleur-de-lys of France in the first and fourth quarters. However, this fairly simple design did not persist. With the ascension of James I to the throne of England the banners of Scotland and Ireland were introduced.

ROYAL STANDARD
1603–1689,
1702–1707

The first Royal Standard of the Sovereign of Great Britain consisted of the old Standard of England in the first and fourth quarters, the Standard of the King of Scotland in the second and the harp of Ireland in the third.

The Standard of Scotland is golden and bears the red 'lion rampant' within a tressure of the same colour, heraldically blazoned as 'Or [for gold], a lion rampant within a double tressure flory counterflory gules'. The exact date of the adoption of this banner is not definite, but it appeared on the great seal of King Alexander II, who married the daughter of King John in the early part of the 13th century. There are some who say that this banner is more properly the flag of Scotland than is the Cross of St. Andrew, but the weight of evidence points to the latter being Scotland's National Flag. The symbol of a harp as a badge for Ireland is somewhat obscure. It is generally accepted that the early Standard of Ireland had three golden crowns on a blue background. It seems that Henry VII substituted the harp for the Irish crowns, but neither the crown nor harp nor any other device for Ireland appear in the standard borne by any sovereign until the reign of James I.

With the execution of Charles I and the establishment of the Commonwealth under Cromwell, standards of a completely new design were adopted. The first, known as the Commonwealth

Standard, had a red field with the Cross of St. George and the harp of Ireland on a blue field surrounded by a wreath of laurels. From 1653 to 1659, the period of the Protectorate, a standard known as

Cromwell's Standard came into being. This consisted of quarters one and four, the Cross of St. George; two the Cross of St. Andrew; three the Irish harp; with an escutcheon of the arms of Cromwell, a white lion rampant. With the return of Charles II the Stuart Standard was reverted to.

CROMWELL'S
STANDARD

In subsequent years the Royal Standard underwent many changes and became more and more involved and complicated until in 1801 it changed to what was very nearly its present form—with the lions of England in the first and fourth quarters, the lion of Scotland in the second and the harp of Ireland in the third, with a little escutcheon in the centre, bearing the Arms of Hanover.

ROYAL STANDARDS

1689–1694   1707–1714   1714–1801

When Queen Victoria came to the throne in 1837 the Arms of Hanover were removed leaving the Royal Standard of Great Britain in its present form (Plate 4, 1). Note is very often made that Wales is not represented in the Royal Standard. The Standard of Wales is an old one; it was assumed in 1248 by Owen Glendower when Owen Gwynned was killed. Owen Gwynned was a descendant of Llewellyn ap Griffith whose standard it originally was. The standard was a quartered coat, gold and red, with four lions passant countercharged. The question of incorporating the Arms of Wales into the Royal Arms has been considered but has never been confirmed; they are displayed in the Standard of the Prince of Wales (Plate 4, 4).

In 1960 when arrangements for Her Majesty's forthcoming visit to India were being considered, it was felt that a new personal flag of distinctive design would be more appropriate for use in the nations of the Commonwealth. The Royal Standard had become associated in the public mind with the United Kingdom.

Accordingly a banner or square flag consisting of her Majesty's initial 'E' in gold ensigned with the Royal Crown all within a chaplet of golden roses on a blue field was authorised. This flag was fringed with gold (Plate 5, 1) and was used during the Queen's visit to India in 1961; subsequently it was felt that for those Commonwealth countries of which she is Queen it would be appropriate if the new device described above were used by Her Majesty in conjunction with the arms of the country she was visiting. Flags have accordingly been designed for Sierra Leone, Canada, Australia, New Zealand, Jamaica, Trinidad and Tobago, and Malta (Plate 5, 2–8). The details of these flags are given later when the flags of these countries are described.

When Her Majesty visits a Commonwealth country for which a personal flag has been approved, the appropriate flag is used instead of the Royal Standard. It must be appreciated that these personal flags do not in any way replace the Royal Standard of Great Britain—this is the banner of the Sovereign of the United Kingdom of Great Britain, whereas the personal flags which have been described are the personal flags of Queen Elizabeth II with her cypher upon them.

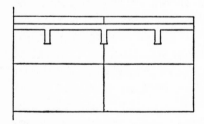

The standards used for the children and grandchildren of the Sovereign have a white label placed along the top of the Royal Standard. The inset diagram illustrates how it is placed. In the case of the children the label has three points and in the case of the grandchildren it has five points. When the eldest son of the Sovereign is created Prince of Wales he has an additional difference in the

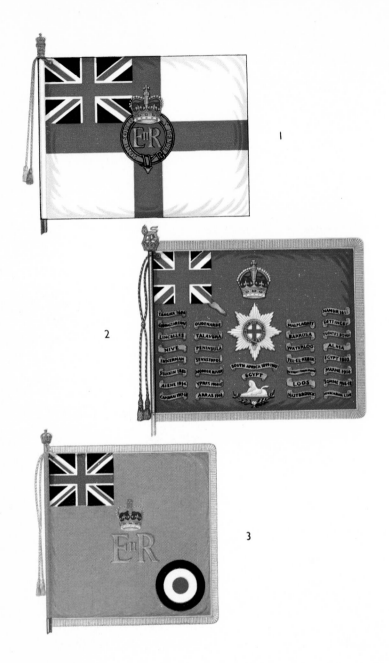

Plate 7   f.p. 27

COLOURS OF THE ROYAL NAVY, THE ARMY
AND THE ROYAL AIR FORCE

Plate 7

COLOURS OF THE ROYAL NAVY, THE ARMY
AND THE ROYAL AIR FORCE

1 A Queen's Colour of the Royal Navy (p. 33)

2 Queen's Colour of the 3rd Battalion of the Coldstream Regiment of Foot Guards (p. 40)

3 Queen's Colour of the Royal Air Force in the United Kingdom (p. 41)

centre, namely a small shield bearing the Arms of Wales described above. This shield is ensigned with the Prince's coronet (Plate 4, 4).

In 1968 a personal flag or banner was created for Prince Charles of Wales. This consists of the traditional Arms of Wales, which are on his standard, but having in the centre the coronet of the Prince of Wales displayed on a green shield. This flag is designed to fulfil the same purpose as the Personal Flag of Her Majesty the Queen, described on page 26.

PERSONAL FLAG
OF PRINCE
OF WALES

H.R.H. Prince Philip, Duke of Edinburgh, and H.M. Queen Elizabeth the Queen Mother and other members of the Royal Family have their own personal standards—that of the Duke of Edinburgh is shown on Plate 4, 2, and consists of the Duke's Arms which are quartered thus: (1) yellow, three blue lions crowned passant and nine red hearts (Denmark); (2) blue, a white cross (Greece); (3) white, two vertical black stripes (Mountbatten); (4) white, on a rock in natural colours, a black castle (Edinburgh).

In the standard of H.M. Queen Elizabeth the Queen Mother the Royal Arms are placed in the hoist whilst in the fly are those of Her Majesty's family (Bowes-Lyon). This is a splendid example of the use of canting or punning arms. It is a quartered coat: in the first and fourth quarters on a white field is the blue lion rampant while in the second and third quarters are three bows 'proper' of Bowes on an ermine field (Plate 4, 3).

THE ARMED FORCES OF GREAT BRITAIN—
MINISTRY OF DEFENCE

The Defence (Transfer of Functions) Act 1964 came into force on April 1st of that year. Until this date the Royal Navy, the Army and the Royal Air Force had been controlled by the Board of Admiralty and the Army and Air Councils. The new Act transferred the control of all three services to the Secretary of State for

Defence under whom the Defence Council exercises command and administrative control; the government office is known as the Ministry of Defence.   This new Act has resulted in the demise of the Board of Admiralty, and the Army and Air Councils.   It is not the province of this work to go into the organisation of government departments more than is necessary to explain their effect on the flags of the armed services.   With few exceptions the flags and ensigns used by the Navy, Army and Air Force remain the same.   The main changes are that the flags of the Army and Air Councils have disappeared and in future the flag formerly flown by the Board of Admiralty will be used only by the Sovereign who has now assumed the office of Lord High Admiral, and that the authority formerly vested in the Admiralty for issuing, on behalf of the Sovereign, warrants for ships to wear special privilege ensigns has been transferred by Royal Proclamation to the Secretary of State for Defence. (*See* Merchant Shipping Act 1894, page 254).

The historic flag of the Lord High Admiral was used by the Lords Commissioners of the Admiralty, known as the Board of Admiralty, the body constituted to carry out the functions of the Lord High Admiral.   This flag, which flew from the Admiralty in Whitehall for 114 years, was hauled down at a ceremony on March 31st 1964.   Exactly when this flag, which is known as 'the Anchor Flag', came into being is uncertain, but the anchor as the badge appeared on the Lord High Admiral's seals at a very early date.

The earliest instance of the anchor on a flag occurs in the well-known engraving supposed to be the *Ark Royal*, Lord Howard's flagship in 1588, which shows the anchor in the head of a streamer flown from the foretop.   Among flags surveyed at Deptford in 1633 is included a silk 'red ensigne with ye Lo. Admiralls badge'. There seems to be little doubt that this was the official anchor and cable.   Beyond the fact that the flag was red there is no evidence as to the exact design of the anchor upon it.   The oil painting by Van der Velde the Younger of the Royal visit to the Fleet at the Nore in 1672 shows the *Royal Prince* wearing the Admiralty flag at the fore, the Royal Standard at the main and the Union Flag at the mizzen.

The design of the Admiralty Flag is of a yellow horizontal anchor on a red field—very similar to the existing design. When in 1685 James II ascended the throne and retained the office of Lord High Admiral in his own hand, he placed the anchor vertically surmounting it with a crown—but this was the only occasion when such a flag was used.

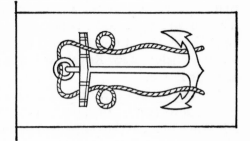

FLAG OF THE LORD HIGH ADMIRAL

The suite of flags worn by the *Royal Prince* in 1672, shown in the painting by Van der Velde (mentioned on page 28), is now only worn by the Royal Yacht when the Sovereign is embarked, although formerly it was the practice of H.M. ships to use these flags on any special occasion.

An extract from the log of H.M.S. *Centurion*, commanded by the Honourable Augustus Kepple, dated October 30th 1750, states: 'Being His Majesty's [George II] birthday hoisted the Anchor and Hope, Standard & Union at the fore, main and mizzen mastheads and fired a salute of 21 guns'. This extract from the log gives another piece of interesting information that the familiar name for the Anchor Flag was the 'Anchor and Hope', probably a corruption of Anchor and Rope (rhyming slang). This name 'Anchor and Hope' is commemorated in the names of some inns in the south of England—notably a hostelry in the High Street of Lymington, Hampshire, and another at Shooter's Hill, Kent.

In the past the Admiralty Flag was flown from any ship in which two or more of the Lords Commissioners of the Admiralty were embarked; but as the Sovereign has now assumed the office of Lord High Admiral, he, or she, will be the only person to use this historic flag. Thus it will, with one exception, only be seen flying from a ship which is carrying the Sovereign. The exception is that it will continue to be flown by ships of the Royal Navy at their launching.

In the Ministry of Defence there are no flags for the Secretary of

State of Defence, or for any of the departments of the Ministry. The Union Flag is flown at one end of the building of the Ministry of Defence, and at the other end the White Ensign, the Union Flag and the Ensign of the Royal Air Force, to represent the Navy, Army and Air Force.

The flag of the Chief of the Defence Staff is a horizontal tricolour, proportions two by one, dark blue at the top, then red, then Royal Air Force blue; in the centre is superimposed his badge, a white and blue eagle (R.A.F.), two red swords (Army), and a blue foul anchor (Royal Navy), all on a white ground encircled by laurel leaves in gold and surmounted by the Royal Crown in proper colours (Plate 6, 4). The flag of the Vice-Chief of the Defence Staff is similar, but with the emblem in black outline.

The flags of the Unified Commanders-in-Chief are vertical tricolours of the same colours as those of the Chief of the Defence Staff, proportions three by two.

Royal Navy The early history of ship ensigns has been described in Chapter One. The Red, White and Blue Ensigns of Great Britain came into being in the early part of the 17th century as tactical flags for use in the Royal Navy which was normally divided into three squadrons, the red, white and blue. A Royal Proclamation dated September 18th 1674 granted to merchant ships the right to wear the Red Ensign. The White and Blue remained solely for the use of H.M. ships until the year 1864 when they were abolished as they had become unnecessary and were puzzling to foreigners.

The Order in Council dated July 9th 1864 abolishing Squadronal Colours reads as follows:

Under the Regulations established by Your Majesty's Order in Council of the 25th. July, 1861, for the governance of the Royal Naval Service, the Flag Officers of the Fleet, whether Admirals, Vice-Admirals, or Rear-Admirals, are classed in Squadrons, of the Red, White and Blue, and are (with the exception of the Admiral of the Fleet) authorized to fly their flags of the colour of the Squadron to which they belong, this regulation necessitating the adoption of ensigns and pendants of a corresponding colour in every ship and vessel employed under their orders, each vessel is therefore supplied with three sets of colours, and the frequent alterations that have to be made when the Fleet is distributed as at present, under the Orders of many Flag Officers, is attended with much inconvenience from the uncertainty and expense which the system entails.

The increased number and size of merchant steam-ships render it a matter of importance to distinguish on all occasions men-of-war from private ships by a distinctive flag; the latter vessels bearing at present the same red ensign as your Majesty's ships when employed under an Admiral of the Red Squadron. It also appears desirable to grant (under such conditions as we may from time to time impose) the use of a distinguishing flag to such ships of the merchant service as may be employed in the public service, or whose commanding officer (with a given proportion of the crew) may belong to the Royal Naval Reserve. We therefore most humbly submit that Your Majesty may be pleased by your Order in Council to prescribe the discontinuance of the division of Flag Officers into the Red, White, and Blue Squadrons, and to order and direct that the White Ensign with its broad and narrow pendants, be henceforth established and recognized as the colours of the Royal Naval Service, reserving the use of the Red and Blue colours for such special occasions as may appear to us or to officers in command of Fleets and Squadrons to require their adoption: the White flag with a Red St. George's Cross to be borne by Admirals, Vice-Admirals, and Rear-Admirals on their respective masts: Commodores of the first class to carry a White broad pendant with the Red Cross at the main-top-gallant-mast-head, Commodores of the second class a similar pendant at the fore-top-gallant-mast-head, and senior officers when two or more vessels are present to bear the broad pennant [sic] at the mizzen-top-gallant-mast-head. The Blue Ensign and Union Jack, with a White border, to be carried by all vessels employed in the service of any public office; by vessels employed under the Transport Department, and the Civil Departments of the Navy (with the Seal or Badge of office to which they belong as at present), and, under our permission, by ships commanded by Officers of the Royal Naval Reserve Force, and fulfilling in other respects the conditions required to entitle them to the privilege. The Red Ensign and the Union Jack, with a White border, continuing as at present the national colours for all British ships, with such exceptions in favour of Yachts and other vessels as we may from time to time authorize to bear distinguishing flags.

The White Ensign is charged with the red Cross of St. George, with the Union Flag in the upper canton next to the mast (Plate 3, 7).

It is laid down in *Queen's Regulations and Admiralty Instructions*, 1956, Article 1236, that 'Her Majesty's ships, when lying in home ports and roads, are to hoist their Colours at 0800 from 25th March to 20th September inclusive, and at 0900 from 21st September to 24th March inclusive; but when abroad, at 0800 or 0900 as the Commander-in-Chief shall direct; and they shall be worn if the weather permits or unless the Senior Officer present sees objection thereto, or directs otherwise, throughout the day until sunset when they are to be hauled down.' These instructions apply in like manner to the use of the Union Flag at the jackstaff.

In large ships the guard and band are paraded, and as the ensign is slowly hoisted the National Anthem of Great Britain is played. Should the ship be lying in a foreign port, then the anthem of that country is played, as are the anthems of any warships of other countries that are present.

In small ships the bugle sounds the 'General Salute', or 'Alert' is piped on the Boatswain's pipe.

At sunset no guard or band is paraded, but the bugle sounds 'Sunset' (Retreat), or the pipe 'Alert', as the ensign is lowered.

When at sea Her Majesty's ships wear their ensigns continuously by day and night. Her Majesty's ships do not, on any account, lower their flags to any foreign ships whatsoever, unless the foreign ships shall first lower their flags to them.

The Jack is not worn when ships are: (1) under way (at sea), except when dressed with masthead flags; (2) in dock or when undergoing a dockyard refit.

There are certain Royal Naval establishments, e.g. civil and medical, at which the Union Flag is normally flown. However, when H.M. ships are dressed on ceremonial occasions, the White Ensign in addition is flown at the gaff or yardarm or from a separate mast.

During a period of hostilities the medical establishments continue to fly the Union Flag but in addition fly the flag of the Red Cross at the gaff or yardarm.

It is a serious offence for any vessel to wear improper colours, the authority being the 73rd Section of the Merchant Shipping Act, 1894 (*see* page 254).

In action a warship always displays not less than two White Ensigns; if one should be shot away, then there is no danger of the ship being regarded as having surrendered.

One yacht club alone, the Royal Yacht Squadron, is authorised to use the White Ensign (*see* page 263).

While on the subject of ensigns, a few words concerning their use ashore will not be out of place. The following is an extract from an Admiralty memorandum dated February 18th 1936:

The White and Blue Ensigns of His Majesty's Fleet are purely maritime flags, and in general their use on shore is incorrect. There has, however, been a customary extension of the use of the White Ensign from the harbour ship used as a Fleet establishment to barracks and other buildings on shore serving the same purpose. . . .

It is common also for the White and Blue Ensigns to be used on cenotaphs and other memorials to naval personnel.

With these exceptions the use of these ensigns on shore is improper . . . the White Ensign is nothing else but the national colours of a ship of war in commission and no past service in the Navy or other connection with the Navy make it correct to hoist it on private buildings on shore.

However, with the permission of the Admiralty, the White and Blue Ensigns may be used on shore for decoration purposes during periods of national rejoicing, provided they (1) are hung out, (2) are suspended on a line, or (3) form part of a set of small flags on a shield or the like on a wall, as part of a display of flags; they should not, however, be flown at the head of a flagstaff.

Although there is no mention of the use of the Red Ensign (Plate 3, 6) on shore in Section 73 of the Merchant Shipping Act of 1894, it would appear that no objection would be raised if it were used for decoration purposes in the manner described above.

The White Ensign used for ceremonial purposes known as the Queen's Colour, was an innovation of 1924. There are a certain number of them for use by Naval Guards of Honour. Each has a field three feet, nine inches long and three feet at the hoist, and is made of silk. It has no fringe, and is secured to the staff by a gold-and-white cord with tassels in the usual way. The staff is topped by a gilt Royal Crown (Plate 7, 1) set upon a mace-shaped base which is charged with three silver foul anchors. In the centre of the flag is a crimson circle, bearing the Royal Cypher and surrounded by the Garter, which is ensigned with the Royal Crown. This is the only White Ensign which is charged with a badge.

The highest ranking officer in the Royal Navy is the Admiral-of-the-Fleet who flies the Union as his proper flag. An Admiral flies the English National Flag of St. George; a Vice-Admiral a similar flag but with a red disc, the diameter of which is half the depth of the white canton in which it is placed (Plate 6, 2); and a Rear-Admiral has an additional red disc which is positioned in the lower canton next to the mast. Commodores 1st and 2nd Class have now been merged in the single rank of Commodore, whose Broad Pennant has one red ball in the canton and is the same as that of a former Commodore 2nd Class (Plate **6**, 1).

During World War II a special Broad Pennant was introduced and flown by the Royal Naval Reserve Commodores of Convoys. This pennant is white with a blue St. George's Cross. On November 2nd 1959 the privilege of flying this Broad Pennant was granted to Commodores on the active list of the Royal Naval Reserve; there are normally two such Commodores.

Space only permits a very brief account of the interesting history of the Masthead Pennant (pendant) now an integral part of the 'Colours' of a warship (*see also* Chapter One). This flag appears to have had its origin in the oft-times very long 'streamers' that dated from the 13th century and were used as a decoration. Pepys tells us in 1674 that it was customary for men-of-war of all nations to fly a masthead pendant so that they might not be mistaken for merchant-men. There seems to be no basis for the legend that during the Dutch wars of the 17th century the Dutch ships hoisted a broom. At least the many paintings and drawings by the Van der Veldes and other artists of the battles of these wars show both English and Dutch ships with pendants.

During the period that Squadronal Colours were used there were red, white and blue pendants, but now there is only the white, and

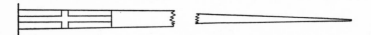

MASTHEAD PENNANT

according to *Queen's Regulations* all Her Majesty's ships and Establishments which are commanded by a Naval or Marine Officer (unless they are the ship of a flag officer) fly the pennant continuous-ly, by day and night during the period that they are in commission. As has been stated flag ships fly the appropriate flag of the flag officer accommodated in the ship.

In order to celebrate the home-coming of a ship at the completion of her commission, it has long been an unofficial custom to increase

Plate 8

COLOURS OF THE ROYAL MARINES, THE ARMY AND THE ROYAL AIR FORCE

1 Regimental Colours of the 40th Commando, Royal Marines (p. 37)

2 Regimental Colours of the 3rd Battalion of the Coldstream Regiment of Foot Guards (p. 40)

3 Queen's Colours of the Royal Air Force College, Cranwell (p. 41)

Plate 8

COLOURS OF THE ROYAL MARINES, THE ARMY AND THE ROYAL AIR FORCE

1 Regimental Colours of the 40th Commando, Royal Marines (p. 37)

2 Regimental Colours of the 3rd Battalion of the Coldstream Regiment of Foot Guards (p. 40)

3 Queen's Colours of the Royal Air Force College, Cranwell (p. 41)

Plate 8   f.p. 34

COLOURS OF THE ROYAL MARINES,
THE ARMY AND THE ROYAL AIR FORCE

greatly the length of the pennant to anything from fifty to eighty
yards or more—a figure of one quarter of a mile has been mentioned
in connection with 'dandified' ships, such cases necessitating something in the nature of an inflated football bladder being attached to
the end in order to keep it afloat when trailing astern.   It is usually
referred to as the 'Paying-off Pennant'.

The Church Pennant has a field divided horizontally red over
white over blue, bearing the red Cross of St. George on a white
background at the hoist.   It is
hoisted to indicate that the ship's
company is engaged in Divine Service.   The earliest known use of
the Church Pennant is to be found
in Article 10 of the *Additional*

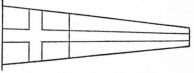

CHURCH PENNANT

Instructions of 1778.   There is, however, a tradition, a picturesque
one, that its use dates from the days of the Dutch Wars, when
services were held in ships of both sides before battle.   In order
that these services should not be interrupted, a pennant, composed
of the St. George's Cross and the Dutch tricolour sewn together,
was hoisted by all ships; it was not until it had been hauled down
that the battle would commence.

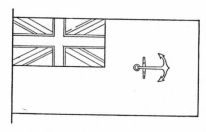

ROYAL FLEET AUXILIARY

Royal Fleet auxiliary vessels
wear the Blue Ensign defaced with
an Admiralty pattern anchor (without cable) in the fly.

In 1951 the Admiralty announced
the granting of a Broad Pennant for
the Commodore (a courtesy title)
of the Royal Fleet Auxiliaries.
The field is dark blue, and bears in
the centre thereof an Admiralty pattern anchor (without cable) in
gold, with its axis parallel to the hoist, within a circle composed of
cable-laid rope, also in gold (Plate 6, 3).   It was flown for the first
time on October 7th 1951, in the R.F.A. *Fort Dunvegan*.

The Royal Naval Auxiliary Service (RNXS) was formed on
November 5th 1962, out of the Royal Naval Minewatching Service
(RNMWS).   The Admiralty Ferry Crew Service was incorporated

in the RNXS in 1963 as a separate branch. In peace time the RNXS is a completely volunteer service, and its role is to provide Port Parties at the minor ports of the United Kingdom and to assist the Naval Control of Shipping Organisation.

The RNXS has been granted its own ensign for use both ashore and afloat. This is the Blue Ensign defaced with the badge of the service. This badge is the same badge as that of the old Mine-watching Service, i.e. a representation of a mine falling into the sea, but the inscription under the Naval Crown has been altered to RNXS. The Senior Officers' Burgee is a dark blue swallow-tailed flag with the same badge.

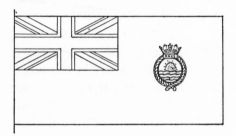 

RNXS ENSIGN   RNXS SENIOR OFFICERS' BURGEE

The plain Blue Ensign (Plate 3, 8) is worn by British merchant men commanded by an officer of the Royal Naval Reserve, having a certain number of R.N.R. officers and ratings on board, and holding an Admiralty Warrant which is issued in accordance with the conditions laid down in *Queen's Regulations and Admiralty Instructions*.

During the early part of 1950 it was decided that Commodores R.N.R., whether on the active or retired list, may, when afloat, use the Blue Ensign in their own right, provided that Admiralty permission has been obtained.

The Blue Ensign, defaced with the appropriate charge or badge in the fly, is now distinctive of Public Offices, the Consular Service, the Colonial Governments and their ships, and a variety of other services.

Towards the end of 1942 the Sea Cadet Corps, the voluntary pre-entry training organisation for the Royal and Merchant Navies, was granted permission by the Admiralty to use the Blue Ensign with the badge of the Corps in the centre of the fly.   This badge has been described as follows: 'Within a circle, the words "SEA CADET CORPS" and a six-pointer star, and ensigned with a Naval Crown, a foul anchor; beneath the whole upon a scroll the motto "READY AYE READY".'   The circle and scroll are light blue, edged with gold; the crown is also gold, but the anchor, star and lettering are white, and the dark blue field of the fly shows through behind the anchor.

A certain number of yacht clubs have an Admiralty Warrant to use the Blue Ensign, and a number have an Admiralty Warrant to use the Blue Ensign and Red Ensign defaced by the badge of the club.   A list of such clubs is to be found in the 'Navy List' (see also Chapter Fourteen).

In the famous 'Sea Regiment', the Royal Marines, the Army principle of two Colours, Queen's and Regimental, is carried out. The Queen's Colour is the Union, and bears in the centre the foul anchor with the Royal Cypher interlaced, ensigned with the Royal Crown and 'GIBRALTAR' above; in base is the globe surrounded by a laurel wreath, and underneath the famous motto of the Corps, 'PER MARE PER TERRAM' (By Land by Sea).

The Regimental Colour is blue.   In the centre is the foul anchor interlaced with the Royal Cypher, 'G.R.IV', ensigned with the Royal Crown and 'GIBRALTAR' above; in base is the globe encircled with the laurel wreath and with the motto beneath it.   In the dexter canton is the Union, and in each of the other three corners is the Royal Cypher of the reigning Sovereign ensigned with the Royal Crown.   An illustration of the Regimental Colours of the Royal Marine Commandos will be found on Plate 8, 1.   It will be noted that these not only bear the Royal Cypher of the new reign and the new design of Royal Crown but also the numerical designation of the Commandos to which they were presented.

The significance of the globe and motto is evident.   The laurel wreath was won at the capture of Belle Isle on June 7th 1761, and the honour 'GIBRALTAR' for the capture and defence of the Rock in

1705. When H.R.H. the Duke of Clarence (afterwards King William IV) presented Colours to all four Divisions in 1827, he said that the King, George IV, had 'directed that whatever King or Queen they might serve under hereafter, though the Cypher of the reigning sovereign must appear on their Standard, still in those of the Royal Marines, the Cypher G.R. IV was for ever to appear'.

Senior Royal Marine Officers have distinguishing flags for use in miniature on motor-cars; these all have a dark blue field, three by two.

The Commandant-General's is rectangular with, in the centre, a yellow foul anchor surmounted by the Royal Crest in proper colours.

That of Lieutenant- or Major-General is a burgee, i.e. it has a

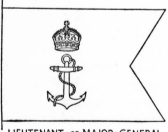

triangular piece cut out of the fly, and has a similar anchor, but ensigned with the Royal Crown, both in white.

A Brigadier displays a triangular flag charged with the white foul anchor.

COMMANDANT-GENERAL

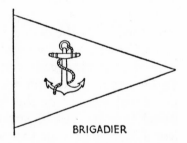

LIEUTENANT-or MAJOR-GENERAL

BRIGADIER

Flags and Colours of the British Army   The story of the development of the flags, or as they are now termed the Colours used in the army is not clear-cut like the story of the flags and ensigns of the Royal Navy, and to this day there is no universal rule; each branch of the Army, infantry, cavalry, etc. have their own individual pattern of flag.

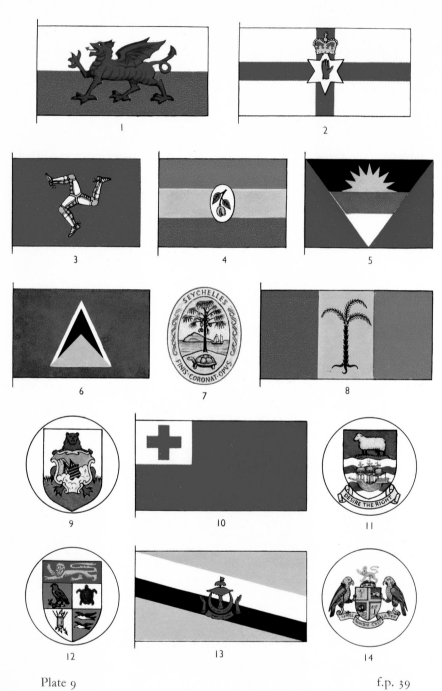

Plate 9

FLAGS OF THE DEPENDENCIES
OF GREAT BRITAIN

Plate 9

FLAGS OF THE DEPENDENCIES OF GREAT BRITAIN

As has been explained, the Cross of St. George was first used as the distinguishing emblem of the soldiers of Edward I, and it came to be the banner that marked the King or Commander and the rallying point of the whole army. But in feudal times the different 'Companies' marched under the banner of the baron or knight who recruited them and whose retinue they formed.

The introduction of standing armies in the 16th century and their organisation into regiments led to the introduction of 'Regimental Colours'. The infantry were the first to adopt these, and at first each company of a regiment had its own Colour, or ensign as they were then called. These early ensigns were very similar to those used in ships: the field was in the regimental colours with the Cross of St. George in the canton, and a device that denoted the rank of the commander of the company. After the restoration of Charles II the pattern was changed and the basic ensign consisted of the Cross of St. George (sometimes with a fimbriation) on a field of the colour of the regiment.

One of the earliest reports that we have of British Army flags is that which informs us that at the Battle of Edgehill (1642) the Royal Foot-Guards of Charles I lost eleven out of their thirteen Colours. There is also a Royal Warrant dated February 13th 1661 authorising Colours for the Foot-Guards.

The junior officers in the British Army were called ensigns until 1871 when they became second lieutenants. The rank of 'ensign' was derived from their former title of ensign-bearers and to this day a second lieutenant in the Brigade of Guards is known colloquially as an ensign. Although this term is no longer official in Great Britain the rank of ensign, equivalent to sub-lieutenant in the Royal Navy, is still retained in the navy of the United States of America.

There appear to have been no very definite regulations controlling the Colours of the Army until the year 1747, when the present pattern was evolved. And although up to now only the Colours of the infantry have been mentioned, the other arms of the Army, the cavalry, artillery etc., soon followed suit and adopted Colours of their own, although these were often of a different type from the rectangular banner of the infantry.

4

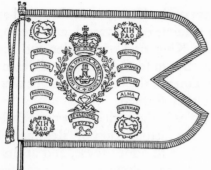

GUIDON OF THE 11TH HUSSARS

When ensigns came to be called 'Colours' is also not clear, but now there are three types that are in use in the British Army. They are:

(1) *The Standard*, carried by the Household Cavalry and the Dragoon Guards, rectangular in shape, thirty inches in length by twenty-seven inches in breadth.

(2) *The Guidon*, carried by the Royal Dragoons, Royal Scots Greys and the Inniskilling Dragoon Guards, pennant shaped, forty-one inches long and twenty-seven inches in breadth, slit in the fly.

(3) *The Queen's Colour and the Regimental Colour*, carried by the Foot-Guards and the Infantry of the Line. There is an interesting point here: in the case of the Guards the Queen's Colour consists of an ensign-type flag with the Union in the Canton, and the Regimental Colour the Union, whereas in the case of the Line Regiments the reverse is the case, with the Queen's Colour the Union and the Regimental an 'ensign type'. Finally it should be noted that the 'Rifle Regiments' have no Colours.

All these flags are made of silk, beautifully embroidered with a golden fringe. The staff on which the Colour is carried is known as a 'Colour Pike'. The Colours bear in addition to the badges of the regiment the battle honours of the unit that they represent. The Colours of the British Army are all regarded with the greatest respect and veneration. Examples of these lovely flags are shown on Plates 7 and 8.

The British Army also has a number of other flags. In 1938 His late Majesty King George VI approved a badge for the Army which consisted of the Royal Crest superimposed on two crossed swords, all in full colour. This badge displayed on a red field is the flag of the Army; unfortunately it appears to be very rarely used.

THE FLAG OF
THE ARMY

Appointments held by senior officers are shown by flags flown on their motor-cars. The flags for the Adjutant-General, the Quartermaster-General and the Master-General of the Ordnance are square, divided horizontally red over blue with the Royal Crest on each side. A General Officer Commanding in Chief flies the distinguishing red, black and red horizontal of the Headquarters of the Army.

Since World War II the senior officers of the British Army have adopted the practice of the Army of the U.S.A. of displaying either flags or badges on their motor-cars which carry stars denoting the rank of the officer: five for a Field Marshal, four for a General, three for a Lieutenant-General, two for a Major-General and one for a Brigadier.

Royal Air Force As the Royal Air Force was only formed in recent times its flags have no long history and generally are similar in pattern to those of the Royal Navy. Thus the Royal Air Force's principal flag is its ensign; the field of this is blue, of a shade known as Royal Air Force blue; in the canton is the Union and in the fly the distinguishing mark used on aircraft of the Royal Air Force—a target of red, white and blue, the blue being outside and the red in the centre (Plate 3, 9).

The colours of the Royal Air Force are red, dark blue and air force blue. The red represents the Army (Royal Flying Corps) and dark blue the Royal Navy (Royal Naval Air Service), the two arms from which the Royal Air Force sprang; the lighter blue represents the Royal Air Force in the air.

As in the Royal Navy and the Army the Royal Air Force has 'Colours' for use on ceremonial occasions; these were approved in principle by the late King George VI in December 1947. They comprise: (1) The Queen's Colour for the Royal Air Force in the United Kingdom; (2) the Queen's Colour for individual units; and (3) the standard for individual operational squadrons; all three are made of silk and are similar to the Colours used by the Navy and the Army. The Queen's Colour for the Royal Air Force is in the form of the Royal Air Force Ensign, with the Royal Cypher in gold, ensigned with the Royal Crown in proper colours in the centre. Examples of the Colours are shown in Plates 7 and 8.

Distinguishing flags are flown by senior officers of the Royal Air Force—these flags are also flown in the bows of Royal Air Force marine craft on ceremonial occasions. The Marshal's flag is air force blue, in the centre a broad red horizontal band between two narrow ones, with a dark blue border top and bottom. That of the Air Chief Marshal has seven stripes of equal width, dark blue top and bottom, with, between, three air force blue and two red stripes. The Air Marshal and the Air Vice-Marshal's flags are similar with dark blue borders, the former having on the air force blue centre a red stripe the same width as the dark blue stripes, and the latter two thin red stripes half the width of the dark blue. The Air Commodore's flag has a swallow-tail or broad pennant having one very narrow red stripe in the centre of a light blue field, with dark blue edges top and bottom. Group Captains and Wing

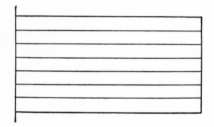

AIR CHIEF MARSHAL'S FLAG

ROYAL OBSERVER
CORPS BADGE

Commanders have triangular flags: the Group Captain has one red stripe in the centre, the same width as the dark blue edgings, and the Wing Commander two red stripes each half the width of that of the Group Captain. The field of all these flags is the air force blue.

It is of course impossible for an aircraft to display a flag whilst flying, but when Her Majesty, or any other member of the Royal Family is travelling by air their standard is hoisted on a small staff over the aircraft during the period when they are embarking or disembarking. In a similar way the Royal Air Force Ensign is flown when important personages are travelling by air.

Attached to the Royal Air Force is the Royal Observer Corps. This Corps has its own ensign which is similar to that of the Royal

Air Force except that the red, white and blue target is replaced by a special badge. This badge was approved by the late King George VI in 1945. The badge consists of the figure of an Elizabethan coast-watcher holding aloft a torch, within a wreath of laurel, surmounted by the Royal Crown and in the base a scroll containing the motto 'FOREWARNED IS FOREARMED'.

As there is a special ensign for British merchant ships, so there is a British Civil Air Ensign. This ensign is of light air force blue; it is charged with a dark blue cross edged with white with the Union in the canton (Plate 6, 7). This ensign may be worn by any British aircraft registered in the United Kingdom when it is grounded and by air transport undertakings which own such aircraft on, or in proximity to, buildings used by them.

THE QUEEN'S REPRESENTATIVES, DEPARTMENTAL AND PROVINCIAL FLAGS AND FLAGS OF CIVIC DEPARTMENTS

Her Majesty's Ambassadors and Ministers (and in their absence, Chargés-d'Affaires) fly the Union Flag with the Royal Arms on a white circular background, surrounded by a garland, in the centre (Fig. 1, page 44). This flag is flown over our Embassies and Legations on certain prescribed days in the year, and it is also used when the holders are afloat. Two flags are used by the Consular Service. When ashore, Consuls-General, Consuls, Vice-Consuls etc. are distinguished by the Union Flag, with, in the centre a Royal Crown on a plain white circular background (Fig. 2). When on duty afloat, the Blue Ensign is flown, with the full Royal Arms in colour in the fly and without any white background (Fig. 3). The Consular Blue Ensign, being a personal distinguishing flag, must be flown at the bow, and not at the stern, which is the accepted position for the national colours. No further flag is necessary, but if, for some special reason it is desired to wear a flag at the stern, then this should be the Red Ensign.

The flags of the representatives of the Queen in Commonwealth countries and colonies, and where applicable the Heads of State of those countries, which have elected to become republics within the framework of the Commonwealth, are dealt with later.

A Lord Lieutenant of a county flies the Union Flag, charged in the centre with a golden sword, placed horizontally, point towards the fly, and with the Royal Crown above (Plate **6**, 8).

There exist in Great Britain a large number of Civic Bodies. Some, such as Her Majesty's Customs, and other ministries are official government departments; then there are a number of semi-official departments, such as Trinity House, and the Nationalised

(1) The Diplomatic Service on shore and afloat. (Ambassadors, Ministers, Chargés-d'Affaires, etc.)

(2) Consular Officers on shore.

(3) Consular Officers afloat.

Industries. An increasing number of counties and towns have adopted coats of arms from which they have evolved flags. Finally, there are the purely civilian organisations, the charitable and the sporting. It is only possible within the scope of this work to give a selected number of examples of all these varied flags.

Vessels employed by the Ministry of Agriculture and Fisheries in fishery research work wear the Blue Ensign with, in the fly a weird-looking fish in white, surmounted by a Royal Crown, the whole enclosed in a yellow circlet.

The Ministry of Transport Ensign is shown on Plate **6**, 6.

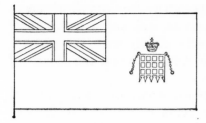

FLAG OF H.M. CUSTOMS

The badge of Her Majesty's Customs is a plain portcullis and chains in gold surmounted by a Royal Crown; this is placed in the fly of the Blue Ensign which is worn by Customs vessels and is flown ashore at Custom-houses.

The Cinque Ports have a most complicated flag. It is in the proportions of four by two, and is quartered, the first and fourth quarters being dark blue. In the first quarter are three representations of Dover Castle in yellow, one on top and two, side by side, below. In the fourth quarter is a single representation of the same castle, also in yellow, but much larger in size. The second quarter is halved. The left-hand half is yellow, and bears a yellow horizontal anchor with its flukes towards the fly, ensigned with a peer's coronet, complete with its scarlet cap and tassel, but the exact rank of the peer, whether Baron, Marquess, Viscount, Earl or Duke, is not clearly indicated. The coronet and anchor are surrounded by a narrow border of red. In the red right-hand half, in pale, are the well-known three lions and ships dimidiated, i.e. the fore-halves of the lions are conjoined to ships' sterns, in yellow. The third quarter is also halved. The left-hand half is yellow, and is charged with a sailing-ship in red, while the other half is red, with a repetition of the three lions dimidiated with the ships' sterns (Plate 6, 5).

This flag has long since become the personal flag of the Lord Warden. It is flown upon Walmer Castle, his official residence. This office was once held by the late Sir Winston Churchill, K.G. This flag was frequently seen flying over his private residence— Chartwell in Kent—and he flew it on his motor-car. The office is now held by Sir Robert Menzies.

The Corporation of Trinity House, London, is one of those peculiar bodies that are found in few places other than Great Britain. It is the authority responsible for the lighthouses, lightships, and buoyage, or, as the old term has it, the sea marks, of England and Wales. It is also the Chief Pilotage Authority of the United Kingdom. Although it provides a public service, and some of the funds to do this are collected by the Commissioners of Customs (Light Dues), it is a private and not a government organisation, although working very closely with the government departments concerned—the Admiralty and the Board of Trade.

The badge of the Corporation, which is used in differing dimensions and with different embellishments in all the five flags of Trinity House, consists of a white field charged with the red Cross of St. George, in each quarter of which there is a representation of a sailing-ship of the period of Queen Elizabeth I, in black, sailing on a blue heraldic sea towards the hoist. The flag of the Master (in modern times an office held by a Prince of Royal blood—at present H.R.H. the Duke of Edinburgh) consists of this badge, in the proportions two by one, on which are superimposed in the centre the complete display of the armorial bearings of the Trinity House Guild or Fraternity, granted in 1573: 'Argent, a cross Gules between four ships, each under full sail, Sable; on each ensign a cross of the first; and each quarter representing a sea piece. Crest, a demi-lion rampant guardant and regally crowned Or, holding in the dexter paw a sword Argent, hilted and pommelled Gold'. An esquire's helm and mantling of white and red complete the design (Plate 6, 10). It is flown at the main masthead whenever the Master is embarked and also at the Trinity House, Tower Hill, London, when he is present.

A personal flag for the Deputy Master was officially approved and adopted on June 10th 1952. It is similar to the Master's flag; however, in this case the field is three by two and the charge in the centre thereof consists of a gold-lined red disc bearing the aforementioned crest only, in generous proportions.

This flag is flown at district depots whenever the Deputy Master is present and at the main masthead when he is embarked, having the status of a 'command' flag; it is also flown at Trinity House on Trinity Monday if the Master is not present.

It was flown in the Trinity House vessel *Patricia* for the first time on July 14th 1952, when the Deputy Master, Captain Gerald Curteis, M.V.O., R.N. (now Captain Sir Gerald Curteis, K.C.V.O., R.N.), embarked and left Harwich for the Olympic Games at

Helsinki. En route, at Oslo, H.R.H. Prince Philip, Duke of Edinburgh (who had been elected an Elder Brother of Trinity House the preceding month) joined the vessel and his Personal Standard was broken at the masthead. At the express wish of the Prince, the Deputy Master flew his personal flag at the yardarm—the vessel having one mast only—thus giving the new flag a 'flying start'.

On important occasions the Royal Yacht is escorted by the *Patricia* or one other of the Corporation's vessels—an ancient privilege of which it is justly proud. In an Admiralty letter dated June 21st 1894, permission was granted 'for the Elder Brethren of Trinity House to fly the White Ensign of H.M. Fleet on board their Steam and Sailing Vessels on all occasions upon which Ships are dressed, and while escorting Her Majesty in company with Royal Yachts and Ships of War'.

Thus, at the Coronation Naval Review in 1953 the *Patricia* flew the Deputy Master's flag at the main masthead (the Master having previously embarked in the Royal Yacht for the occasion) and the White Ensign at the fore masthead; she wore the Trinity House Ensign at the stern and a small edition of the Trinity House Jack at the jackstaff. In accordance with custom these flag arrangements obtained throughout the period during which she was employed on escort duties.

The Ensign of the Corporation is the Red Ensign defaced with the badge of the Corporation (*see* page 46) in the fly (Plate **6, 9**).

All Trinity House vessels, tenders and lightships wear this Ensign; it is also flown at (a) all the Corporation's lighthouses, (b) the Trinity House throughout the year, except on those occasions when special distinguishing flags are flown, (c) district depots in addition to the Burgee (*see* below), always providing the necessary facilities exist for so doing.

The Trinity House Jack consists of the badge of the Corporation in the proportions five by four. Strictly, this is the flag of Trinity House (*see* below) and should only be called ' Jack' when flown as a diminutive at the jackstaff of vessels belonging to the Corporation. An Elder Brother has, since June 26th 1928, been entitled to fly this flag at the masthead when he is afloat on official duty in the service of the State or of the Corporation of Trinity House.   Among those who have made use of this privilege are H.R.H. Prince Philip, Duke of Edinburgh, Admiral of the Fleet Earl Mountbatten of Burma, Field Marshal the Earl Alexander of Tunis, and Sir Winston Churchill.

This flag is also flown at the Trinity House on special occasions

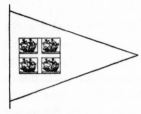

such as the birthdays of members of the Royal Family; a diminutive of it is worn at the jackstaff when (a) vessels are moored alongside or at anchor; (b) ships are dressed.

The Burgee (or Cornet) consists of a red triangular flag charged with a rectangular panel similar to that on the Ensign.   It

TRINITY HOUSE: BURGEE

is flown at (a) the masthead in tenders when they are in port; also when they are under way with the District Superintendent on board; (b) all district depots.

Another distinctive suite of flags is that of the General Lighthouse Authority for Scotland and the Isle of Man, namely the Commissioners of Northern Lights.   The Board is constituted in accordance with an Act of Parliament passed in 1786.   Their flag has a white field, two by one, with the Union Flag (1606 pattern) in the first quarter, and a representation of a lighthouse, in blue, in the fly.   There appears to be no record of the date of origin; however, in the absence of the St. Patrick's Cross in the Union, it seems probable that it was adopted before 1801.

It is flown at the main masthead when the Commissioners are embarked; in addition, they fly their 'Pennant' at the fore masthead.   The title of the last mentioned is rather misleading in that this flag functions much in the same way as a house flag or yacht

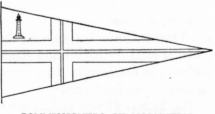

COMMISSIONERS OF NORTHERN
LIGHTS: PENNANT

burgee.   It is blue and bears a white cross, charged with a very narrow red cross; in the first quarter, the lighthouse in white.   The Ensign is the Blue Ensign defaced with the lighthouse in white;

this is worn in tenders and flown on lighthouses and depots on shore (Plate **6**, 11).   It was adopted in 1855.

In 1863 the Port of Dublin Corporation, which was not only the General Lighthouse Authority in Ireland but also the Corporation for preserving and improving the Port of Dublin, was granted permission to use the Blue Ensign defaced with a badge in the fly. This consisted of a lighthouse on a circular blue background, surrounded by a scroll bearing the words 'IRISH LIGHTS DEPART-MENT'.   The General Lighthouse Authority became a separate body in accordance with the Dublin Port Act of 1867, and was designated the Commissioners of Irish Lights.   At the same time the design of the badge on the Blue Ensign was changed, as shown on Plate **6**, 12.

The flag of the Commissioners is white, three by two, charged with the red Cross of St. George; each quarter comprises a seascape —first and fourth showing a lighthouse on a rock, second and third a lightship, all proper.   There seems to be no record of the date of adoption of this flag.   Similar charges, only placed within a circle, are displayed on the blue triangular field bearing the St. George's Cross, of the 'Pennant'. This is flown at the main masthead, but is replaced with the Commissioners' flag whenever they are embarked.

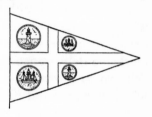

COMMISSIONERS OF IRISH
LIGHTS: PENNANT

The Commissioners' flag is also flown at all lighthouse stations in the Republic of Ireland; however, those in Northern Ireland fly the Blue Ensign defaced, as described above.

The City of London has a white flag with the red Cross of St. George bearing in the canton the red sword of St. Paul. These are the arms of the City and date back at least to 1381 and perhaps 1359.

The badge of the newly constituted Greater London Council differs from that of the old London County Council badge in that the Cross of St. George and mural crown has been replaced by a Saxon crown in gold.   The lower part of the shield retains the six wavy bars of blue and white representing water.

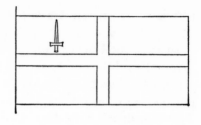

FLAG OF THE GREATER
LONDON COUNCIL

FLAG OF CITY OF LONDON

Another well-known flag is that of the city of Glasgow whose arms had been used for centuries before they were matriculated on October 25th 1866.   As described in the patent, they are: 'Argent, on a mount in base vert an oak tree proper, the stem at the base thereof surmounted by a salmon on its back also proper, with a signet ring in its mouth or, on the top of the tree a red breast, and in the sinister fess point an ancient hand-bell, both also proper.'

The bird is St. Serf's robin, restored to life by St. Mungo.   The tree is the bough with which the monastery lamps were relighted when he made it burst into flame; the fish and the ring are emblems drawn from the romantic legend of Queen Langueth, and her remarkable deliverance by the saint who sent the monk to catch the fish that swallowed the ring which she had given her lover, and of which her husband demanded the return; and the bell is the consecrated one he brought from Rome on the occasion of his last visit.

Edinburgh has a black triple-towered castle on a rock displayed on a white field; by the castle is the old chapel of St. Margaret.

Hampshire, which should properly be called Southamptonshire, has the three red roses of Southampton.

LYMINGTON'S FLAG

Many smaller towns have in recent years acquired coats of arms, and from these have developed a borough or council flag; as an example the new borough flag of Lymington,

Hampshire, is illustrated. It consists of an air force blue field, proportions five by three charged with the Arms of Lymington.

It is when we come to the flags of our City Companies that we realise that once upon a time the Companies did send into battle contingents distinguishable by their insignia, and displayed them as 'Barge Flags' during water processions and pageants on the River Thames. The Grocers marched under their cloves, the Fish-mongers under their dolphins and crowned fishes, the Drapers under their crowned clouds and sunrays, the Goldsmiths under their leopards' faces, the Merchant Taylors under their tents, the Ironmongers under their gads and swivels, the Mercers under the head of the Virgin wearing her crown, the Vintners under their three casks, the Clothworkers under their hooks and teasel, the Skinners under their three crowns and ermine field, the Salters under their covered salt-cellars and the Gardeners under what looks rather like Adam digging with an iron spade.

The Honourable Company of Master Mariners received the Royal Charter in 1930 and a grant of livery two years later. To commemorate the occasion the Anglo-American Oil Company pre-sented it with its first flag.

The House Flag of British Rail is similar to that flown from the ships of British Rail and used by the Shipping Division (*see* page 258), except that the field is flame red.

HONOURABLE COMPANY OF
MASTER MARINERS

A well-known flag to those who go to sea is that of the Royal National Lifeboat Institution (page 52). A handsome flag is that granted by the Admiralty in 1957 to the National Maritime Museum. It consists of a conventional anchor placed vertically with similar but small anchors on each side of the shank, in gold on a red field. This was originally the badge of the old Navy Board, 1546–1832, and was used as a defacement on a Red Ensign or Jack of that Board.

Nearly all the Harbour Commissioners round our coasts have

ROYAL NATIONAL LIFEBOAT
INSTITUTION

FLAG OF NATIONAL MARITIME
MUSEUM

their own flags; many of them have warrants to wear the Blue
Ensign on their harbour craft.   The port of London Authority has
for its badge a sea-lion grasping a trident in yellow.   The House
Flag is the banner of St. George bearing in the centre the Port of
London Authority's Arms with a yellow-edged red ring inscribed
'PORT OF LONDON AUTHORITY'.   The arms look quaint; they con-
sist of St. Paul, the Patron Saint of London, sitting on the Tower
of London, holding in his right hand a drawn sword.

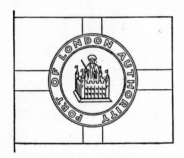

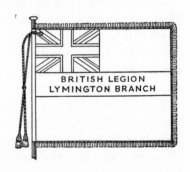

PORT OF LONDON AUTHORITY:
HOUSE FLAG

After the end of World War I an Association open to all who had
served in the Royal Navy, the Army or the Royal Air Force was
formed.   After World War II the scope of the Association was extended to include personnel of the Merchant Navy, and a women's
section was founded.   This Association is called the British Legion
and there is scarcely a town throughout the country without its
'Legion branch'. Each of these branches, and also each of the

branches of the Women's Legion, have their standards, and there is also the Headquarters Standard. They are all of a standard pattern, that of the Headquarters consisting of a Blue Ensign, dimensions three feet, nine inches in length and three feet in breadth. Across the centre of the standard is a broad gold stripe inscribed with the words 'BRITISH LEGION' and underneath the word 'HEADQUARTERS'. In the case of the branches the word 'Headquarters' is replaced by the name of the branch, i.e. 'SOUTH-AMPTON BRANCH'. The branch standards may be further embellished with scrolls in the top or bottom part, denoting that the branch has been awarded the Jellicoe or Haig Cup, or with stars in the same places, denoting winners of the Certificate of Merit.

The standards have a gold fringe and are decorated with cords and tassels which should be of such a length that when the pole of the standard is held horizontally they hang level with the outer edge of the fringe.

Winners of the Haig Cup are permitted to wear a pennant above the standard.

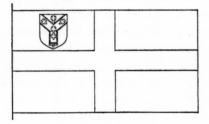

CHURCH FLAG

And last, but by no means least—the Church of England. For many years there was controversy as to the proper flag to hoist over a church. A common practice was to hoist the flag of St. George. A pronouncement by the Earl Marshal on February 11th 1938 settled this by laying down that as far as any church within the Provinces of Canterbury and York is concerned, the Cross of St. George may be flown, with in the first quarter the arms of the See in which the particular church is ecclesiastically situated. Descriptions of these arms will be found in *Crockford's Clerical Directory*.

Chapter Three

THE DEPENDENCIES OF
GREAT BRITAIN

Formerly the British Commonwealth was called the British Empire and consisted of 'colonies' directly governed by Great Britain, all of which acknowledged the Sovereign of Britain as their Head of State. But this has changed in recent years and the Commonwealth has become a free association of twenty-six sovereign independent states and a number of dependencies for whose administration, in varying degrees, Britain, Australia and New Zealand are responsible.

Some of the independent countries have retained their allegiance to the Sovereign of Great Britain, whom they recognise as their Sovereign; in these the Head of State is the representative of the Sovereign and holds the rank of Governor-General. Others of the independent countries have elected to be republics and in these the Head of State is a President who is elected by the country itself.

Governor-Generals continue to use the dark blue flag with the Royal Crest of the lion and crown in full colour, in the centre and the name of the country underneath (*see* page 71). The Presidents of those countries which are republics have standards of varying design.

The independent countries of the Commonwealth have close and special relations with Great Britain, but they have no formal ties and are completely independent in all senses of the word, responsible both for their own internal and external affairs. In view of this and the fact that many have adopted flags that do not in any way resemble the flags of Great Britain, the descriptions of their flags are given in subsequent chapters according to the continent on which they are situated.

As stated above there remain a number of dependencies for whose

Plate 10

FLAGS OF CANADA

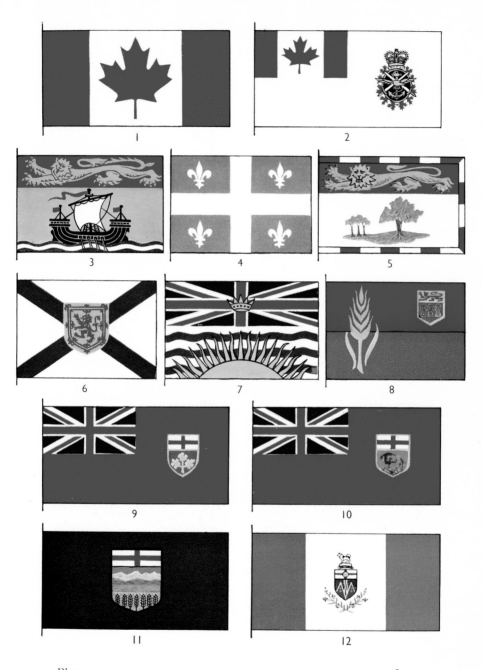

Plate 10   f.p. 54

FLAGS OF CANADA

administration Great Britain is in some measure responsible.   They differ considerably—some are associated states, some protected states and some colonies, but broadly speaking it can be said that all are responsible for their own internal government, whilst Great Britain is responsible for their external relations and foreign policy.

Strictly speaking the Union Flag of Great Britain is the flag of a colony, but nearly all have and use as their National Flag a Blue (and in a few cases a Red) Ensign, defaced with the badge of the colony which is generally placed on a plain white disc.   The Governor, or Lieutenant-Governor flies the Union Flag, with the distinctive badge of the colony or dependency on a disc surrounded by a garland of laurel, complete with berries, superimposed on the centre of St. George's Cross.

Although some retain their old 'colonial flag' most of the asso-ciated states and protectorates have flags of an individual design. All these flags, and those of the colonies, will be described, but before doing this there are three special 'states', part of the British Isles and closely linked to Great Britain, and yet with a large degree of independence, namely the Channel Islands, the Isle of Man and Northern Ireland; and also Wales.

WALES differs from all the other dependencies in that she is not independent but is governed by the British Parliament at West-minster.   Nevertheless, she has a distinctively national character, her own language, widely though not universally spoken, her own Prince, whose standard has been described in Chapter Two, and finally her own flag of which Welshmen are very proud.   This is the Red Dragon (Y Ddraig Goch) of Cadwallader displayed on a field divided horizontally white over green—the livery colours of Llewellyn, and later those of the Tudors (Plate 9, 1).   This flag received official recognition when it was announced in the House of Commons on February 23rd 1959 that Her Majesty the Queen had been pleased to command that in future only the Red Dragon on a white and green field was to be flown on Government buildings in Wales and where appropriate in London.

There are two other versions of the flag of Wales, one very similar to that described above, except that the dragon is standing on a 'mont vert' (green mountain).   The other also has a field

5

white over green divided horizontally and carrying in its centre the old Royal Badge of Wales, which dates from before the year 1800. This is the same red dragon, but Her Majesty Queen Elizabeth II

approved on March 11th 1953 that it should be augmented by a scroll carrying the words 'Y DDRAIG GOCH DDYRY CYCHWYN' in green letters on a white ground, the whole surmounted by the Royal Crown. This more elaborate flag is some-times used on special occasions as an alternative to the Red Dragon Flag described above.

Many churches in Wales flew a very beautiful, though unofficial, flag from about 1936 until the end of 1954. It consisted of a black cross on a golden field and is said to have been taken from

ROYAL BADGE
OF WALES

the arms of the manors of Llawhaden and Pebidiog (anciently known as Dewisland), of which the early Bishops of St. David's were barons. The Representative Body of the Church in Wales adopted a distinctive flag in ac-cordance with the Grant of Arms re-ceived from the College of Arms and dated December 9th 1954. It com-prises a white field charged with a royal blue St. George's Cross, and in the centre thereof a Celtic Cross in gold. This flag may be flown on any church within the Province of Wales.

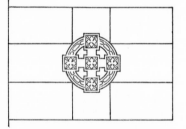

WELSH CHURCHES

NORTHERN IRELAND differs from Wales in that she has her own parliament and governs herself internally. Her National Flag is the Union of Great Britain, but she also has her own semi-official flag which in 1953 the Government assented to any citizen of Northern Ireland flying on any festive occasion or other occasions of rejoicing. This flag consists of a red St. George's Cross on a white field with in the centre the six-pointed white star (for the six counties, Antrim, Armagh, Down, Fermanagh, Londonderry and Tyrone). In this star is the red hand of Ulster (a right hand). One of the earliest references to this hand is in the description of the regimental flag used by Gordon O'Neill in 1646, which had a white field bearing a red hand with the motto 'PRO REGE ET PATRI PUGNO'. The star is surmounted by the Royal Crown (Plate 9, 2).

The Arms of Northern Ireland consist of a white shield bearing the red St. George's Cross and the badge described above, and the flag of the Governor of Northern Ireland consists of these arms on a yellow disc surrounded by a garland in the centre of the Union Flag of Great Britain.

The flag of the ISLE OF MAN is red with in the centre the 'three legs of Man' which are white with gold embellishments (Plate 9, 3). This device is the Arms of Man adopted by the native kings of the island in the 13th century. In the past some versions have shown the legs running in an anti-clockwise direction; however, a recent Government specification for the flag is that it is to be double-sided with two badges per flag which read clockwise. A Government circular of July 1968 instructs that in future the Manx Flag is to be flown from all public buildings and Government flagstaffs. It is felt that as the island has its own National Flag it is more appropriate that it be used rather than the Union Jack, and that this practice is no reflection on the Sovereign who bears the title of Lord of Man. The Lieutenant-Governor's flag is the Union with the Arms of Man, surrounded by a wreath, in the centre. This is flown from Government House when he is in residence. Manx ships are permitted to wear the Manx Flag in addition to the Red Ensign required by the Merchant Shipping Act.

The CHANNEL ISLANDS are very involved, for there are two separate principal authorities, Jersey and Guernsey. Alderney and Sark are dependencies of Guernsey, but, nevertheless, as described later, they all have their own flags, used in addition to the Union Flag of Great Britain.

JERSEY STATE FLAG

Jersey uses a white flag charged with a red diagonal cross. Although this flag has yet to receive the formal recognition of H.M.

Government it appears to have been established as the island's territorial flag for well over a century. Space will not permit a detailed account of its origin. Major N. V. L. Rybot, D.S.O., F.S.A., dealt with this very thoroughly in an article entitled 'The So-Called Jersey Flag' in *The Mariner's Mirror*, Vol. 37, No. 1, pp. 82–84, January 1951. This flag is flown on all official occasions on public buildings, as well as on business establishments. The Bailiff flies a diminutive of it on his motor-car. This flag is to all intents the same as the so-called flag of St. Patrick (*see* page 22).

In passing it is interesting to recall that when the Channel Islands were occupied by Germany during World War II, this flag was *worn as an ensign* by ships carrying passengers and cargo between the islands—the use of the Red Ensign being, for obvious reasons, out of the question!

JERSEY   GUERNSEY

The Lieutenant-Governor flies the Union Flag with a badge superimposed in the centre of the St. George's Cross. This badge consists of a red shield charged with three lions (sometimes referred to as leopards) passant guardant in gold (taken from the Seal), on a white circular background encircled by a garland.

The Lieutenant-Governor of GUERNSEY and its Dependencies, Alderney and Sark, flies the Union Flag with a similar badge, but in this case there is a sprig of golden leaves projecting from the top of the shield.

The State and Island Flag of Guernsey, the red Cross of St. George on a white field, is claimed by some to have been the official flag since 1907. However, it was announced in December 1935 that King George V 'was graciously pleased to sanction the continued

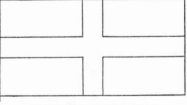

GUERNSEY STATE FLAG

use of the flag bearing the St. George's Cross on a white ground, as a distinct flag for Guernsey.' Unfortunately, those responsible for

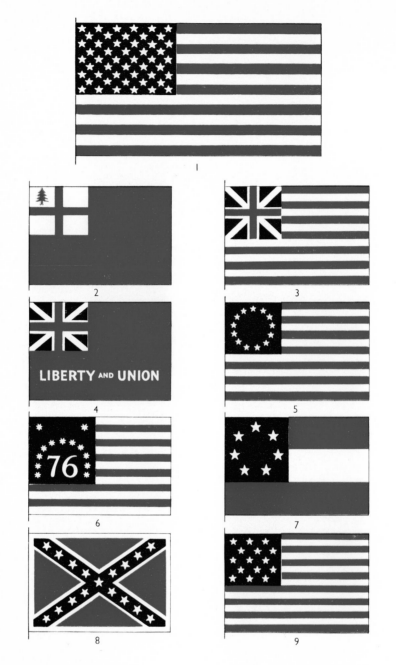

Plate 11   f.p. 59

FLAGS OF THE UNITED STATES OF AMERICA

Plate 11

FLAGS OF THE UNITED STATES OF AMERICA

advising the King omitted to include in their draft two important
words, namely, *on land*, the use of this flag *afloat* having been reserved
as the flag proper for a British Admiral in an Order-in-Council
dated July 9th 1864.   It can be flown by all and sundry in the island.

This flag also did duty as an ensign during World War II in the
same circumstances as the flag of Jersey, as recorded previously.

ALDERNEY also uses the St. George's Cross flag, but in the centre
thereof there is a device consisting of a golden lion wearing a red
crown and having a red tongue and claws and holding a sprig of
leaves; the background is green having an ornamental border in
gold.   This flag, which was approved by King Edward VII in
1906, is hoisted on official buildings only.

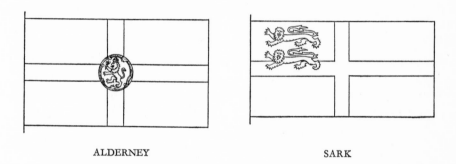

ALDERNEY   SARK

Although there is no official flag for SARK, the Seigneurial flag
has been used by the reigning Seigneur, or Dame, for many years.
It might be described as being a cross between a State flag and a
medieval personal banner denoting Territorial Sovereignty.   The
field is white with the red Cross of St. George, the first quarter being
'Gules, two lions—or leopards—passant guardant, Or'—known
heraldically as 'Normandy Ancient'—the lion in the base impinging
on the dexter arm of the cross.

In the last few years there have been considerable changes in the
form of government amongst the islands of the West Indies:
Jamaica, and Trinidad and Tobago which became independent in
1962 have been joined by Barbados; a number of the other islands
have become 'States in Association with Great Britain', whilst

others have retained their old status quo.   The 'States in Association' are Antigua, Dominica, Grenada, St. Christopher-Nevis-Anguilla, St. Lucia and St. Vincent.   All these states, with the exception of Dominica and St. Vincent, have adopted new and distinctive flags.

The new flag of ANTIGUA is proportioned three by two, and has a red field, in the centre of which a triangle is formed by joining the top of the hoist and top of the fly to the centre of the foot, or bottom.   This triangle is divided into three unequal horizontal stripes, black over light blue over white.   In the centre of the top stripe is a golden rising sun with rays (Plate **9,** 5).   Antigua has also acquired a new coat of arms in place of the old one which showed a landscape and calm sea.   The chief of the shield is black with a sun with nine rays; this rises from a sea of three white and three blue wavy bars.   From a green mount in the base rises a stone tower.   The crest is a pineapple in proper colours, and the supporters are two deer.   A scroll carries the motto 'EACH ENDEAVOURING, ALL ACHIEVING'.

ARMS OF
ANTIGUA

DOMINICA has decided to retain the Blue Ensign, defaced by her new badge which replaces the old badge which showed a sailing-ship, wearing a Red Ensign secured to a wharf; in the background were hills and a rising sun.   The new badge consists of the new Arms of Dominica; in these the shield is divided quarterly, the first and fourth quarters gold and the second and third blue.   In the first quarter is a coconut tree, in the second a toad, in the third a Carib canoe, and in the fourth a banana tree.   The crest is a lion, passant guardant, and the supporters two parrots.   The motto translated is 'AFTER THE GOOD LORD WE LOVE THE SOIL' (Plate **9,** 14).

DOMINICA: DETAIL
OF ARMS

GRENADA has chosen as her new flag a horizontal tricolour, blue at the top, then yellow, then green.   In the centre of the yellow stripe is an oval escutcheon, bordered in brown, carrying a branch of a nutmeg tree, complete with fruit. The proportions of this flag are three by two (Plate **9**, 4).

The islands of ST. CHRISTOPHER (or ST. KITTS), NEVIS and ANGUILLA have combined to form one state and have a vertical tricolour, light green at the hoist, then yellow and light blue. In the yellow stripe is a black palm-tree with three branches (Plate **9**, 8). Its proportions are two by one. A simplified flag, the tri-colour without the palm trees is flown by the ordinary citizens for everyday use. At the time of writing the relationship of An-guilla to the combined state is not

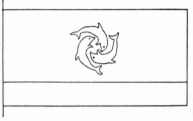

ANGUILLA

certain, and Anguilla has adopted a flag of her own; this is a white flag with a narrow pale blue stripe along the bottom, and in the centre of the white three pink dolphins arranged in a circle.

ST. LUCIA's flag has a plain blue field, proportions eight by five and carries a device consisting of a white and black triangular shape with, in its base, a golden triangle (Plate **9**, 6).

ST. VINCENT

ST. VINCENT has decided to retain the Blue Ensign, defaced by her badge as her National Flag. The badge has a blue disc with a sand-coloured base on which stands a yellow altar, on the dexter side a female figure robed in white bearing an olive branch, and on the sinister a kneeling female figure, also in white, presumably making a sacrifice. The motto is 'PAX ET JUSTICIA'—'Peace and Justice'.

In addition to the West Indian Islands that are states in associa-tion with Great Britain there are a number of other islands in the Western Atlantic that are still 'colonies'. Of these BERMUDA is of interest as she uses the Red Ensign, instead of the Blue used by other dependencies. On this Red Ensign are placed the Arms of Bermuda without any background. The arms consist of a white shield with a green grassy mound in the base on which is seated a red lion affronté.   The lion supports a scrolled shield upon which is represented the wreck of the *Sea Venture*, which in 1609, under the command of Admiral Sir George Somers, came to grief on the Sea Venture Flat.   The Flat is actually a sunken reef and not a high island as shown in the coat of arms (Plate 9, 9).   The arms as described above, placed on a disc and surrounded by a garland in the centre of the Union Flag, make the flag of the Governor.   Why Bermuda uses a Red Ensign as her National Flag when all other dependencies use a Blue is not known officially.   It may have been that the first settlers came to the island in merchant ships which would be wearing the Red Ensign.   Bermuda has one more un-usual custom, and that is that the old 1606 Union Flag is still flown from Gates Fort at the extreme eastern end of the Island over-looking the 'Town Cut', the main shipping channel to St. George, the original capital of Bermuda, and a place of great historical interest.

The flag badge of the BAHAMAS consists of a seascape with a ship, flying the Union Flag at the peak of the mizzen, chasing two pirate ships, surrounded by a garter bearing a motto the meaning of which is 'Commerce restored by the defeat of the pirates', sur-mounted by a crown, with 'BAHAMAS' on a scroll beneath.   This badge on a white disc is used to deface both the Red and the Blue Ensigns, and also within the customary wreath on the Union Flag as the flag of the Governor.   The defaced Red Ensign is used for ships and vessels and the Blue for civic use ashore.   The flag badge of the Bahamas was originally submitted to the Secretary of State for the Colonies in about 1850, but it was not until January 10th 1964 that it received Royal approval.

The Bahamas received a new constitution in January 1964 and the flag of the Premier of the Bahamas—used only by the Premier when on official visits and from a single staff to indicate that the House of Assembly is in session—has a blue field with the Arms of the Bahamas on a white disc in the centre.   This is similar in general design to the flag badge, except that it is placed on a shield.

BAHAMAS

The appropriate design for the BRITISH VIRGIN ISLANDS comprises a green shield charged with twelve golden oil lamps with red flames, and a female figure, attired in white and wearing sandals, carrying one of these lamps, placed on the Blue Ensign.

BRITISH VIR-
GIN ISLANDS

The CAYMAN ISLANDS were originally a dependency of Jamaica, having been annexed to Jamaica in 1873. On Jamaica attaining independence these islands remained as British Colonies and retained their old badges which are used to deface the Blue Ensigns, and so form the distinguishing flags of these colonies. The badge of the Cayman Islands is the

CAYMAN ISLANDS

arms granted by Royal Warrant dated May 14th 1958, and consisting of a shield having six wavy horizontal stripes, white and blue alternating, and three five-pointed green stars, edged in gold; on a red chief a lion passant guardant also in gold. The crest comprises a green turtle in front of a pineapple plant in gold, on a wreath of the colours, i.e. white and blue. Beneath the shield is the motto 'HE HATH FOUNDED IT UPON THE SEAS' in green lettering on a white scroll, shaded in red.

The blue shield of MONTSERRAT is charged with a black Latin or Passion Cross, erected on a light brown soil. Standing beside it is a female figure, in emerald green attire and wearing sandals, supporting a light brown harp with the left hand. It is positioned on a white disc in

MONTSERRAT

the centre of the fly of the Blue Ensign.

Like the Cayman Islands the TURKS AND CAICOS ISLANDS were formerly dependencies of Jamaica, but are now dependencies of Great Britain and have adopted a new coat of arms in place of the old rather enigmatic one of a sailing-ship and a man making salt. The new badge which defaces the Blue Ensign was granted on September 28th 1965. The new

TURKS AND CAICOS
ISLANDS

coat of arms, from which the flag badge is taken, consists of a golden shield with in chief a queen conch shell and a spiny lobster, and in base a Turk's head cactus proper. The crest is a pelican and the supporters two flamingoes.

BRITISH HONDURAS is famous for its mahogany. This is announced in its arms and in the badge, which is derived from the arms and is used on the Union Flag surrounded by a garland, and without the garland on the Blue Ensign. The badge has a scalloped gold edge, and is divided into three, with in the top left-hand corner the Union Flag, and the top right-hand side the axes and tools of the mahogany-feller. In the centre of the lower part is a barque at sea, under full sail.

BRITISH
HONDURAS

It is understood that discussions about a new constitution, and possible independence for British Honduras are being held, but that as yet no decisions have been reached.

The badge of the FALKLAND ISLANDS is the same as the new arms which were granted in 1948. It consists of a blue shield having three wavy bars in the lower half of which is superimposed the ship *Desire* in gold. In the chief there is a ram in natural colours standing upon tussac grass. The motto 'DESIRE THE RIGHT' in black letters is placed upon a scroll beneath the shield. Used on both the Union Flag and the Blue Ensign, it is encircled by the usual garland in the former case, and on a white circular background in the latter (Plate 9, 11).

The Falkland Islands Dependencies were divided on March 3rd 1962, South Georgia and South Sandwich Islands remaining dependencies, while the area south of 60° South forms a separate colony under a High Commissioner, and is known as the BRITISH ANTARCTIC TERRITORY. A new coat of arms has been prepared for that territory, but so far no flag badge has been approved for superimposing on the Union Flag or Blue Ensign.

ARMS OF BRITISH ANTARCTIC TERRITORY

Sᴛ. Hᴇʟᴇɴᴀ has rather an ugly badge.   On the Union Flag it has
the usual circular background surrounded by a garland, while on
the Blue Ensign it has no background at all.   The scroll round
the shield is yellow with a pink riband stretched
across the top.   On a vivid green sea against blue
sky is an Indiaman, the red Cross of St. George
flying from her stern, sailing between two cliffs, the
nearer one black, the other brown.   St. Helena
has several dependent islands of which the prin-
cipals are Aꜱᴄᴇɴꜱɪᴏɴ Iꜱʟᴀɴᴅ and Tʀɪꜱᴛᴀɴ ᴅᴀ
Cᴜɴʜᴀ.   Before Ascension became a dependency
of St. Helena the island was administered by the Admiralty and
flew the White Ensign.

ꜱᴛ. ʜᴇʟᴇɴᴀ

Gɪʙʀᴀʟᴛᴀʀ has a triple-towered castle (in natural colour) and
a golden key on a red ornamental shield for its
badge.   On the Union Flag the white background
and garland are used, but on the Blue Ensign this
garland is omitted.   The motto 'Mᴏɴᴛɪꜱ Iɴ-
ꜱɪɢɴɪᴀ Cᴀʟᴘᴇ' (Gibraltar was the 'Mons Calpe'
of the ancients), reads: 'The Badge of Mount
Calpe'.   It is hardly necessary to remark that the
key symbolises the Rock as being the key to the
Mediterranean.   In addition to the official flag

Gɪʙʀᴀʟᴛᴀʀ

there is an unofficial flag that is
flown by many of the inhabitants;
this has a white field proportions
two by one, with a red stripe at the
bottom and is charged with the
badge of the three-towered castle
of Gibraltar from which is suspended a golden key.

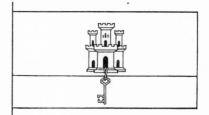

Gɪʙʀᴀʟᴛᴀʀ

The old badge of the Sᴇʏᴄʜᴇʟʟᴇꜱ
was redesigned in April 1961.   It is now oval in shape, with the
seascape comprising a green island and a two-masted schooner in
full sail; on a sandy foreshore is a tortoise in front of a tall palm-tree,
all in natural colours.   This badge has a decorated border bearing
the inscription 'Sᴇʏᴄʜᴇʟʟᴇꜱ' in red and 'Fɪɴɪꜱ Cᴏʀᴏɴᴀᴛ Oᴘᴜꜱ'

('The end crowns the work') in green, all on a white disc (Plate **9**, 7).   The usual garland surrounds the white disc when it appears on the Union Flag, but not when it is borne on the Blue Ensign.

When the state of Malaysia was formed BRUNEI elected to remain as a dependency of Great Britain.   Her State Flag has a yellow field, proportions two by one, with a band (divided horizontally white over black, the white part somewhat broader than the black) running diagonally from near the top of the hoist to near the bottom of the fly.   A red device or 'arms' is placed in the centre of the diagonal band; this consists of a pylon with wings, surmounted by a flag, 'growing' out of a horizontally placed crescent; it is supported by two forearms, and beneath is a scroll with a motto, the translation of which reads: 'ALWAYS RENDER SERVICE WITH GOD'S GUIDANCE' (Plate **9**, 13).

HONG KONG

HONG KONG used to have a harbour scene in its circular badge.   It depicted an island in the background and some tea chests on a quay in the foreground, with a three-masted sailing-ship and a junk anchored in mid-stream.   This badge was superseded in 1959 by one bearing the new arms of the colony (granted by a Royal Warrant, dated January 21st 1959) as shown in the accompanying illustration.   Incidentally, H.R.H. Prince Philip, Duke of Edinburgh, presented these arms on March 7th 1959, during his visit.

Great Britain is responsible, in varying degrees, for the adminis-tration of a number of the many islands in the Pacific Ocean.   Two, the British Solomon Islands and the Kingdom of Tonga are 'protectorates', the remaining dependencies are, with one excep-tion, colonies.   The exception is the New Hebrides Group which is administered by an Anglo-French Condominium Govern-ment.

The KINGDOM OF TONGA has a very distinctive and colourful suite of national flags.   The State Flag has a red field with a rec-tangular white canton charged with a truncated red cross, very similar to the well-known Red Cross of the International Red Cross Society (Plate **9**, 10).   The Flag of the Customs Service is very

Plate 12

FLAGS OF THE UNITED STATES OF AMERICA

(See pp. 88–90)

1 Alabama

2 Alaska

3 Arizona

4 Arkansas

5 California

6 Colorado

7 Connecticut

8 Delaware

9 Florida

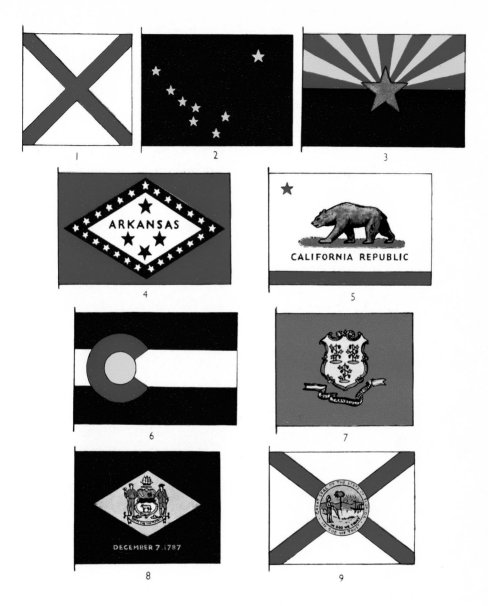

Plate 12   f.p. 66

FLAGS OF THE UNITED STATES OF AMERICA

similar, but it is blue with a broad white stripe along the bottom
edge bearing the letters H.M.C.   The Standard of the Sovereign
of Tonga is a very handsome flag;
it has a quartered field, (1) yellow
charged with three white stars
having six points, (2) red bearing a crown in proper colours,
(3) a bird in flight with an olive
branch in its beak in white on
a light blue ground and (4) yellow
charged with three grey swords.
Overall in the centre of the flag
a white six-pointed star charged
with the red cross from the State Flag.

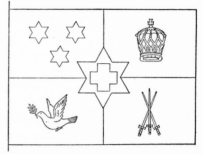

TONGA: SOVEREIGN'S STANDARD

FIJI uses its arms, without any background, on the Blue Ensign,
but on the Union Flag of the Governor the arms are on the usual
white disc surrounded with the garland.   The shield of the arms
has a red chief charged with a golden lion holding
a cocoa pod in its forepaws.   The remainder of
the shield is white and divided into four quarters
by a red St. George's Cross.   In the first
quarter are three sugar canes, in the second a
coconut palm, in the third a flying dove with a
sprig of olive in its beak, and in the last a bunch
of bananas.   The crest is a Fijian outrigger
canoe, the supporters two Fijians wearing the
'Tapa sulu', a kilt of mulberry tree bark cloth.   The motto,
'RERE VAKA NA KALOU KA DOKA NA TUI' is the Fijian for 'Fear
God and honour the King'. The Governor of Fiji is responsible
for the administration of the island of Pitcairn.

FIJI

The High Commissioner for the Western Pacific is situated at
Honiara in the British Solomon Islands Protectorate and is responsible for the administration of the British Solomon Islands Protectorate, the Gilbert and Ellice Islands, the Central and Southern
Line Islands and the New Hebrides which is an Anglo-French
Condominium.   In each of these dependencies there is a Resident,
the representative of the High Commissioner.   The badge of the

High Commissioner of the Western Pacific consists of the Royal Crown above the letters W.P.H.C. on a white disc which, surrounded by a garland, is placed in the centre of the Union Flag.

The BRITISH SOLOMON ISLANDS PROTECTORATE follows the normal custom of using the Blue Ensign on which is displayed the badge of the protectorate. The original rather dull badge consisting of the words 'BRITISH SOLOMON ISLANDS PROTECTORATE' was replaced, first in 1947 by a badge consisting of a red shield which bore a turtle standing erect,

WESTERN PACIFIC
HIGH
COMMISSIONER

and finally in 1956 when the present arms were granted by a Royal Warrant dated September 24th. These arms are a quartered shield, bright blue and white with in chief a golden lion 'passant guardant' on a red field. The quarters of the shield are (1) a Sandfordi eagle perched on a branch, (2) a turtle standing erect, (3) a bow surmounted by two spears, heads upwards, in saltire and two spears, heads downwards, also in saltire, and overall a Melanesian dancing shield, and (4) two frigate birds one above the other. All these charges are in natural colours and placed on a white disc on the Blue Ensign (Plate 9, 12).

The archipelago of islands running south-south-east from Hawaii are known as the 'Line Islands'. There are two groups within this complex which are the responsibility of Great Britain: first the colony known as the GILBERT AND ELLICE ISLANDS, consisting of the Washington, Fanning and Christmas Islands. Their badge, which is used in the usual way on the Blue Ensign and Union Flag, is a shield having blue and white wavy bands in the base, representing the sea, with the sun and a frigate bird in gold set against a red sky.

GILBERT AND
ELLICE ISLANDS
COLONY

The remainder of the Line Islands that are administered by Great Britain, the CENTRAL AND SOUTHERN LINE ISLANDS, are composed of the islands of Malden, Starbuck, Caroline, Vostock and Flint.

And finally the NEW HEBRIDES, administered by the Anglo-

French Condominium.   Their badge is simply the Royal Crown in proper colours placed on a white disc with the lettering 'NEW

HEBRIDES'.   On the Union Flag it has the usual garland but not on the Blue Ensign.   On these islands there is a French Resident as well as the British one, and the French tricolour flies side by side with the British flag.

Chapter Four

NORTH AMERICA

CANADA's first official National Flag was inaugurated by a Royal Proclamation dated February 15th 1965, thus concluding a controversy which had raged for many years.

The new flag is described as a red flag, proportions two by one, containing in the centre a white square the width of the flag, bearing a single red maple leaf; in heraldic terms it is described as 'gules on a Canadian pale argent a maple leaf of the first'. The shade of red is the same as that used in the British Union Flag and Red Ensign (Plate 10, 1).

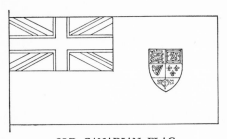

OLD CANADIAN FLAG

Prior to the adoption of this flag, which might be called the 'Maple Leaf Flag', Canada used a Red Ensign defaced with the country's arms. This flag was the Ensign for Canada's merchant ships, and was introduced as such in 1892. In 1924 the Canadian Government approved this flag as 'the distinctive flag for Canada overseas'. In 1945 it was approved for general use. Although this flag never received Royal approval it was to all intents and purposes the National Flag of Canada. It has now been entirely superseded.

In the early part of 1968 an Ensign for the Armed Forces of Canada was introduced. This is a handsome flag; the field is white, and in the canton is the National Maple Leaf Flag of Canada. In the fly is a badge which is very similar to the badge of the Chief of the Defence Staff of Great Britain, i.e. a shield carrying a 'foul' anchor, crossed swords and an eagle in flight, surmounted by the

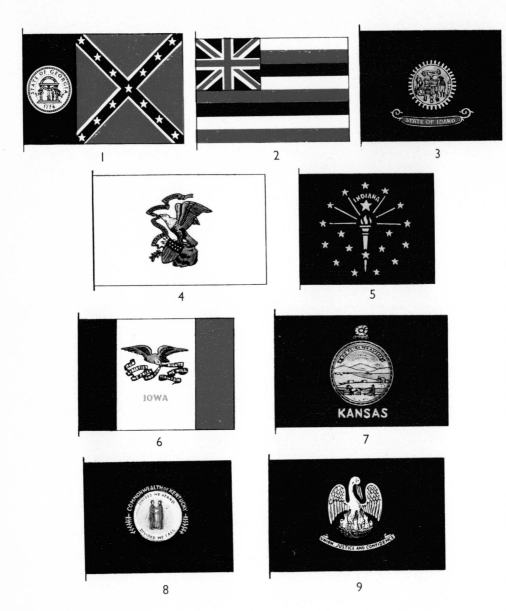

Plate 13   f.p. 71

FLAGS OF THE UNITED STATES OF AMERICA

Plate 13

FLAGS OF THE UNITED STATES OF AMERICA

(See pp. 88–90)

1 Georgia

2 Hawaii

3 Idaho

4 Illinois

5 Indiana

6 Iowa

7 Kansas

8 Kentucky

9 Louisiana

Imperial Crown, and in this case surrounded by a wreath of maple leaves (Plate 10, 2).

At the time of writing it is not quite clear as to how this new ensign will be used as ships of the Royal Canadian Navy will still wear the National Maple Leaf Flag as an ensign, though they have now a new 'Jack'. This is very similar to the Ensign of the Armed Forces, except that the badge in the fly consists only of the anchor and eagle surmounted by a naval crown, all in dark blue.

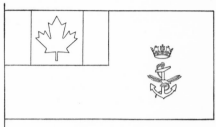

CANADIAN NAVAL JACK

The Royal Canadian Navy retains the white masthead pennant of the same design as the Royal Navy, and also the same distinguishing flags for flag officers as are in use in the British Navy.

The Canadian Army are retaining their old Regimental Colours, and the Royal Canadian Air Force will fly the National Flag as an ensign, with below it the new Ensign of the Armed Forces.

In 1961 Royal Approval was given to the design of the Queen's Personal Flag for Canada (*see* page 26). This consists of the Arms of Canada as granted by Royal Warrant dated November 21st 1921, with the Queen's device of the crowned 'E' upon a royal blue ground, surrounded by a chaplet of gold roses, placed in the centre of the flag (Plate 5, 2).

GOVERNOR-GENERAL OF CANADA

The Governor-General uses the usual blue flag.

A distinctive flag for Anglican Churches in Canada was adopted in 1955. It is a red St. George's Cross on a white field, each quarter being charged with a green maple leaf. If he so wishes, a diocesan bishop may use this flag with the diocesan arms superimposed on the centre of the St. George's Cross. The General Synod displays its own arms in the same manner on the flag.

6

Each of the ten Canadian provinces has its own arms, and also in recent times nearly all have adopted a provincial flag, which in each case embodies these arms. These flags and arms are described below. Each province has its Lieutenant-Governor who uses the Union Flag with the arms of the province in the centre on a white disc and surrounded by a green garland.

The Arms of ALBERTA were granted by Royal Warrant dated May 30th 1907. The upper part of the shield is white with a red St. George's Cross; in the base is a wheatfield with a landscape of prairie fields and mountains in the distance. The flag, or banner as it is called, has an ultramarine blue field with in the centre the arms of the province in full colour. The proportions of the flag are two by one (Plate 10, 11).

The shield of the Arms of BRITISH COLUMBIA was granted by Royal Warrant dated March 31st 1906 and the crest and supporters have become part of the achievement by usage. The shield is white with three wavy blue bars and rising from the base a sun 'in his splendour'. In chief is the Union Flag with in its centre an antique crown in gold; the crest is the Royal Crown surmounted by a lion 'statant guardant'; the supporters are on the dexter side a wapiti and on the sinister a mountain sheep. The flag is the shield, stretched horizontally to the proportions five by three (Plate 10, 7). The Provincial Flag was authorised by Order in Council dated June 20th 1960.

MANITOBA has a green shield with a buffalo or bison standing on a rock. In chief is a red St. George's Cross on a white field. The flag is the Red Ensign defaced by the shield described above. The new flag was proclaimed on May 12th 1966 (Plate 10, 10).

NEW BRUNSWICK was granted her arms by Royal Warrant dated May 26th 1868, and they consist of a golden shield with in the base blue and white wavy bars representing the sea on which a black 'lymphad' (galley) with a white sail and red flags and oars in action sails towards the dexter side. In chief 'gules' (red) a golden lion passant guardant. These arms, like those of British Columbia, drawn out horizontally to proportions three by two make the Provincial Flag which was adopted by proclamation dated February 24th 1965 (Plate 10, 3).

The official Provincial Flag of NEWFOUNDLAND AND LABRADOR is still the Union Jack, but in addition to this, Newfoundland uses a Blue Ensign for Government vessels and a Red for merchant ships; both ensigns are defaced by a badge which is circular and shows Mercury, the God of Commerce and Merchandise, presenting to Britannia a fisherman who is kneeling and offering

BADGE OF
NEWFOUNDLAND

the gifts of the sea. In the top of the circle are the words 'TERRA NOVA' and in the bottom the legend 'HAEC TIBI DONA FERO',

ARMS OF
NEWFOUNDLAND

'I bring you these gifts'. The Arms of Newfoundland, which were granted as long ago as January 1st 1637, are entirely different from the flag badge and consist of a chocolate-coloured shield (still called 'gules' heraldically) with a white St. George's Cross. In the first and fourth quarters is a golden crowned lion 'passant guardant', and in the other two a white unicorn. The crest is a moose and the supporters are two natives. The motto is 'QUAERITE PRIME REGNUM DEI', 'Seek ye first the Kingdom of God'.

NOVA SCOTIA's flag, as befits her origins, consists of the blue St. Andrew's Cross on a white field, with in the centre on an escutcheon the Royal Arms of Scotland, a gold shield on which is a red lion rampant within a double red border or 'tressure flory counter-flory gules' (Plate 10, 6). The Arms of Nova Scotia have on the shield the same basic design as that on the flag with a crest and supporters and the motto 'MUNIT HAEC ET ALTERA VINCIT', 'One defends and the other conquers'.

ARMS OF
NOVA
SCOTIA

The arms of ONTARIO are a green shield with in the top a red St. George's Cross on a white field, and in the base three leaves of maple. The crest is a bear, and the supporters are on the dexter side a moose and on the sinister a Canadian deer. The motto in

English is 'Loyal in the beginning, so it remained'.   The flag is the
Red Ensign defaced with the shield of the arms (Plate 10, 9).

The Arms of PRINCE EDWARD ISLAND are on a white shield with
on a green mound an oak tree and three saplings; the upper part is
one of the golden lions of England on a red field, and the motto
'PARVE SUB INGENTI', 'The small under the protection of the great'.
The flag consists of the shield drawn out horizontally to the proportions of six units to four with a red and white fringe a quarter of
a unit thick (Plate 10, 5).

QUEBEC's Arms were adopted in 1939 and consist of a shield
equally divided horizontally into three parts, blue at the top, then
red and then gold.   In the top blue panel are three golden fleurs-de-
lis, in the centre an English golden lion and in the base a maple sprig
with three leaves.   The motto reads 'JE ME SOUVIENS', 'I re-
member'.   The field of the flag is sky blue charged with a white
St. George's Cross, and in each quarter is a white fleur-de-lis
(Plate 10, 4).

SASKATCHEWN has a green shield with in the bottom three golden
sheaves of wheat and in chief a red lion on a golden field.   The flag,
the proportions of which are three by two, is divided equally into
two horizontal parts, red on top with the shield of the arms in the
fly, and green below.   A golden 'stylised' ear of corn is in the hoist
(Plate 10, 8).

YUKON
TERRITORY

NORTH-WEST
TERRITORIES

The Arms of the YUKON and the
NORTH-WEST TERRITORIES are as yet
not officially adopted.   That of the
Yukon is described heraldically as
'Azure on a Pallet wavy Argent a
like Pallet of the field issuant from
the base two Piles reversed Gules
edged also Argent each charged
with two Besants in pale on a Chief
Argent a Cross Gules surmounted of a Rounded Vair'; and that of
the North-west Territories 'Per bend wavy Gules and Vert Billety
Or in sinister Chief the Mask of an arctic Fox Argent on a Chief
indented also Argent a Barrulet wavy Azure'.

The Yukon Territory has now adopted a flag.   It is a white flag,

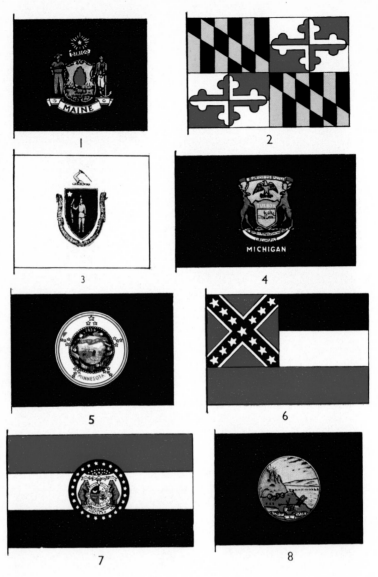

1

2

3

4

5

6

7

8

Plate 14   f.p. 75

FLAGS OF THE UNITED STATES OF AMERICA

Plate 14

FLAGS OF THE UNITED STATES OF AMERICA

(See pp. 88–90)

1 Maine

2 Maryland

3 Massachusetts

4 Michigan

5 Minnesota

6 Mississippi

7 Missouri

8 Montana

proportions two by one with a green vertical stripe to the hoist, and a blue stripe to the fly. The centre of the flag is charged with the full Arms of Yukon which are the badge described above, surmounted by a mameluke (dog) standing on a mount of snow proper (i.e. black and white); beneath is a wreath of fireweed, the floral emblem of the Yukon (Plate 10, 12).

One of the most widely known transport companies is the Canadian Pacific. They operate a number of services which all have flags of the same basic design (Plate 39, 6) but each having its own colour scheme: CP Rail, red; CP Air, orange; CP Ships, green (Plate 39, 6); CP Transport, blue; CP Hotels, grey; and CP Telecommunications, yellow ochre.

As has been stated in Chapter One, page 3, it is now generally believed that the first flag to fly in what is now the UNITED STATES OF AMERICA was the Raven Flag of the Vikings who, under Leif Ericsson, are reputed to have landed in the vicinity of the Cape Cod peninsular in about the year 1000 A.D.

The first voyage of Columbus in 1492 was made possible by King Ferdinand and Queen Isabella of the Kingdoms of Leon and Castile. He discovered islands in the West Indies and took possession of one of them, San Salvador, in the name of his sovereigns on October 12th of that year. Two flags were carried ashore for the ceremony: the Royal Banner displaying the Arms of Castile and Leon quartered, and a special white one, having a swallow-tailed fly, charged with a Latin Cross in green, with the letters 'F' and 'Y' (for Fernando and Ysabel) in gold on either side of the lower portion of the vertical limb, each surmounted by a golden crown. These are generally recognised as being the first European flags in America.

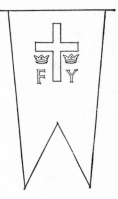

FLAG OF COLUMBUS

The first flag to be flown on the mainland proper was that of the Kingdom of England, the red Cross of St. George on

a white field, which John Cabot hoisted near Cape Breton in 1497.

Ponce de Leon landed in Florida in 1512, and planted the Castile-Leon flag. Twelve years later Verrazano the Florentine raised the lilies of France on behalf of King Francis I in North America. They were again hoisted in 1534; this time by the French explorer, Jacques Cartier, when he landed and claimed that portion of land which later became Quebec.

In 1609 Hudson arrived in the *Half Moon* at New Amsterdam (later to be called New York) wearing the flag of the Dutch East India Company, a horizontal tricolour, orange (on top), white, and light blue with the letters 'V.O.C.', in black, on the white stripe, these being the initials of the Vereenigde Oost-Indische Compagnie (*see* page 90).

In 1621 these letters were replaced by the monogram of the Dutch West India Company—'G.W.C.'—(Geoctroyeerde West-Indische Compagnie), the 'G' being on the left outer bar of the 'W', and the 'C' on the right.

The Pilgrim Fathers landed on Plymouth beach, now Massachusetts, on Christmas Day 1620. The famous *Mayflower* in which they sailed wore the British Union Flag (1606–1801 pattern, Plate 3, 4) at the main, and the red Cross of St. George on a white field, at the fore.

As Charles I, on May 5th 1634, had restricted the use of the Union Flag to the Royal Navy, the National Flags of England and Scotland, those of St. George and St. Andrew respectively, were used for public departments and the merchant services; and when in 1643 the colonies of Plymouth, Massachusetts Bay and New Haven became the United Colonies of New England they adopted as their flag the Red Ensign of Britain as it was then, with the addition of a green pine tree in the first quarter of the St. George's Cross in the canton (Plate 11, 2). Many old flag books show the New England flag as the Blue Ensign, but it is now generally agreed that this is not correct, and that the red was the first flag. Although New England came into being in 1643 the flag described above does not appear to have come into general use until 1686. By the year 1707 many of the colonies were using flags of their own; these were probably the forerunners of the State Flags of the present time.

The first Congress met at New York in October 1765, and the organised opposition to the Stamp Act gained such force that in 1766 the Act was repealed. But the issue could not be too long delayed, and in December 1773 came the Boston Tea Party.

With that began the war and the making of many flags. Massachusetts had its tree; New York its black beaver on a white field; South Carolina its handsome silver crescent on blue, designed by Moultrie, which was soon afterwards replaced by the very unpleasant yellow with a rattlesnake on it; Rhode Island, best of all, had the white bearing the blue anchor of hope; there is no need to give them all, but they were so various, and so disfigured with mottoes, that none would, or could without jealousy, be adopted as a national flag. A national flag was wanted; what was it to be?

The answer came on January 1st 1776, when a flag was hoisted at Prospect Hill in Somerville, or, as some writers would have it, at Cambridge, where General Washington had his headquarters— less than two miles away.

This flag is known as the Great (or Grand) Union Flag or the Cambridge Flag (Plate 11, 3). It had seven red and six white horizontal stripes, and in the first canton the British Union Flag. It appears to have been designed and adopted for use in naval vessels and on fortresses, not as a battle flag for the army, as some have suggested. Strange to say, there has yet to be found a record of its having been officially adopted by the Continental Congress, in spite of the fact that it soon became known variously as the 'Congress Flag', the 'Union Flag', and as the 'Colours' of the United Colonies.

As to what facts actually governed the first design of the 'Cambridge' flag much speculation exists. In the United States there seems to be a belief that a clear-cut origin will never be discovered; this is a great pity, for, after all, it is still less than two hundred years since the hoisting of the flag took place.

Several reasons have been given for it. Here are two.

The thirteen stripes stood for the thirteen states which were revolting against the Mother Country, while the Union was inserted to prove that loyalty still existed, and that there was still a hope that the colonies would not be forced to break away.

The British Red Ensign was used, six white stripes being placed thereon, so that the colonists should have a distinctive flag.

To complicate the issue, the Cambridge Flag was very similar to the ensign of the East India Company. Some writers state that it was the same, but this appears incorrect, as all old illustrations show the East India flag as having nine horizontal stripes, five red and four white, whereas the Cambridge Flag had thirteen stripes, seven red and six white; both flags had the Union Flag of Britain in the upper canton.

Probably the reason this design was chosen was the simple one that flags with horizontal stripes were very common; Bowles, in his *Naval Flags* of 1790, shows numerous such flags.

During the period 1776–95 merchant ships, with which are included privateers, wore an ensign consisting of thirteen stripes with no Union Flag or other device in the upper canton. There are a number of old prints showing such ships in the National Maritime Museum at Greenwich, and the interesting thing is that while in the majority the ensign is shown as being of red and white stripes, there are quite a few where the stripes are red, white and blue—almost green in one case. Whether this is due to artistic licence or inaccuracy, or whether the flag was the design of the master of the ship, remain unanswered questions, but it is interesting to note that Hawaii has a flag whose field is striped red, white and blue (Plate 13, 2).

It was obvious, however, that this new flag would not do, for it most undoubtedly had a drawback in the Union which could not be explained away.

No surprise will therefore be felt that some change was soon asked for. The stripes did very well—nothing could be better— but what was to replace the Union in the upper canton?

Surely the obvious reply must have been white stars, and as there were thirteen states, there should be thirteen stars.

So the Continental Congress on June 14th 1777 'Resolved, that the Flag of the United States be thirteen stripes alternate red and white, that the Union be thirteen stars white on a blue field, representing a constellation.'

It will be noted that the resolution does not give specific details, such as the proportions of the field and its blue canton containing the thirteen stars. The design of the flag is reputed to be that illustrated on Plate 11, 5, but documentary evidence proving that this is indeed the case has yet to be brought to light. The first Stars and Stripes to be flown in battle by land forces seems to have been the famous 76 Flag flown in the battle of Bennington, August 16th 1777. Its outer stripes were white and the stars had seven points (Plate 11, 6). There are some who consider that this was the first Stars and Stripes to have thirteen stars, but the evidence is uncertain.

In spite of all that has been written—and it is considerable—about George Washington's Arms being responsible for the Stars and Stripes, or the part Mrs. Betsy Ross of Philadelphia is supposed to have played in the construction of the first flag, we cannot perhaps do better than quote the well-known American authority, M. M. Quaife, who wrote, in 1942, as follows: 'Homer, alive, attracted but scant attention; when safely dead, and assured of immortality, numerous Grecian cities eagerly claimed him as their son. A like obscurity shrouds the birth of the Stars and Stripes. No one bothered at the time to record the name of its creator, or claim the honour for himself.'

The thirteen states were New Hampshire, Massachusetts, Rhode Island, Connecticut, Delaware, Maryland, Virginia, North Carolina, South Carolina, Georgia, New York, New Jersey and Pennsylvania. Vermont joined in 1791 and Kentucky (which was part of Virginia formed into a separate state, just as Tennessee was afterwards formed out of North Carolina) in 1792. Here were, therefore, fifteen states, and not thirteen, and to meet the new conditions Congress on January 15th 1794, enacted that 'from and after the 1st day of May 1795, the flag of the United States be fifteen stripes and the Union be fifteen stars' (Plate 11, 9).

There was little difficulty in dealing with an increase among the stars, though every additional star weakened the artistic effect, but by 1818, when five other states had been brought in, and the future had others in store, it became evident that the original idea of a stripe for each state would simply ruin the appearance of the flag by making it look like a piece of shirting; and on April 4th of that year Congress enacted that the stripes should be reduced permanently to the original number of thirteen, and that the Union, should then have twenty stars, and that for each new state admitted a star should be added on the next Independence Day, July 4th, following its admission to the Union. Readers have not infrequently asked for a list showing how the number of stars was increased and when each successive design was brought into use. Since the original design came into use on June 14th 1777, there have been twenty-seven official changes in the number of stars, the last being on July 4th 1960 (*see* Table on page 81, *also* Plate 11, 1).

Before proceeding, we must first retrace our steps and give a brief account of the ephemeral flags of the Confederacy.

When the eleven Southern states seceded from the Union in 1860 and formed the Confederation, the Government made no change in the Stars and Stripes, and did not omit the stars which represented its enemies.

The first Confederate Flag was adopted on March 5th 1861, and was known as the 'Stars and Bars' (Plate 11, 7). It consisted of a field, horizontally red over white over red. A large square canton covered the left-hand halves of the top and middle stripes. It was blue and had a circle of seven white stars upon it. This flag also did duty as the Ensign of the Confederate Navy.

It soon became evident that the Confederate armies needed a more distinctive flag for use in the field, and so the Battle Flag was designed and adopted (Plate 11, 8).

On May 1st 1863 it was decreed that the Stars and Bars should be superseded by a new flag. This had a white field, two by one, with the aforementioned Battle Flag as a square canton which occupied two-thirds of the depth of the hoist, and became known as the Second Confederate Flag. Nearly four weeks later the Secretary of the Navy signed an order (dated May 26th 1863) instructing warships to hoist this flag as the Ensign, and the Battle Flag mentioned above as a Jack. However, the proportions of the Ensign were three by two, not two by one.

DESIGN	NUMBER OF STARS	DATE WHEN BROUGHT INTO USE		ADDITIONAL STATES REPRESENTED
1st	13	June 14th 1777		—
2nd	15	May 1st 1795		Vermont and Kentucky
3rd	20	July 4th 1818		Tennessee, Ohio, Louisiana, Indiana, and Mississippi
4th	21	„	1819	Illinois
5th	23	„	1820	Alabama and Maine
6th	24	„	1822	Missouri
7th	25	„	1836	Arkansas
8th	26	„	1837	Michigan
9th	27	„	1845	Florida
10th	28	„	1846	Texas
11th	29	„	1847	Iowa
12th	30	„	1848	Wisconsin
13th	31	„	1851	California
14th	32	„	1858	Minnesota
15th	33	„	1859	Oregon
16th	34	„	1861	Kansas
17th	35	„	1863	West Virginia
18th	36	„	1865	Nevada
19th	37	„	1867	Nebraska
20th	38	„	1877	Colorado
21st	43	„	1890	North Dakota, South Dakota, Montana, Washington, and Idaho
22nd	44	„	1891	Wyoming
23rd	45	„	1896	Utah
24th	46	„	1908	Oklahoma
25th	48	„	1912	New Mexico and Arizona
26th	49	„	1959	Alaska
27th	50	„	1960	Hawaii

In certain circumstances—i.e. in bad or indifferent visibility—the Second Confederate Flag was extremely difficult to recognise at a distance, so on March 4th 1865 a large red stripe was added to it down the edge of the fly. At the same time it was decided to alter the proportions of the field to three by two, slightly reduce the size of the canton, and make the width of the red stripe equal to one half of the flag, measuring from the canton.

The way that the National Flag of the United States developed has been explained on pages 77–80, and it can be seen from the table above that by the year 1912 it had acquired forty-eight stars, but although the number of the stars and stripes had been fixed this did not apply to the other details of the flag. For instance the proportions of the flag were not laid down, neither were there any instructions which defined how the stars were to be arranged in the canton, with the result that there were many variations of the flag. This chaotic state of affairs was ended by President Taft who by executive orders, dated June 24th and October 29th 1912, limited flags to certain sizes, defined the proportions and furnished a plan, which was published by the Navy Department, showing the exact configuration of the National Flag. The dimensions prescribed in these orders were:

Hoist (breadth of flag)	1 unit
Fly (length of flag)	1·9 units
Hoist of canton	7/13 unit
Fly of canton	·76 unit
Width of each stripe	1/13 unit
Diameter of each star	·0616 unit

There have been some minor variations since, but the basic design introduced under President Taft has been retained, although it was not until 1934 that the exact shades of colour were standardised.

The forty-ninth and fiftieth stars were added for Alaska and Hawaii (Plate 11, 1) on July 4th 1959, and July 4th 1960, respectively. However the proportions of the flag and its canton remain as heretofore.

This flag is something more than the National Flag to the citizen of the United States of America—it is the symbol of the nation to which he or she owes allegiance, just as we owe ours to the Throne. The *Pledge to the Flag* is as follows: 'I pledge allegiance to the Flag of the United States of America, and to the Republic for which it stands, one nation under God, indivisible, with liberty and justice for all.' The *Flag Code*, which is a very strict one, consists of a comprehensive set of rules governing the display and use of the flag.

There are a very large number of official flags in use in the United States; the space available will allow for the mention of but a few of them.

Plate 15

FLAGS OF THE UNITED STATES OF AMERICA

(See pp. 88–90)

1 Nebraska

2 Nevada

3 New Hampshire

4 New Jersey

5 New Mexico

6 New York State

7 North Carolina

8 North Dakota

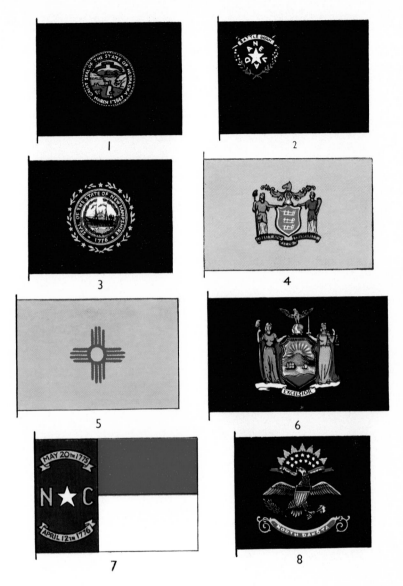

Plate 15   f.p. 82

FLAGS OF THE UNITED STATES OF AMERICA

The President's Standard is dark blue; in the centre thereof is a representation of the Seal of the President of the United States surrounded by a circle of small white five-pointed stars—one for each state (Plate 1, 1). That of the Vice-President has a white background with a slightly different spread-eagle device in the centre, encircled with thirteen small dark blue five-pointed stars.

U.S. SECRETARY OF
DEFENCE

Heads of Executive Departments with civilian status have four stars, one in each of their respective flags.

The Secretary of Defence flies a blue flag charged with a central device, in proper colours, which is taken from the Seal of his Department; in each corner of the flag there is a small white five-pointed star.

The Ensign of the U.S. Navy and also the U.S. Merchant Navy is the National Flag. The dark blue canton with the fifty stars is used by the Navy as the Jack; it is called the 'Union Jack'. Naval vessels in commission fly the Warship Pennant at the masthead.

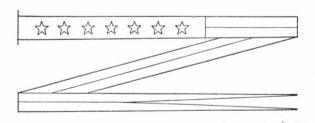

U.S. WARSHIP PENNANT

This is dark blue at the hoist and is charged with seven five-pointed stars; the remainder is divided horizontally, red over white, with a long slit in the fly.

The flag of the Secretary of the Navy is dark blue with in the centre a large white foul anchor with four white stars, one in each

corner.　Each of the Flag Officers of the Navy has his distinguishing flag.　Fleet or five-star Admirals have five stars disposed in a

U.S. SECRETARY OF NAVY

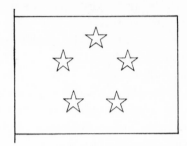

U.S. FLEET ADMIRAL

pentagon on a dark blue field; that of an Admiral has four stars
in a diamond formation, the Vice-Admiral's three stars are in

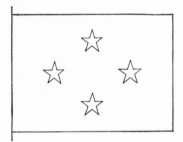

U.S. ADMIRAL

a triangle, and the Rear-Admiral's
two vertically one above the other.
The Broad Pennant of the Commodore has one star.　The colour of the
field of all sea-going Admirals is dark
blue with white stars; the flags of
Vice-Admirals and Rear-Admirals not
eligible for a command at sea have
white flags with blue stars.

In addition to the flags described
above the Navy has a Ceremonial Flag or Colour.　This has a
dark blue field with a golden fringe; in the centre there is a three-

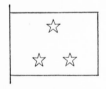

U.S. VICE-ADMIRAL

U.S. REAR-ADMIRAL

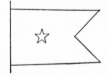

U.S. COMMODORE

masted ship, a conventional anchor and the American eagle, the
whole enclosed in a cable-laid rope (Plate 1, 4).

The Army of the United States has very many flags. The flag of the Secretary of the Army has a red field with the four white stars in the corners and in the centre the bald-headed American eagle with a breast plate of red and white vertical stripes.

U.S. SECRETARY OF ARMY

The flags of the Army can be roughly divided into four main categories, (a) Colours, (b) distinguishing flags, (c) flags of individual high ranking officers, (d) guidons.

Colours are defined as a specific flag indicative of the spirit and tradition of the United States, or the office, position or organisation represented. The following are among those authorised to bear Colours, the President and Vice-President of the United States, Cabinet Members and senior officials of the Armed Forces such as the Chairman of the Joint Chief of Staff, etc.

Regiments and separate battalions whose organisation is fixed by the tables of organisation are authorised Colours symbolic of their branch and history. These are known as Colour Bearing Organisations. Other branches of the Army have distinguishing flags.

When the term Colour, in the singular, is used this implies the National Colour. This is the National Flag, but with a golden fringe and proportions modified to four by three (length to breadth). Colours, in the plural, implies both the National and Organisational Colour paraded together. All Colours are silk flags with gold fringes. The colours of the fields of the flags are laid down according to the branch of the Army to which the organisation belongs, i.e. Armour, yellow; Artillery, scarlet; Infantry, dark blue, and so on. In the case of distinguishing flags, they bear the insignia of the branch and unit identification in numbers and symbols. If the unit is designated 'Colour-bearing', then the colour of the field is the same as that of the distinguishing flag but the device consists of the bald American eagle with on its breast the arms of those units with an authorised coat of arms, and beneath on a scroll the designation of the unit, i.e. 1st Infantry, 5th Artillery etc.

The Ceremonial Flag, or Colour, of the Army has a white field with a complicated device in the centre and a gold fringe (Plate 1, 2).

Guidons are swallow-tailed flags and are used as markers for companies, batteries etc. The design is generally similar to the distinguishing flag of the unit, and of the same colour and bearing the insignia of the unit in the centre.

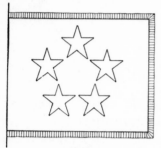

U.S. GENERAL
OF THE ARMY

Senior Officers in the Army have a red flag with the number of stars in white appropriate to their rank. A five-star General, whose title is General of the Army, has his stars arranged in the form of a pentagon. The others have their stars displayed in a horizontal line; thus, a General has four, a Lieutenant-General three, a Major-General two and a Brigadier-General one.

The flags of the Air Force of the United States follow the same general pattern as those of the Army, except that the colour of the field is generally blue instead of red. Thus the Secretary of Air Force has a dark blue flag with four white stars, one in each corner, and in the centre the Arms of the Air Force in full colour.

There are distinguishing flags for all the many Air Commands, Major Air Divisions, Wings etc. The flags of the Senior Officers of the Air Force are similar to those of the other services; they are dark blue in colour and in order to distinguish them from those of the Navy the stars are arranged in the same pattern as those of the Army.

The Ceremonial Flag of the Air Force is very similar to that of the Secretary of the Air Force except that it does not have the four stars in the corners; the Arms of the Air Force in the centre are circled by thirteen white stars and on a scroll beneath is the title 'UNITED STATES AIR FORCE' (Plate 1, 6).

The United States Marine Corps is in a very special position and has its own series of flags, the basic colour of which is red. The Standard of the Corps is thus a red flag with in the centre the Arms of the Marines, a gold anchor over which is a globe and the crest the

Plate 16

FLAGS OF THE UNITED STATES OF AMERICA

(See pp. 88–90)

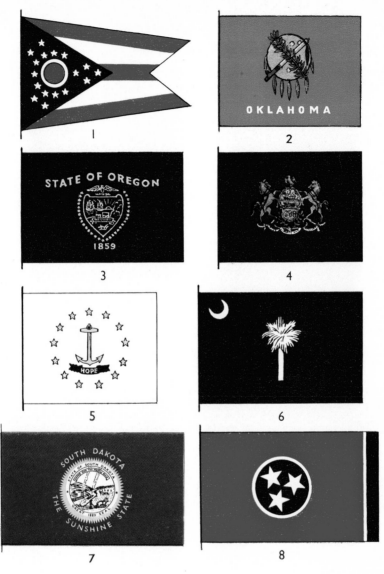

1

2

3

4

5

6

7

8

Plate 16 f.p. 86

FLAGS OF THE UNITED STATES OF AMERICA

American eagle; beneath on a scroll 'UNITED STATES MARINE CORPS' (Plate 1, 3). The flag of the Commandant is similar to the Standard, but it has no scroll and has four white stars disposed symmetrically round the arms in the centre. The other senior officers have red flags, but the stars are disposed in the same fashion as those of the Navy so as to distinguish them from the Army.

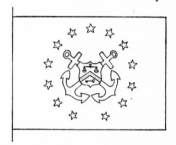

U.S. MARINE CORPS COMMANDANT U.S. SECRETARY OF TREASURY

Although the organisation is on naval lines, the Coastguard Service of the United States is strictly a civilian service and comes under the Secretary of the Treasury who has a blue flag with a badge in the centre of a shield and two crossed anchors surrounded by a circlet of thirteen stars; these charges are all white.

The Coastguard Ensign is an interesting flag. It has sixteen red and white vertical stripes, starting with a red one at the hoist. In the fly is a crossed anchor badge with the motto 'SEMPER PARATUS', 'Always prepared', and the date '1790' in dark blue. In the white canton is a modification of the Arms of the United States with the eagle in blue.

The Senior Officers of the Coastguard Service have blue flags

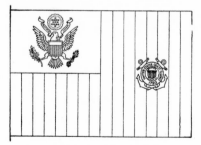

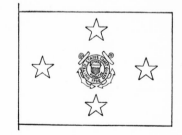

U.S. COASTGUARD ENSIGN U.S. COASTGUARD COMMANDANT

with the same device that is in the fly of the ensign, and stars indicative of their rank, four for the Commandant, three for the Assistant-Commandant and two for the Rear-Admiral. The Colour of the Coastguards is white with in the centre the same arms that are in the canton of the ensign, with the motto 'SEMPER PARATUS, 1790' below, and above: 'UNITED STATES COAST GUARDS' (Plate 1, 5).

The Customs Service Ensign is similar to that of the Coastguards except that it has the badge of the Customs in the fly.

Yachts fulfilling certain requirements are authorised to wear the Yacht Ensign in lieu of the Stars and Stripes. It is clearly distinguishable from the latter in that the blue canton contains a large white anchor inclined at an angle of forty-five degrees, encircled by thirteen white five-pointed stars.

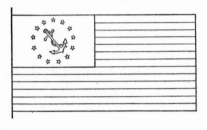

U.S. YACHT ENSIGN   U.S. POWER SQUADRON

In addition to the Yacht Ensign there is a special ensign for the U.S. Power Squadron.   The field of this ensign, the proportions of which are three by two, consists of seven blue and six white stripes arranged vertically.   The canton is red and in it is placed an inclined anchor and thirteen white stars, the same as that in the Yacht Ensign.

Each of the states has its own flag.   Some of them are very beautiful; some of them are plastered with devices which can only be compared with the ugly badges used by some colonies of the British Commonwealth.   It is interesting to note that two of them, namely those of the States of Massachusetts and Oregon, have a different charge on the reverse side of the field.

The illustrations of the flags of each state are given in Plates 12–17.

The red cross on the flag of ALABAMA is said to have its origin in the Confederate Battle Flag (Plates 11, 8 and 12, 1).

ALASKA, admitted as the forty-ninth state of the American Union on January 3rd 1959, chose a dark blue flag with the constellation of the Great Bear and the North Star (Plate 12, 2).

The central star in the flag of ARKANSAS commemorates the Confederacy, and the other three stand for Spain, France and the United States of America, to which the state successively belonged (Plate 12, 4).

HAWAII was admitted as the fiftieth state in the Union and adopted a flag of unique design; the field consists of eight horizontal stripes of equal width, white (top), red, blue, white, etc., with the Union Flag of Great Britain in the upper canton. This design was originally adopted on May 31st 1845, and became the Territorial Flag when Hawaii was annexed by the United States of America, but the origin of the design is obscure. The eight stripes are held to represent the eight islands of the group, but there are different theories about the Union Flag. It will be recalled that Captain James Cook discovered the islands in 1778, and subsequently it is suggested that the British explorer George Vancouver presented the King of Hawaii with the Union Flag to fly over his palace. Another version is that the King made a vague concession of Hawaii Island to Vancouver and that the British flag was flown until news of the 1812 War was received; at about that time the King decided to have a flag of his own and an English sea captain, George C. Beckley, designed the present eight-striped flag bearing the British Union Flag (Plate 13, 2).

One of the most striking of the state flags is that of MARYLAND, for it is pure heraldry and is taken from the Arms of the Baltimore family (Plate 14, 2). Although adopted officially on March 9th 1904, it is said to have been in use long before American Independence.

MINNESOTA used to have an unusual flag in that it was white on the obverse and blue on the reverse; this made it very expensive, and in 1957 the flag was revised and became deep blue on both sides, with the State Seal emblazoned in bright colours on a white circle in the centre (Plate 14, 5).

The flag of NEW MEXICO is a simple, yellow flag with a device, the ancient Zia sun symbol, in red, the colours of the flag being those of Aragon and old Spain (Plate 15, 5).

The Anglo-Dutch origins of the CITY OF NEW YORK are recalled by its flag, the field of which consists of three vertical stripes of equal width, blue (at the hoist), white and orange—the colours of the flag of the Dutch East India Company flown by Hendrik Hudson when he founded New Amsterdam, which was to become New York. The City Seal is superimposed on the centre white stripe. When this flag is used by the Mayor of New York five blue stars, each with five points symbolising the five boroughs of the city, form an arc above the centre charge.

The flag of OHIO (Plate 16, 1) is of unusual shape. The seventeen stars mark the fact that Ohio was the seventeenth state to join the Union; some other states have adopted the same idea.

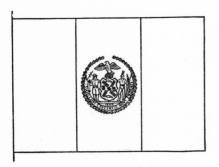

NEW YORK CITY

DISTRICT OF COLUMBIA

Formerly the flag of SOUTH DAKOTA, like that of Minnesota, was different on each side, but in 1963 the State Legislature approved a new design, which has both sides the same. This flag consists of a sky-blue field with in the centre the Great Seal of South Dakota; this seal can have either a white or a sky-blue background, with the seal outlined in dark blue. Thus South Dakota has, in fact, two official State Flags. Surrounding the seal are a serrated sun and the words 'SOUTH DAKOTA' and 'THE SUNSHINE STATE' (Plate 16, 7).

The flag of the State of WASHINGTON can be recognised at once as it is the only green flag in the whole fifty (Plate 17, 5).

A reference should here be made to the flag of the District of Columbia, which was approved on October 15th 1938. Of simple

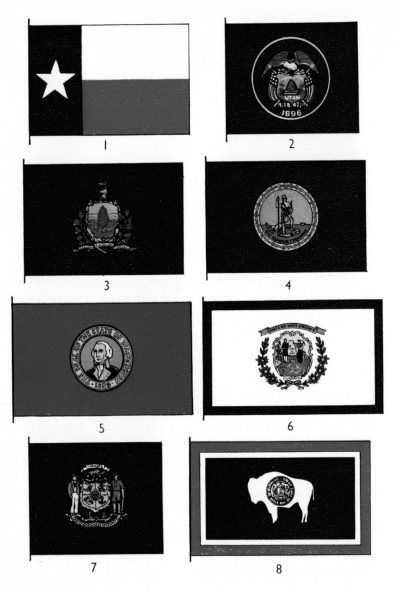

1

2

3

4

5

6

7

8

Plate 17   f.p. 91

FLAGS OF THE UNITED STATES OF AMERICA

Plate 17

FLAGS OF THE UNITED STATES OF AMERICA

(See pp. 88–90)

1 Texas

2 Utah

3 Vermont

4 Virginia

5 Washington

6 West Virginia

7 Wisconsin

8 Wyoming

and distinctive design, the field is white with two red horizontal stripes and three five-pointed stars of the same colour on the upper white stripe, taken from the Arms of George Washington.

We now pass to the Dependencies of Guam, Panama Canal Zone, and the Virgin Islands. They each have a distinctive flag which is flown with the Stars and Stripes—the latter always occupying the position of honour i.e. on the *left* hand of the observer.

The flag of GUAM is dark blue with a red border, and in the centre on an oval shield the Seal of Guam on which is depicted an estuary, an outrigger canoe and a coconut tree with the word 'GUAM' overall in red block letters.

GUAM   PANAMA CANAL ZONE

The flag of the Governor of the PANAMA CANAL ZONE is also dark blue, but with no border, and in the centre the Seal of Panama, which is a large white circle charged with a shield having a Spanish galleon end on in full sail, and above thirteen vertical stripes, seven white and six red, from the Arms of the United States, and beneath on a scroll the motto 'THE LAND DIVIDED, THE WORLD UNITED'.

The VIRGIN ISLANDS possess a white flag with the spread-eagle device in the centre thereof between the letters 'V' and 'I' as shown in the accompanying illustration.

VIRGIN ISLANDS

Finally we come to the island of PUERTO RICO (Rich Port). When Columbus discovered it on November 19th 1493, he took possession of it on behalf of Spain and named it San

Juan Bautiste (St. John the Baptist). In accordance with a decree
dated November 8th 1511, King Ferdinand,
who with Queen Isabella, was Sovereign of Spain
at that time, granted a seal. This consisted of a
green circular shield charged with the silver
lamb of St. John, resting on a copy of the Bible
in red and bearing between a yoke and a cluster
of arrows the initials 'F' and 'I', each surmounted by a crown, all in gold; and a motto,
'JOANNES EST NOMEN EJUS'—'John is his name'—in silver.

PUERTO RICO

The border surrounding the shield consists of two each of
the following emblems: a red lion rampant with golden crown
(Leon), a golden castle (Castile), a cross potent in gold
(Jerusalem), and the Royal Banner, as shown in the illustration on
this page.

Puerto Rico continued to be a Spanish possession until the ter-
mination of the Spanish-American War in 1898, and became a
dependency of the United States of America on April 11th of the
following year in accordance with the Treaty of Paris. It has been
a self-governing commonwealth within the United States of
America since July 25th 1952.

In choosing a distinctive flag, it was decided to revive one which
had been adopted by the Puerto Rican patriots of 1895, who
were affiliated with the Cuban Revolutionary Party which was
the spearhead of the movement
for the independence of both
countries from Spain. It is similar
to that of Cuba except that the
five horizontal stripes of equal
width consist of three red ones
and two white, and the equilateral
triangle at the hoist is blue, charged
with a large white five-pointed star.
The proportions of the field are
eight by five.

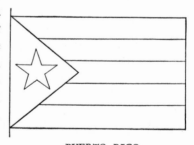

PUERTO RICO

AMERICAN SAMOA adopted a distinctive flag early in 1960, and it
was flown for the first time at Pago Pago on April 27th of that

year—the sixtieth anniversary of the first raising of the Stars and Stripes there in 1900. The field, proportions two by one, is blue and has a red-bordered white triangle extending from the fly to the hoist. On this an American bald eagle in proper colours is in flight towards the hoist, looking downwards and grasping in his right talon a Pue (Samoan chief's symbol), and in his left a Nifo Oti (Samoan dancing knife), both in gold.

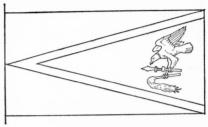

AMERICAN SAMOA

The blue and red used in this design are the colours used on the Stars and Stripes; the American eagle holding in his talons the symbols of Samoan authority and culture indicates the protection and friendship of the United States.

Before passing on to the flags of Latin America, mention should perhaps be made of the Organisation of American States which was formed in Washington on April 14th 1890, and later became known as the PAN AMERICAN UNION. It now comprises twenty members, namely, Argentina, Bolivia, Brazil, Chile, Colombia, Costa Rica, Dominican Republic, Ecuador, El Salvador, Guatemala, Haiti, Honduras, Mexico, Nicaragua, Panama, Paraguay, Peru, United States of America, Uruguay, and Venezuela.

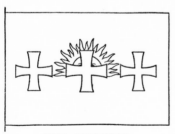

THE AMERICAS

This organisation was formed 'to achieve an order of peace and justice, to promote their solidarity, to strengthen their collaboration, and to defend their sovereignty, their territorial integrity, and their inpendence'.

In 1932 a distinctive flag was adopted; this has a white field charged with three crosses of a reddish-purple shade (the middle one is slightly larger than the other two), and a rising sun in bronze behind the middle cross. The three crosses are said to symbolise ships of Columbus and

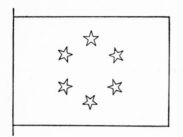

TRUST TERRITORY OF THE
PACIFIC ISLANDS

the rising sun the 'Bronze sun of the Incas'. It is usually flown on April 14th Anniversary—Pan American Day; this flag is known as the Americas'.

A large number of islands in the Pacific, formerly owned by and administered by Spain, Germany and Japan, are now controlled by the United States under a mandate from the United Nations. In order to foster a sense of nationhood amongst these the United States has sponsored a special flag for this TRUST TERRITORY OF THE PACIFIC ISLANDS. This flag has a field of medium blue with six white stars arranged in a circle.

Chapter Five

LATIN AMERICA
AND THE CARIBBEAN

MEXICO became an Empire in 1821, and a National and Merchant Flag, a vertical tricolour of equal stripes of green, white and red, was adopted soon after that.   It is said that green represented hope, the white peace, and the red union.

The badge of Mexico is an eagle holding a snake in its beak and standing on a prickly pear.   A wreath of oak and laurel surrounds the eagle.   These arms owe their origin to an Aztec legend to the effect that the Aztecs could not settle until they found a place on an island in a lake on which grew a cactus.   On this cactus plant there would be an eagle holding a snake in its beak.

MEXICO

The National Flag (Plate 19, 9), Naval Ensign, Merchant Flag, and President's Standard now have this eagle badge in the centre of the white stripe of the tricolour.   The Jack is square and of unusual design.   Its field is divided diagonally from the upper fly to the lower hoist, white over red; positioned centrally over the dividing line, a wide green stripe bearing a white anchor, axis parallel to the hoist, in the centre thereof.   There are three yellow eight-pointed stars, one each in the upper and lower hoist, the other in the lower fly.   The Masthead Pennant is divided vertically into three sections, green (at the hoist), white and red.

A square edition of the National Flag is used by the Secretary of State and a similar one, but swallow-tailed, by the Under-Secretary of State.   Many officials use similar flags with distinguishing marks added.   For example, that of the Secretary of State for the Navy is

similar to the former but has in addition a large white anchor on
the green stripe, whereas the Commander-in-Chief of the Navy has
four white five-pointed stars, one under the other, in place of the
anchor. Admirals, Vice-Admirals and Rear-Admirals with an
independent command have similar stars, three, two and one
respectively, on the green stripe. However, if they have no
independent command they fly similar flags but swallow-tailed.

Ambassadors and Ministers have a square white flag with the
eagle badge in the centre. The Consular Officer's flag is similar,
but is swallow-tailed.

The Governor of a State flies a square-shaped tricolour without
a badge, but the colours are placed horizontally, with the green on
top and the red at the bottom.

The General commanding a Division has the same flag as the
Governor of a State, but has the eagle badge added in the centre
of the white stripe. The Brigade Commander flies a similar flag,
but has it swallow-tailed.

The vertical tricolour is used by the Customs and vessels carrying
mails. The former mount a black foul anchor in the white stripe,
the latter the letters 'C.M.', also in black.

Central America starts with GUATEMALA.

The Spanish dominion in Mexico ended with the surrender of
the capital by O'Donoju—which is the Spanish way of rendering
the pronunciation of O'Donoghue—and in the same year, 1821,
Guatemala obtained its freedom. When it hauled down the
Spanish flag it was much bigger than it is now, Honduras, Salvador,
Nicaragua and Costa Rica having split off from it
in 1839. The republic was established in 1847.

The Merchant Flag consists of three vertical
stripes of equal width, blue, white and blue
(Plate 19, 6). The National Flag and the Ensign
are similar to the Merchant Flag, but in each case
the centre stripe is charged with the badge
shown in the accompanying illustration in
full colours. This badge shows a white scroll

GUATEMALA

charged with the inscription 'LIBERTAD 15 DE SEPTIEMBRE 1821',
which is placed in front of two crossed swords and two crossed

rifles with bayonets fixed.   A quetzal (*Paramocrus mocinno*) is perched on the scroll, its colouring a bright metallic green with a vivid red breast.   The design is surrounded by a laurel wreath which is tied with ribbon of the national colours.

The old Naval Ensign was a horizontal tricolour, the top stripe being half red, half blue, the centre stripe white, and the bottom stripe half yellow, half blue.   Later on it appeared with seven stripes, blue, white, red, yellow, red, white and blue.

El Salvador is the smallest of the Central American republics. She formed part of Spain's dominions until September 15th 1821, when she joined the Federation of the Central American States, but became independent when she eventually broke away in 1838.

However, the old Federation flag (horizontally blue over white over blue) was retained until 1865.   In that year a new flag was adopted, consisting of five dark blue and four white horizontal stripes, with a red canton charged with fourteen white five-pointed stars.   On September 15th 1912 this was superseded by the old Federation flag mentioned above.   Four years later a slightly modified version of the arms of the old Federation was placed in the centre of the white stripe to form the National Flag, Naval Ensign and President's Flag (Plate 19, 5).

The arms consist of a triangular shield; thereon are five conical mountains rising out of the sea (the five volcanoes of the Central American isthmus). In the centre is a pole, and thereon is a cap of liberty.   The sun's rays appear in the background with the inscription '15 DE SEP-TIEMBRE DE 1821'; on each side are two of the old Federation flags, and underneath a scroll bearing the legend 'DIOS, UNION Y LIBERTAD'—the 'Y' is sometimes omitted.

EL SALVADOR

A wreath of laurel tied with dark blue ribbon encircles the design, while in a circle outside the whole are the words 'REPUBLICA DE EL SALVADOR EN LA AMERICA CENTRAL'.

The legend only from the scroll is placed in block lettering on the white stripe of the Merchant Flag (Plate 19, 4).

A blue flag charged with a white diamond, the major and minor axes of which are the same as the length and hoist respectively, does duty as the Jack.

The horizontal blue over white over blue flag of 1838 is also used

HONDURAS

as a basis for the flags of HONDURAS. The National and Merchant Flags have five blue five-pointed stars arranged two, one and two on the central white stripe (Plate **19**, 8). The Naval Ensign has a badge in the centre of the white stripe; there are different designs of this badge, but the type illustrated, either with or without the five stars, is the one in general use. The details include an oval compartment containing the triangle from the Arms of the United Provinces, the water around which represents the two oceans. Surrounding the oval are the name of the country and motto 'LIBRE, SOBERANA, E INDEPENDIENTE'—'Free, Sovereign, and Independent', with the date of independence, September 15th 1821. Surmounting the oval is a quiver of arrows between two cornucopias, and below are oak and pine trees with various tools, which include a square, wedge, hammer etc.

The Masthead Pennant is vertically blue, white and blue, with the five blue stars from the Merchant Flag on the white stripe.

Columbus discovered NICARAGUA in 1520, and it remained under Spanish rule until 1821. Then, for a while, it belonged to the Federal Union of five Central American States which broke up in 1838. The National Flag, Naval Ensign and Merchant Flag are of the same blue, white and blue, with the badge of Nicaragua on the white stripe (Plate **19**, 10). This badge consists of a triangle, which bears a landscape con-

NICARAGUA

sisting of five conical mountains rising out of the sea. A pole rises out of the middle mountain, a red cap of liberty being placed thereon. The sun is rising between the two right-hand mountains.

Plate 18

FLAGS OF LATIN AMERICA AND THE CARIBBEAN

1

2

3

4

5

6

7

8

9

10

Plate 18

FLAGS OF LATIN AMERICA
AND THE CARIBBEAN

Encircling the triangle is the legend, 'REPUBLICA DE NICARAGUA—AMERICA CENTRAL', in gold lettering.

The flag which is illustrated on Plate **18**, 9, is the National and Merchant Flag of COSTA RICA. This was adopted in 1848. This flag is used by private citizens. The State Flag used by Government Departments and the Naval Ensign have on the central stripe a white circle charged with the Arms of Costa Rica, which are rather complicated. The shield bears a landscape design of two seas separated by three mountains, and on each of the seas a ship is sailing. The sun is rising on the horizon. The mountains represent the volcanoes of Barba, Irazu and Poás, while

COSTA RICA

the two seas allude to the fact that Costa Rica has outlets to both the Atlantic and Pacific Oceans, and in general symbolise the international nature of her trade. On the top portion of the shield are five white five-pointed stars, a relic of the old Central American Federation; above, on two scrolls, are the inscriptions 'AMERICA CENTRAL' and 'REPUBLICA DE COSTA RICA'.

PANAMA became a separate republic in 1903, and the famous canal was opened to commerce in 1914. There is a canal zone extending for five miles on either side, which is under the jurisdiction of the United States of America.

The flag was designed by the first President, Manuel Amador Guerrero, and it was hoisted for the first time on November 3rd 1903. Of simple and commendable design, it serves as the National Flag, Naval Ensign and Merchant Flag (Plate **20**, 1).

South America begins with the three republics of Colombia, Ecuador and Venezuela, whose flags consist of three horizontal stripes, yellow over dark blue over red. These colours have their origin in the banner which Francisco Miranda carried during the period of revolution which finally led to the break-away from Spain.

COLOMBIA, which was formerly New Grenada, gained its independence in 1819 under Simon Bolivar.

The National Flag consists of three horizontal stripes, yellow over dark blue over red, the first mentioned occupying the upper half of the field. However, when the Arms of Colombia are super-imposed on the centre of the flag it becomes the Naval Ensign and the President's Flag (Plate **18**, 7). They are displayed on a white background encircled with a narrow red border. The foregoing circular charge is placed on the rectangular dark blue field of the Jack.

COLOMBIA

These arms consist of a shield, with a white 'fesse' in the middle, charged with a red cap of liberty. Above the fesse, on a blue ground, is a pome-granate between two cornucopias, all in yellow. In the base of the shield is a landscape between two oceans with a sailing-ship on each. This is repre-sentative of the Pacific and Atlantic Oceans, divided by the Isthmus of Panama, which was at one time Colombian territory. On each side of the shield are two tricolours, while the crest is a condor holding up the shield with a rope of laurel in green.

Originally nine golden stars were placed under the arms, and were symbolical of the nine states of Colombia, but when the states were revised and increased to fourteen these stars were omitted.

The Masthead Pennant is sky blue with the national colours, yellow over dark blue over red, in the head.

In order to make a clear distinction between the Naval Ensign and the Merchant Flag, the charge on the centre of the last men-tioned consists of a white eight-pointed star on a dark blue oval having a red rim (Plate **18**, 8). A similar flag, with the addition of a large black conventional anchor at the hoist on the yellow stripe, is worn by merchant ships commanded by an officer of the Naval Reserve.

A blue-bordered diminutive of the National Flag serves as the Customs Flag.

The Air Ensign has a sky-blue field with the National Flag in the upper quarter next to the mast. In the centre of the fly is an ingeniously contrived 'target' comprising the national colours. The white star from the Merchant Flag is placed upon three horizontal stripes, red over dark blue over yellow, and surrounded by an annulet, the upper half of which is yellow and the lower quarter is dark blue (nearest the hoist) and red.

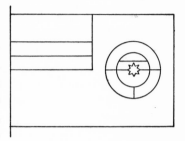

COLOMBIA: AIR ENSIGN

The flag of ECUADOR which is illustrated on Plate **19**, **2** is the National and Merchant Flag. This flag is also flown by private citizens. The State or Government Flag, the Standard of the President and the Naval Ensign all carry the Arms of Ecuador in the centre (Plate **19**, **3**).

The arms consist of an oval shield which contains a landscape showing a snow-capped mountain rising out of the sea with a

ECUADOR

steamer thereon and the sun with four of the signs of the Zodiac in the sky. They were adopted upon the Declaration of Independence in 1822. The snow-topped mountain represents the Chimborazo, the highest peak in the country, of historic importance during the War of Independence; the steamer stands for commerce, while the four signs of the Zodiac are those of March, April, May and June—memorable months in the history of the country. Above the oval is the condor of the Andes, below is a fasces, and on each side are two tricolours, the heads of which are fashioned like halberds.

The Jack has a rectangular blue field bearing a white foul anchor surmounted by a condor in flight, and the Masthead Pennant is divided vertically into three sections, yellow (at the hoist), dark blue and red.

The name VENEZUELA, 'Little Venice', was originally given by Columbus to the Gulf of Maracaibo, where the native settlements were built on piles in the water.   Venezuela obtained her independence in 1830.

The Merchant Flag, which is also used by private citizens as the National Flag, is shown on Plate **20, 5**.   Like the flag of Ecuador it has horizontal stripes of yellow, blue and red, but in the Venezuelan flag these stripes are of equal width, and in the centre of the blue are seven white five-pointed stars, arranged in an arc.

The Government or State Flag and the Naval Ensign are the same as the Merchant Flag with the addition of the Arms of Venezuela in the upper or yellow stripe, placed in the hoist.

In the present arms, which date from 1930, the shield has a blue base charged with an untamed white horse, and a chief divided vertically into two, red and yellow, charged with a sheaf of golden corn and two tricolours in saltire with swords, respectively.

The shield is flanked by a green wreath of palm and laurel, and below an elaborate scroll was inscribed '19 DE ABRIL DE 1810— INDEPENDENCIA' and '20 DE FEBREO DE 1850 —FEDERACION', with 'E.E.U.U. DE VENE- ZUELA' (standing for the 'United States of Venezuela') beneath.   Two horns of plenty form the crest.   On April 15th 1953, the official name of Venezuela was changed to 'Republica de Venezuela', in accordance with Article 1 of the Constitution, and substituted

VENEZUELA

in all cases where formerly 'E.E.U.U. de Venezuela' was used, including the scroll referred to above.

These arms are borne in the centre of the President's Flag, which consists of a square field, divided horizontally, yellow over blue over red.   In addition, there are four white five-pointed stars, one each above and below the arms on the yellow stripe and one on either side on the blue stripe.   The aforementioned arms occupy one-half the depth of the field.

The Masthead Pennant is divided horizontally, yellow over dark blue over red.

Blue rectangular flags bearing a large white conventional anchor

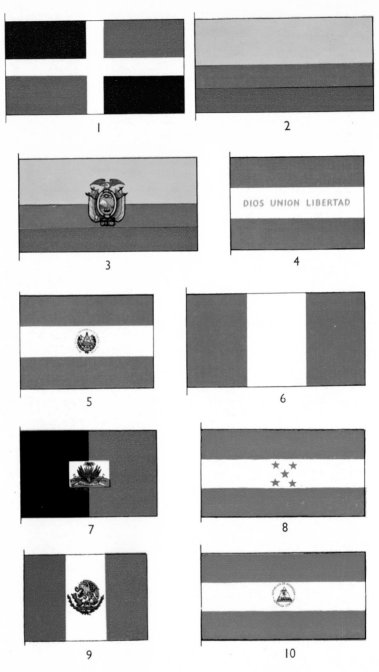

1

2

3

4 DIOS UNION LIBERTAD

5

6

7

8

9

10

Plate 19

FLAGS OF LATIN AMERICA
AND THE CARIBBEAN

Plate 19

FLAGS OF LATIN AMERICA AND THE CARIBBEAN

in the centre thereof are flown by the Minister of Defence and the Commander-in-Chief of the Navy. However, the former has additional charges, namely, the shield from the arms in the upper hoist and four white five-pointed stars—one on either side of and one above and below the anchor. Admirals, Vice-Admirals and Rear-Admirals fly yellow pennants with blue five-pointed stars on the centre line, three, two and one respectively.

GUYANA, which was formerly British Guiana became independent on May 25th 1966 and adopted a handsome and unusual new flag in place of the old badge of a full-rigged ship which was displayed on the Red Ensign of Great Britain. The new flag, was designed by Whitney Smith, Director of the Flag Research Center, Massachusetts, U.S.A. The heraldic description of the flag is 'Vert on a pile throughout issuant from the dexter or fimbriated argent a pile gules fimbriated sable upon the same base'. Translated into ordinary language this means that the field of the flag is green, and that there is a golden triangle issuing from the hoist to the fly, bordered with white and within this a smaller triangle which is red, bordered with black (Plate 20, 7). Guyana has adopted no other flags for any special services and this flag fulfils all duties.

PERU in its long history has had troublous times and many flags, but since 1825 the basic design of her flags has been one consisting of three vertical stripes, red, white and red. This is used today as the Merchant Flag, and is flown as the National Flag by the ordinary citizens (Plate 20, 3). With version (a) of the arms on the centre of the white stripe it becomes the State or Government Flag; with version (b) it is the Naval Ensign (see page 104). The shield is halved horizontally; the top half is again halved, vertically this time; the blue or dexter half is charged with a llama, and the white or sinister has a cinchona tree. The base is red, charged with a gold cornucopia disgorging gold coins.

The edges of the shield and the partition lines are bordered with a narrow gold edging.

The crest comprises a laurel wreath. In version (a) the shield is placed within a wreath of palm and laurel, and in (b) it is flanked on each side with two flags.

Again version (a) is placed in the centre of a square red-bordered

8

PERU (*a*)   PERU (*b*)

white flag which does duty as the Jack.   The President flies a
white rectangular flag with version (*b*) in the centre thereof and a
golden sun in each of the four corners.

The Masthead Pennant is divided into three sections, red (at the
hoist), white and red.

BOLIVIA was formerly Upper Peru, and took its name from
Bolivar in 1825.   Like Peru, it has had a troubled history, and is
now without a coastline of its own.

A horizontal tricolour, red, yellow and green, with the arms in
the centre of the yellow stripe, is the State Flag, Naval Ensign,
and President's Flag.   Merchant ships wear the plain tricolour
(Plate 18, 3); private citizens also display a similar flag.

The present arms, and the tricolour, were adopted by law
on July 14th 1888.   The former consists of an oval cartouche,
encircled with a border, the upper half of which is yellow, and

bears the name 'BOLIVIA' in crimson;
the lower half is blue and is charged with
nine golden stars representing the nine
departments into which the country is
divided.   In the centre is a landscape with
the sun shining over a mountain—the
mountain of Potosim, famous for its
mineral wealth—a house, a breadfruit-tree,
a corn-sheaf, and a llama, these symbols
representing the riches of the country,

BOLIVIA

mineral, vegetable and animal.   Behind the oval are two crossed
cannon and four rifles with fixed bayonets, two on each side.   On

one side is a cap of liberty, and on the other an axe, while three of the national flags also appear on each side. On the top is a wreath with a condor alighting thereon.

BRAZIL may be regarded as Portuguese South America. It is true that the Spanish flag was hoisted by Pinzon at Cape St. Augustine in January 1500, but Cabral had the Portuguese up at Porto Seguro in the following April, and his 'Terra da Vera Cruz', as it was then named, was the real beginning of Brazil. The Spanish Flag consisted of the red and yellow horizontal stripes from the Arms of Aragon; that of Portugal had a white field charged with the white shield, bordered red, which is still to be seen on her present flag (*see* Plate **23**, 12). Then Portugal was captured by Spain, and the Spanish flag went up; the Dutch arrived at Bahia, and hoisted their tricolour, which, at different places on the coast, remained for twenty years until Portugal, emancipated from Spain, resumed possession of her American colonies. In 1808 these became the refuge of the Portuguese king whose eldest son threw off the parental yoke in 1822; and they became an Empire with a flag of its own. This, the flag of Brazil, was decreed in 1889 and was modified in June 1960 and again on February 22nd 1968. The Brazilian National Flag, Ensign and Merchant Flag is green with in the centre a yellow diamond or lozenge which has in its centre a blue circle representing the night sky of Brazil. Across this is a white stripe with the motto 'ORDEM E PROGRESSO'. Originally there were twenty-one stars in the blue circle; an additional one was added by the decree of 1960, and a twenty-third by the decree of 1968—one star for each of the states of Brazil and one for the Federal District (Plate **18**, 4).

The same decree of February 1968 which added a star to the National Flag also officially changed the name of the country from 'ESTADOS UNIDOS DO BRASIL' (the United States of Brazil) to 'REPUBLICA FEDERATIVA DO BRASIL' (the Federal Republic of Brazil), and this new title now appears on the scroll beneath the coat of arms. These arms, which upon a green field form the President's Flag (Plate **18**, 5), consist of in the centre a blue circle containing the Southern Cross, with round the edge twenty-two stars, representing the states; formerly there were twenty stars.

BRAZIL:
ADMIRALTY FLAG

The field of the Jack is dark blue, divided into quarters by a cross of twenty-one white five-pointed stars, five in each arm and one in the centre. This is the basic design used for the Minister of Marine's Flag, the Admiralty Flag and Admirals' flags. Thus, the former has a simplified version of the badge on the President's Flag, in the first quarter; the Admiralty Flag is similar, but has in addition a pair of white anchors in saltire, in the third quarter.

We now pass to the third type, namely Admirals' flags. In the flag of an Admiral the first quarter contains five small white five-pointed stars in the form of a pentagon: an Admiral commanding a squadron has four similar stars arranged in a square diamond form; a Vice-Admiral a triangle of three stars; while a Rear-Admiral shows but two stars side by side.

The dark blue Masthead Pennant has twenty-one small white five-pointed stars positioned on the horizontal axis at the head.

CHILE has a very handsome flag, the design of which dates from 1817; it does duty as the National Flag, Ensign and Merchant Flag (Plate 18, 6). The Jack is square, dark blue in colour, and is charged with a small white five-pointed star. The Masthead Pennant is

CHILE: JACK

divided horizontally, white over red, charged with a blue panel at the hoist, bearing a small white five-pointed star.

The President's Standard bears the arms on the National Flag. These date back to 1834, and consist of a shield, half blue and half red, the blue being on top, while overall is a white star. Above are three plumes of red, white and blue, the feathers of the rhea, the representative of the flightless birds in South America. The dexter supporter is a 'huemal' (sometimes called a 'guemal'), a furciferine deer which is found only in the mountain ranges of Chile; the sinister supporter is a condor of the type found in the Andes. The motto 'POR LA RAZON O LA FUERZA'—meaning 'By Right and Might'—was used during Chile's War of Independence.

CHILE: ARMS

The Ministers of State and Generals have a blue flag with a red cross, edged with white, whose upright limb is off centre and nearer the hoist, a white five-pointed star being in the upper canton; the Minister of National Defence hoists plain dark blue on which are the arms in gold; the Commander-in-Chief of the Fleet has dark blue with four white stars, one in each corner; a Vice-Admiral has a dark blue flag with three white stars, one above two, while the Rear-Admiral, if in command, flies a dark blue flag with two white stars, one above the other. If he is not in command, he shows the same two stars, but upon a red flag. Brigadier Generals and Governors of Provinces are distinguished by a red flag with a white cross, the upper left-hand quarter being dark blue and bearing the star. The Consular Flag is of similar design, but is shaped like a yacht's burgee.

The ARGENTINE Republic, which takes its name as a synonym from the silver river, La Plata, was discovered by the Spaniards in 1516, and began its struggle for independence at the same time as Chile, obtaining it in 1816.

The State Flag, which is flown by Government Departments, and the Ensign (Plate 18, 1) consists of three horizontal stripes of equal width, light blue over white over light blue (the pre-independence colours), having the 'Sun of May', with straight and wavy rays alternating, in gold, in the centre of the middle stripe.

This charge on a square white field with a light blue border is the Jack (Plate 18, 2), and the Merchant Flag, which is used by private citizens as the National Flag, is the same as the State Flag, described above, without the 'Sun of May' in the centre.

The Masthead Pennant is divided horizontally, light blue over white over light blue.

The President's Standard is light blue, with a badge in the centre and a white five-pointed star in each of the four corners.

ARGENTINE

This badge consists of an oval shield, divided into halves, the top being light blue and the lower white.   Overall are two hands grasping a staff on which is a red cap of liberty.   Above is a golden sun, and the shield is surrounded by a laurel wreath, which, unlike most wreaths used in a similar position, partly obscures the face of the sun.

The flag of the Minister of Marine is also light blue; in the centre thereof a white anchor charged with the 'Sun in May' emblem, all within a narrow white rectangular frame.   That of the Chief of Naval Operations is also blue but carries five white five-pointed stars, one in the centre and one in each corner of the field.

Naval command flags have a light blue rectangular field.   An Admiral, if Commander-in-Chief afloat, has a white star in each corner, but otherwise he has three white stars placed diagonally across the field; a Vice-Admiral has two stars in a diagonal position, and a Rear-Admiral one star placed centrally.

After a century of domination, first by the Spaniards and then by the Portuguese, URUGUAY achieved its independence in December 1828, and adopted its National Flag.   The field was white, with nine horizontal blue stripes, with El Sol de Mayo—the Sun of May— in a white canton.

By a law of July 11th 1830, the number of stripes was reduced to five white and four blue—one for each of the nine political divisions forming the republic.

The sun has golden rays, straight and wavy alternating.   This symbolises Uruguay's independence, while the white and blue stripes are indicative of her former association with Argentina.

This flag has remained the National Flag to the present day.   It also does duty as the Naval Ensign and the Merchant Flag (Plate **20**, 4).   The Masthead Pennant is striped horizontally white over blue over white and has a white panel at the hoist charged with the 'Sun in May' emblem.

The Jack consists of three horizontal stripes of equal width, blue, white and blue, and overall a red diagonal stripe from the top of the hoist to the bottom of the fly.   This flag was originally designed and used in 1811 by the national hero, José Gervasio Artigas, when fighting for Uruguay's independence.

Although Uruguay is a republic it has no official President; senior members of the Cabinet take it in turn to carry out the duties of a President, and while discharging this office use the 'Presidential Flag' which has a white field charged with the Arms of Uruguay. These arms are quartered: the first quarter is blue, and bears the golden scales of justice; the second is white, and has a representation of the 'Cerro' of Montevideo, with a fortress upon its

URUGUAY: ARMS

summit. This is the symbol of power. The third is also white, and is charged with a horse, the symbol of freedom and liberty, while the fourth quarter is blue and bears a golden bull as the symbol of wealth. These arms date from 1829. The wreath which surrounds them and which is tied with a light blue ribbon is half olive and half laurel, and was added in 1906. The shield is ensigned with the 'Sun of May'.

The Minister of National Defence flies a white flag charged with a blue foul anchor between two blue five-pointed stars, and the Inspector-General of the Navy a white flag bearing the blue anchor at the hoist and one blue five-pointed star in the centre of the fly.

A Vice-Admiral has a white flag charged with three blue stars, one and two; and a Rear-Admiral's flag is similar but has two stars only.

PARAGUAY gained its independence from Spain about the middle of 1811, through a bloodless revolution led by Dr. Francia. Towards the end of that year a horizontal red, white and blue tricolour charged on the one side with the King of Spain's Arms, and those of Asunción on the other, was adopted. Francia, who was President from 1816 until 1840, is reported to have been particularly interested in the design of this flag; he also revised the charges, which were adopted by law at the end of 1842.

These remain in use today on the tricolour, which is not only the National Flag but also the Ensign and Merchant Flag (Plate **20, 2**).

This flag is unique in that it is the only South American flag having a different charge on each side of the field.

These charges are positioned in the centre of the white stripe; that on the obverse side being the national arms, whereas that on the reverse side is the Treasury Seal. In each case the charge is placed on a white disc with a red, white and blue rim. The former has a yellow five-pointed star within a palm and olive wreath, tied at the bottom with red, white and blue ribbon, encircled with the words 'Republica del Para-

Obverse   Reverse

guay' in black block letters; on the latter, a yellow lion seated and supporting a staff carrying a red cap of liberty and, above, the inscription 'Paz y Justicia'—'Peace and Justice'—in blue, take the place of the yellow star and wreath.

Both charges have the land and sky as a centre background.

The Masthead Pennant is striped horizontally red over white over blue, with a white panel bearing a yellow five-pointed star at the hoist.

The Jack has a square white field with an unusual saltire; this is red from the top of the hoist to the bottom of the fly, and blue from the top of the fly to the bottom of the hoist. The centre of the saltire is charged with a yellow five-pointed star.

The President's Standard is blue, and bears a large white disc with a red, white and blue rim, the red being outside and the blue inside. This disc bears a large yellow five-pointed star, surrounded by a laurel wreath, as shown in the arms. There is a yellow five-pointed star in each corner of the flag. The Defence Minister flies a blue flag. In the centre thereof is a yellow anchor and in each corner of the field there is a small yellow five-pointed star. Without the anchor it becomes the flag of the Chief of Naval Staff, and with the four stars only, that of the Commander-in-Chief of the Navy.

A Vice-Admiral flies a blue flag with three small yellow stars placed diagonally across the field from the top of the hoist to the bottom of the fly. A Rear-Admiral, when in command, is known by a similar flag, but there are only two yellow stars, also placed diagonally across the field.

Turning to the Army, a General has a blue flag, thereon a red cross with a narrow white edging. The first quarter is red, however, and bears a yellow five-pointed star in the centre.

The Diplomatic Service is known by a red flag, charged with a blue cross edged with white, the first quarter being blue with a yellow five-pointed star in the centre.

The Consular Service flies a flag with a white cross thereon, the top two quarters being red and the bottom two quarters blue, while in the first quarter is the yellow star.

Three former West Indian Colonies of Great Britain have become independent countries within the British Commonwealth of Nations; they are Barbados, Jamaica, and Trinidad and Tobago.

BARBADOS, the most recent of these, acquired independence on the 30th November 1966 and her new National Flag was hoisted on that day. It has three vertical stripes, ultramarine blue, gold and ultramarine blue, proportions three by two, in the centre a black trident head, or broken trident, of generous proportions (Plate **20**, 6).

JAMAICA became independent within the Commonwealth on the night of August 5th–6th 1962 and adopted a new National Flag. This consists of a diagonal cross or saltire in gold; the triangles thus enclosed are black at the hoist and fly, and green at the top and bottom (Plate **20**, 8).

Her Majesty the Queen's new Personal Flag for use in Jamaica was first flown on her visit to the West Indies in the spring of 1966. It consists basically of the Arms of Jamaica and is illustrated on Plate **5**, 7. The Governor-General uses the standard blue Governor-General Flag.

The independence of TRINIDAD AND TOBAGO within the Commonwealth was celebrated at a ceremony held on August 31st 1962, when the new National Flag was hoisted. This has a red field with a broad diagonal black stripe, bordered on each side with white stripes running from the top of the hoist to the bottom of the fly (Plate 20, 9). The National Flag is used as the Ensign for her merchant ships, but the Coastguard Ensign has a white field with a red St. George's Cross with in the canton a replica of the National Flag, fimbriated in white. These new flags replace the old British Blue Ensign which was defaced with the old elaborate badge.

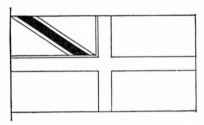

TRINIDAD AND TOBAGO
COASTGUARD ENSIGN

TRINIDAD AND
TOBAGO: BADGE

Her Majesty the Queen has also adopted a Personal Flag for Trinidad and Tobago which, like that for Jamaica, was first used during the visit paid in 1966. This has a handsome and elaborate design and is illustrated on Plate 5, 8.

When Columbus made his first journey to the New World, he first landed at Guanahani, an island in the Bahamas, and called it San Salvador. Then he sailed on to CUBA, which remained a Spanish Colony until 1898.

It was the Venezuelan General Narciso López who, in 1848, made the first serious attempt to help Cuba break away from Spanish rule. He carried *La Estrella Solitaria*—'The Lone Star'— banner, Cuba's present flag.

The field consists of five horizontal stripes of equal width, three blue and two white, with a red triangle, charged with a five-pointed star, at the hoist.

The long struggle for independence continued for half a century until, as a result of the Spanish-American War, it was taken under the protection of the United States in 1898. Cuba became an independent republic in 1902, and López's flag was adopted as the official flag. Today it is the National Flag, Naval Ensign and Merchant Flag; it is illustrated on Plate 18, 10.

The Masthead Pennant is divided horizontally blue over white, with a small red triangle charged with a white five-pointed star thereon at the hoist.

The Jack is divided into horizontal halves. The upper half is again divided, but vertically, red (at the hoist) and white, the red portion being charged with a white five-pointed star, while the lower half of the Jack is blue. This was the flag used by Carlos Manuel de Céspedes during the ten years' war 1868–1878.

The President's Flag has a light blue rectangular field bearing three small white five-pointed stars near the upper edge and three similar stars along the lower edge. In the centre is a representation of the arms. These arms consist of a shield which is halved vertically. On its dexter side are two white diagonal stripes running from left to right on a blue ground—the national colours. The other half contains a design in full colour, incorporating a royal palm, the most beautiful tree among the Cuban flora, which stands in a valley between two

CUBA

mountains, these representing the island. At the top of the shield is a 'chief', on which the sun is shown rising over the sea, the former representing the tropics, and the latter the Caribbean Sea. On each side is a promontory, symbolical of the coasts of Florida and Yucatan, while a golden key is placed horizontally upon the sea, the conception being that Cuba is the key of the Gulf of Mexico. Behind the shield is a bunch of lictor's rods, the emblem of support and authority, which is topped by the Phrygian cap, for freedom, democracy and equality. The shield is flanked by a wreath of oak and laurel.

The flag of the Minister of Defence is blue; in the centre thereof a large white anchor within a narrow white rectangular frame.

From the eastern point of Cuba Columbus proceeded southeast to what he named 'Hispaniola'—Little Spain—but which was known to the natives as HAITI. This is still the name of the smaller or western part of the island.

The real break-up of Spanish America may be said to have begun with the Treaty of Ryswick, 1697, when Spain ceded Haiti to France. Then it was that the lilies of France superseded the scarlet and gold of Spain.

General Jean Jacques Dessalines, founder of the independence of Haiti, adopted a distinctive flag on May 18th 1803. It comprised the blue and red vertical stripes from the Tricolour: these, he said, represented the Negroes and mulattoes respectively who were fighting side by side for liberty. He was assassinated three years later and Henri Christophe changed the blue stripe to black. However, this ephemeral flag was superseded by one divided *horizontally* blue over red charged with the Arms of Haiti which were designed by President Alexander Sabès Petion, who held office from 1807 to 1818. It was re-affirmed in the Constitution of 1843.

In 1963 Haiti adopted a new flag which is divided vertically, black to the hoist and dark red to the fly. This plain black and red flag is the Merchant Ship Ensign and also the everyday National Flag used by the private citizens. The State Flag and the Warship Ensign have, in the centre, a white rectangular panel containing the arms. These arms have also been slightly modified; the cap of liberty which formerly surmounted the palm-tree has been deleted, and the flags below are now black and red. The arms

ARMS OF HAITI

now consist of a palm-tree on a green mount in the centre; in front of the tree is a drum, with three black and red flags and three rifles with fixed bayonets on each side.   Finally, a cannon on its carriage is placed on each side and beneath, on a white scroll, is the motto 'L'UNION FAIT LA FORCE' ('Union makes Strength') (Plate 19, 7).

The DOMINICAN REPUBLIC occupies the eastern (and larger) side of Hispaniola, and has a very distinctive flag.   It was designed in 1839 by Juan Pablo Duarte, founder of the society called 'La Trinitaria' (The Trinitarians), who were responsible for the formation of the republic in 1844.   This flag is quartered, first and fourth blue and second and third red, while overall is a white cross; it is now the Merchant Flag (Plate 19, 1).

The National Flag and Naval Ensign are the same, but in addition, there is the national arms in the centre of the white cross.   These consist of a shield with blue and red quarterings with a white cross overall, and thereon three pairs of Dominican flags in saltire on which a Bible and a golden cross are superimposed.   Flanking the shield are two branches, a palm and a laurel; above the shield is a blue scroll inscribed 'DIOS PATRIA LIBERTAD' —'God, country, liberty'—the secret password of the Trinitarians, and beneath a red scroll with the words 'REPUBLICA DOMINICANA'.

DOMINICAN
REPUBLIC

The Masthead Pennant is quartered like the Merchant Flag and charged overall with a white cross.

The Jack has a royal blue field with the arms on a white disc in the centre, encircled with seventeen white five-pointed stars.

The President's Flag is white.   The first quarter comprises a diminutive of the National Flag, and the fly is charged with a large anchor in gold. The Army flag is a little startling. Overall it has the white cross.   In the first quarter, which is dark blue, are five white five-pointed stars,

DOMINICAN REPUBLIC:
ARMY FLAG

arranged in a horizontal line.   The second and third quarters are red; the fourth quarter is composed of four equal horizontal stripes, reading from top to bottom, of green, white, red and yellow—representing infantry, aviation, artillery and cavalry respectively.

Naval command flags have a dark blue field, nine by five, with a white 'Greek' cross in the centre thereof.   White five-pointed stars are added to denote rank, thus—Admiral four, Vice-Admiral three, Rear-Admiral two, and Commodore one.

Chapter Six

EUROPE

ALBANIA's colours are red and black, and her emblem is the black double-headed eagle of Scanderberg, the great 15th-century Albanian patriot. Conquered by the Turks in 1431, she regained her freedom in 1913 under the terms of the Treaty of London. Scanderberg chose the eagle as the device on account of an old tradition which says that the Albanians are the descendants of an eagle, and the Albanian name for Albanians is 'Shgipetar' or 'Skipetar', which means 'the descendants of the eagle'.

The shade of red was very deep crimson until about 1934, when it was changed to a bright red. The flags were almost square, the length being very slightly less than the hoist—a most unusual feature. There was, however, one exception—namely, the State Flag, which had the usual proportions of three by two and bore the black eagle surmounted by a crown in gold. After 1945 this flag, but with a red five-pointed star edged with gold in the place of the golden crown, became the National Flag (Plate 21, 2).

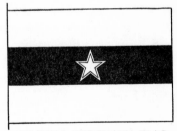

ALBANIA: MERCHANT FLAG

The Merchant Flag consists of three horizontal stripes of equal width, red, black and red, and in the centre of the middle stripe there is a red five-pointed star edged with gold. The proportions of the field are three by two.

ANDORRA, that little state tucked away in the Pyrenees between Spain and France, is in theory a principality whose constitution dates from the year 1278. Judicial powers in civil affairs are vested jointly in two representatives, one appointed by the Spanish

Bishop of Urgel and the other by the President of the French Republic. However, the Andorrans elect their own representatives to the council that governs the country.

The original flag had a field divided vertically, yellow (at the hoist) and red. Later this was changed to a vertical tricolour by adding a bright blue stripe at the hoist and placing a coat of arms in the centre of the yellow stripe. Great difficulty has been experienced in obtaining details of the official flag. The Spanish version shows the shield from the seal, which appears over the entrance of the archway to the Town Hall of Andorra. It is quartered, (1) a bishop's mitre and crozier in gold on a blue field; (2) and (3) seven vertical stripes, four in gold and three in red (probably taken from the arms of Aragon—*see* page 166); and (4) blue with two bulls in gold facing the *fly* and not the hoist as one might have expected (Plate **21**, 3). Another version, the French, is said to have a slightly different quartered shield, ensigned with a golden coronet; yet another variation is sometimes met with, namely a horizontal tricolour, bright blue over yellow over red, the centre stripe being charged with a coronet.

The National and Merchant Flags of AUSTRIA consist of three horizontal stripes of equal width, red, white and red (Plate **21**, 4). These colours came from the Arms of Leopold Heldenthum, the great Duke of Bebenberg, who fought in a battle in which his white surcoat became so stained with blood that the only white portion left was a band round the waist which had been covered up by the sword-belt. Leopold V of Bebenberg will be remembered as the captor of our own Richard Coeur-de-Lion when the latter was on his way home from the Holy Land.

It was decided to adopt this flag after the formation of Austria's first republic on November 12th 1918. After twenty years it was superseded by the 'Hakenkreuz' flag of Germany as a result of the 'Anschluss' of 1938. However, it was restored again at the end of World War II, when the second republic was established on December 19th 1945. The arms of the republic, which were adopted in accordance with the Law of Coats of Arms, Article 1, para. 2, dated May 1st 1945, are shown in the accompanying

Plate 20

FLAGS OF LATIN AMERICA AND THE CARIBBEAN

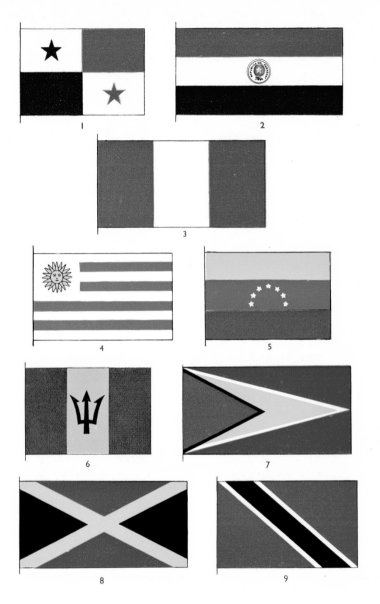

Plate 20   f.p. 118

FLAGS OF LATIN AMERICA
AND THE CARIBBEAN

illustration.   The colours are as follows: eagle—black; tongue—red; crown, beak, legs, claws, sickle and hammer—yellow; chain—steel; shield—red over white over red.

These arms are borne on the middle of the white stripe of all flags and banners flown by the President, State Authorities, Foundations and Institutions. Austria recovered her independence on May 15th 1955, when the State Treaty was signed in Vienna by Great Britain, the United States of America, France and Russia.

AUSTRIA: ARMS

The Austrian States or 'Länder' have their own flags; these are for the most part horizontally striped of two colours, although Carinthia has a three-striped flag, yellow, red and white. There is also some overlapping; for instance Salzburg, Vorarlberg and Vienna all have red over white, while Upper Austria and the Tyrol have white over red.

The National Flag of BELGIUM (Plate **21,** 5) is a tricolour of rather unusual proportions—namely, 3 to 2·60—consisting of vertical stripes of equal width, black (at the hoist), yellow, and red—the old colours of the Duchy of Brabant; the Merchant Flag is the same, but the field is three by two.

These colours were adopted as the National Flag in 1830 when Belgium became an independent kingdom.

A Royal Decree by King Leopold I in 1858 inaugurated the first Royal Standard.   This was the national tricolour charged with the Arms of the Royal House.   It was intended for use afloat, but as the Belgian Navy was disbanded in 1862 it had a very short life, and Belgium was without a Royal Standard until 1921.   The present Royal Standard, like its predecessor, is for use afloat only.   Its design has been governed by a number of decrees.

It is square; the colour of the field is exactly the same as the ribbon of the Order of Leopold, known as 'rouge ponceau'—a shade between crimson and amaranth.   In the centre thereof the Arms of the Royal House, a golden lion rampant (the Lion of Belgium), very similar to the Arms of Leopold I.   Each of the four

9

BELGIUM: ROYAL STANDARD
FOR USE AFLOAT

corners of the field bears the initial of the Sovereign ensigned with the Royal Crown, in gold. The Personal Standards of the Queen, and other *male* members of the Royal Family, are the same except that each has her or his initial under the crown in the corners. Princesses of Belgium have no personal standards.

On land the Royal Family use the National Flag; however, there is one exception, namely King Baudouin uses a diminutive of his Standard as a car flag.

During World War II a 'Section Belge' was formed in the Royal Navy of Great Britain. This section was the nucleus of the re-born Belgian Navy, known as the 'Force Navale'. At first it was under the administration of the Ministry of Communications which in February 1949 was superseded by the Ministry of Defence. In February 1950 a Royal Decree granted to the Force Navale, now the Belgian Royal Navy, a special Ensign of somewhat unusual but handsome design. This is white, proportions three by two, with a saltire formed from the national colours of red, gold and black. In the upper quarter are two crossed cannons surmounted by the Royal Crown, and below a foul anchor (Plate **21**, 6).

BELGIUM:
EMBLEM ON
ARMY
COLOURS

The Jack is a square edition of the National Flag. The Masthead Pennant is divided vertically into three, black at the hoist, yellow and red, the latter is forked and three times the length of the others.

All units of the Army of Belgium have the same basic colours, i.e. the National Flag but square in shape and with a golden fringe. The flag pike or staff is surmounted by an emblem consisting of a rect-angle, the longer sides of which carry in French on one and Flemish on the other the National motto

'L'Union Fait la Force', and also the designation of the unit to which the Colours belong; the short sides carry the initials of the monarch in whose reign the Colours were awarded. This rectangle is supported by a crown with a wreath of oak and laurel, and overall is the lion. The whole device is in gilt bronze.

The flags of the Colours vary in size, those of the infantry being 0.90 metres square, while the standards of the cavalry and artillery are 0·80, and the 'Fanions' or guidons of the auxiliary services are 0·70. Honours and citations are inscribed on the Colour flags in capital letters. The whole is embellished with a golden cord and tassels.

During World War II the Belgian section of the Royal Air Force used the R.A.F. Ensign with the red, yellow and black target (black in the centre), in place of our red, white and blue one.

An official announcement of April 26th 1950, stated that the Belgian Air Force Ensign was to have a field of air force blue, three by two, and in the centre thereof a target comprising the aforesaid colours and separated from the field by a yellow fimbriation. This charge occupied two-thirds the depth of the hoist. In the upper corner of the field was a pair of stylised yellow wings charged with a shield ensigned with a crown of the same colour. The design of this emblem was slightly altered in 1953; the target now occupies approximately one-half the depth of the hoist, as shown here.

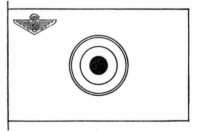

BELGIAN AIR FORCE

The shield on the winged emblem is black, having a narrow red border, and is charged with a yellow lion rampant.

The Minister of Communications administers unarmed vessels owned by the government, such as hydrographic, buoyage, passenger, Dover–Ostend packets etc. They wear an ensign which is the national tricolour defaced with the Belgian lion rampant, black with red claws and tongue, surmounted by the Royal Crown, also black.

BELGIUM: GOVERNMENT
VESSELS

BELGIUM: YACHT
ENSIGN

Merchant ships commanded by officers of the Naval Reserve wear a similar ensign, but in this case there is no crown.

The Yacht Ensign consists of the national tricolour with the Royal Crown, in gold, on the black stripe. It is worn by yachts whose owners are members of the Royal Belgian and one or two other Belgian yacht clubs.

White, green and red are the colours of BULGARIA. White stands for the country's love of peace, green for her main products of agriculture, while red signifies the bravery and endurance of her army. These colours were adopted by the Constituent Assembly in 1878. The Merchant Flag is the same as the National Flag (Plate 21, 7), a horizontal tricolour of equal stripes, white at the top, green in the middle and red at the bottom. The emblem of the state is placed on the white stripe, at the hoist, in accordance with the Constitution of the People's Republic of Bulgaria, dated December 4th 1947. This emblem comprises a golden lion rampant, framed by a wreath composed of ears of corn tied with a ribbon of the national colours, and below a red scroll with the inscription '9. IX. 1944' in gold; above the lion there is a red five-pointed star. The field of the Naval Ensign was composed of the plain horizontal tricolour, having a red upper canton charged with the golden lion rampant, and a white lower canton bearing a large red five-pointed star. However, the present one is white with two narrow horizontal stripes, green over red, in the lower hoist: a large red five-pointed star is placed near the hoist above the

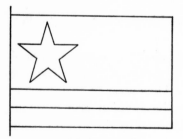

BULGARIA: ENSIGN

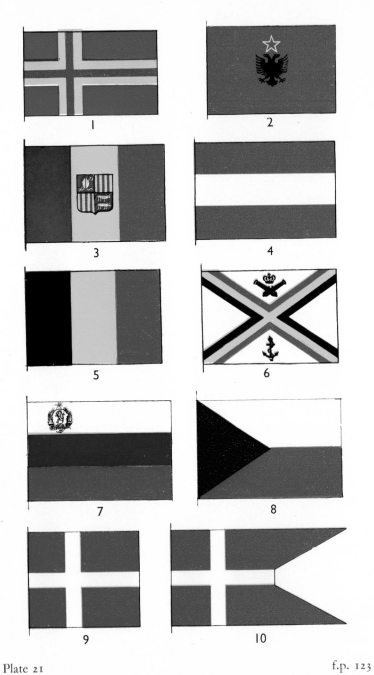

Plate 21

FLAGS OF EUROPEAN COUNTRIES

Plate 21

FLAGS OF EUROPEAN COUNTRIES

two narrow stripes, as shown in the illustration on the previous page. A diminutive of this ensign is positioned at the hoist of the red swallow-tailed Masthead Pennant. The Jack, which used to have a white field bearing a red cross over a green saltire, is now red and bears a large red five-pointed star, fimbriated white, in the centre.

CZECHOSLOVAKIA is one of those countries which has adopted red, white and blue for her national colours, but they are arranged in rather a striking fashion. The top half of the National and Merchant Flag is white, and the bottom half red, while the blue appears as a blue triangle in the hoist (Plate 21, 8). The flag was established by the law of March 30th 1930. Czechoslovakia includes the former Austrian provinces of BOHEMIA and MORAVIA. The ancient colours of the Kingdom of Bohemia were red and white, while blue was contained in those of Moravia.

In accordance with Government Ordnance No. 29, dated October 10th 1954, vessels of the Armed Forces wear an ensign consisting of the National Flag bearing in the upper hoist a red five-pointed star charged with the white lion rampant of Bohemia. This lion wears a golden coronet and has a double tail, as shown in the accompanying illustration.

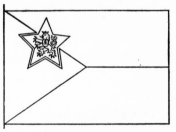

CZECHOSLOVAKIA:
ARMED FORCES

One of the oldest flags that has been in continuous use is the famous 'Dannebrog' of DENMARK, which literally translated means 'Danish cloth', but its symbolic meaning can best be described as 'The spirit of Denmark'. In 1219 King Waldemar was leading his troops into battle against the pagan Livonians. The moment was critical, and the King saw, or thought he saw, a white cross in the blood-red sky, and this is said to have been the origin of the flag. In common with the emblems of other Scandinavian countries, the upright limb of the cross is displaced slightly towards the hoist. The National and Merchant Flag (Plate 21, 9) is rectangular, the proportions being laid down in the decree of July 11th 1848, thus: the width of the cross is one seventh the hoist, the rectangles at the hoist are squares with sides three sevenths of the hoist, and the length of the rectangles in the fly is half as much again as that of the squares. The Ensign and Jack are longer in the fly than the National and Merchant Flag, and they are swallow-tailed to the bar of the cross, which, however, is cut square. In this case the length of the rectangles in the fly is five fourths that of the inner squares, and the length of the swallow-tails is half as much again as the fly rectangles (Plate **21**, 10).

DENMARK: ROYAL ARMS

The Masthead Pennant is red with a forked fly: overall, a narrow white cross.

Mention should perhaps be made of a most unusual custom obtaining in naval vessels, namely, Ensigns and Jacks, *also Masthead Pennants and Admiral's flags*, are half-masted *annually on Good Friday*. Again, Ensigns and Jacks are worn at half-mast on Remembrance Day, April 9th, from 8 a.m. until noon.

The Naval Ensign is also flown at all Royal Danish Air Force Stations, there being no distinctive ensign for this service.

The Royal Standard is the Ensign with the addition upon the centre of the cross of a large white square bearing the Royal Arms,

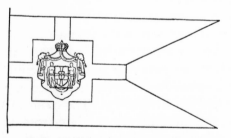

DENMARK: ROYAL STANDARD

DENMARK: ARMS FROM
QUEEN'S STANDARD

with supporters upon a pavilion which is ensigned with the Royal Crown. The Standard of H.M. the Queen is similar except that the supporters to the Royal Arms are not included.

H.R.H. Princess Margrethe, Heir to the Throne, has her own Standard. In this case the charge on the large white square is less ornate. It consists of a shield, bearing the charges from the first quarter of the Royal Arms, surrounded by the collar and pendant of the Order of the Elephant and ensigned with the Royal Crown (*see* illustration). When the white square bears a blue foul anchor surmounted by the Royal Crown, the flag is that of the Minister of Marine.

DEVICE ON H.R.H. PRINCESS MARGRETHE'S STANDARD

There are a number of flags consisting of the Ensign with a special charge in the first quarter. These include the Government Vessels Ensign, the Ministry of Marine, the Mail Flag, the State Railways, the Royal Greenland Trading Company, etc., the distinctive charges being the Royal Crown in white, the Royal Crown over a foul anchor in gold, a post-horn surmounted by the Royal Crown in gold, the Royal Crown over the letters 'D.S.B.', also in gold, and two white arrows in saltire, respectively.

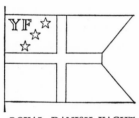

ROYAL DANISH YACHT CLUB ENSIGN

There is also a special ensign worn by yachts whose owners are members of the Royal Danish Yacht Club. This consists of the Warship Ensign with the letters 'Y.F.' in the upper canton: underneath these letters are three stars disposed diagonally, all in gold. The flag of the Ministry of Fisheries has a triangular red field bearing the Royal Crown, a foul anchor and a trident, in gold.

Many Danes have a tall flagstaff in the front gardens of their houses from which they fly the National Flag. However, a streamer is often hoisted as an alternative because, it is said, they dislike a bare flagstaff. This has a red field, and bears the white cross of Denmark. It is a diminutive of the streamer (but without the swallow-tail) used by ships in Tudor times.

The flag of EIRE (Republic of Ireland) is composed of equal vertical stripes, green, white and orange—in that order from the mast (Plate **22**, 10). We read of Irish tricolours being used in 1830 and 1844; however, they did not appear in large numbers until 1848. During that year meetings were held in various parts of Ireland to celebrate the French Revolution, and the Irish tricolour was flown side by side with that of the French. The colours used were green, white and orange, but the order in which they appeared from the mast was anything but constant. Indeed, sometimes orange was placed next to the mast, followed by either white or green.

It is interesting to note that the National Flag at that time had a green field with a golden harp superimposed; this remained until the Rising of 1916. From then onwards the tricolour captured the imagination of the people and was soon accepted by all and sundry as the National Flag.

By 1920 the arrangement of the colours comprising the tricolour appears to have been established, with green at the mast, orange at the fly, and white occupying the centre. This flag was recognised officially on the establishment of the Free State, 1921–22. It was formally confirmed in Article No. 7 of the Constitution of Ireland, 1937, wherein it was stated that 'the national flag is the tricolour of green, white and orange'. It continued as such when the Republic of Ireland Act came into force on April 18th 1949. The proportions of the field are two by one. A set of rules governing the design and display of the tricolour was drawn up and published by the Stationery Office, Dublin. It contains eleven paragraphs, and appears to have been based on the United States of America Flag Code.

The Merchant Flag and Naval Ensign are the same as the National Flag, but the Jack is green, with a golden harp, in generous proportions, superimposed in the centre thereof. The golden harp is also borne on the blue flag of the President, and a similar harp is placed at the head of the white Masthead Pennant.

One Yacht Club in Ireland, the Royal St. George, continues to use the British Blue Ensign. Other Irish clubs use the Irish Blue; this has a blue field with a diminutive of the National Flag of Eire in the upper canton, and generally defaced by a club badge.

FINLAND was part of the Kingdom of Sweden from 1154 until

1809, when after a struggle it was ceded to Russia. In 1581 King John of Sweden conferred on Finland the status of a Grand Duchy and a coat of arms. These arms have remained practically the same to this day. They consist of a red rect-

angular shield bearing a yellow crowned lion rampant with a sword in its right paw which is clad in armour. There are also nine white roses on the shield, which was originally sur-mounted by a ducal coronet but this latter was discarded when Finland became an inde-pendent republic in 1917.

FINLAND

There is considerable uncertainty as to the origin of the present flag of Finland, which is described as an azure blue cross, off-set towards the hoist as is common with most Scandinavian flags, on a white field. The proportions of the standard are eleven by eighteen and the arms, as described above, are placed in the centre of the blue cross. This is the State or Government Flag (Plate **22**, **2**).

Although the original colours of Finland are said to have been red and yellow, there has always been a strong feeling for the present white and blue and there is evidence that these colours were used in many ancient provincial and military flags. After much

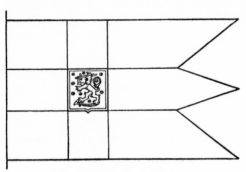

FINLAND: ENSIGN

discussion in the Finnish Legislative Assembly the present flag was adopted for Independent Finland on May 29th 1918.

The State Flag described above with three tails is the Ensign for the Armed Forces of Finland; with the addition of two yellow cannon in saltire charged with two rifles in the first quarter it becomes the flag of the Minister of Defence; and with a thunderbolt over a post horn, in gold, the Post Office flag.

The Jack has a square white field with in the centre the Arms of

Finland; the Masthead Pennant has a forked tail, and the blue cross of Finland in the hoist.

The Merchant Ensign is the same as the State or Government Flag, but without the arms in the centre, and this flag is also used by the ordinary citizens of Finland as their National Flag.

The Flag of the President is similar to the Ensign of the Armed Forces, but has in the canton what is best described as an heraldic 'cross-pattée', in blue, charged with a yellow 'fyflot', or swastika-shaped cross, the Cross of Freedom, Finland's most distinguished order.

DETAIL OF FINLAND'S PRESIDENT'S FLAG

The flag of the ALAND ISLANDS, which have a semi-autonomous status, is light blue bearing a yellow cross charged with a red cross. It was adopted on April 7th 1954, and may only be displayed *on land* (Plate **21**, 1).

During World War II the FAROE ISLANDS were under British protection. They adopted a very distinctive flag, which had a white field bearing a red cross edged (fimbriated) with blue; as with other Scandinavian flags the vertical limb of the cross is nearer the hoist than the fly. These islands were subsequently granted partial Home Rule, and this flag was officially recognised under Article No. 12 of the law concerning Home Rule, passed by the Lagting on December 5th 1947, and ratified by the Danish Government on March 23rd 1948. In accordance with a Royal decree of June 5th 1959, the bright blue border of the cross was changed to an azure-blue one (Plate **22**, 1).

Napoleon I of FRANCE said at Auch in Armagnac, 'The fleurs-de-lis? During eight centuries they have guided France to glory . . . they must always be dear to France and held in reverence by her true children'. And so the 'fleur-de-lis' although no longer displayed on any of the official flags of France is still regarded with esteem by all French citizens.

The origin of the fleurs-de-lis is the legend that King Clovis of France dreamt during the night before the battle of Tolbiac, in the year 496, that the golden toads in one of his standards had been changed into lilies. In spite of this story it was many years before the fleurs-de-lis were recorded on any banner of France. The Standard of the Emperor Charlemagne, who reigned from A.D. 768 to A.D. 814, is reputed to have been red, with three short pointed tails and decorated with a number of golden crosses and roundels. Then there was the 'oriflamme' of St. Denis, which was used inter-mittently from the 11th to the 16th centuries. This took varying forms, but was essentially a plain red banner with tails, sometimes two and sometimes three or four. It was in the year 1191 that King Philippe II first raised a banner decorated with the fleur-de-lis; this was azure blue and liberally sprinkled with golden 'lilies'. During the next two hundred years the flag

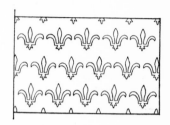

FRANCE: KING
PHILIPPE II'S BANNER

underwent a number of changes, until in the year 1365 during the reign of Charles V it had become a rectangular blue flag with only three golden lilies upon it (Plate **22**, 4).

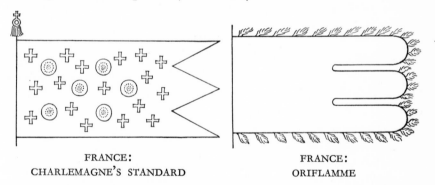

FRANCE:
CHARLEMAGNE'S STANDARD

FRANCE:
ORIFLAMME

There have been different views as to what the stylised fleur-de-lis is supposed to represent, but the general consensus appears to be that it is the flower of the yellow iris, the so-called 'Flag', botanically the *Iris pseudacorus*. Another opinion is that it is the head of a lance shaped like a flower.

Like England, France developed special flags or 'Pavillons' as ships ensigns are called in France; also like England, although at first those for warships and merchant ships were the same, it was

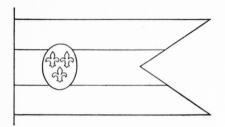 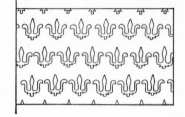

FRANCE: GALLEY ENSIGN   FRANCE: FLEUR-DE-LIS ENSIGN

not long before the warships were distinguished from the merchant ships by different ensigns. One of the earliest was a two-tailed flag, white with red horizontal red stripes top and bottom, carrying in the hoist a blue shield with three gold fleurs-de-lis. This appears to have been the ensign of the galleys, and went out of use when galleys were no longer used as fighting ships in the 17th century. Meanwhile at about this time other French warships started using a plain white ensign, which towards the end of the 17th century became charged with a number of gold fleurs-de-lis; in the course of time they were reduced to three.

The early ensigns of the French Merchant ships in the 16th century were a white cross on a plain blue or a red ground, and these became combined to form a flag which had two quarters red and two blue. In 1689 merchant ships were wearing a new flag, blue with a white St. George's Cross, carrying in the centre a shield with three fleurs-de-lis. The exact significance of this flag is not clear, for very soon an order was issued requiring all merchant ships to carry the Royal Arms and also an ensign. Great latitude was allowed in the design of the ensign, as long as the white ensign of the warships was not used. Most merchant ships seem to have flown a white ensign with some simple device in the canton.

The French Revolution in 1789 swept all these flags away, and they were replaced by the blue, white and red tricolour which with variations in detail has persisted to this day. There seems little doubt that the origin of the tricolour is to be found in the colours of Paris, red and blue, to which was added the historic white of France. Although one authority gives the date of the introduction of the tricolour as October 1789, it seems that this is wrong, and

Plate 22

FLAGS OF EUROPEAN COUNTRIES

1. Faroe Islands: National Flag (p. 128)
2. Finland: State or Government Flag (p. 127)
3. France: Tricolour, National Flag, Ensign and Merchant Flag (p. 130)
4. France: The Bible (Standard of Charles V) (p. 123)
5. West German Federal Republic: National and Merchant Flag (p. 157)
6. West German Federal Republic: Government Authorities Flag (p. 159)
7. East German Democratic Republic: State Flag (p. 158)
8. Greece: National and Merchant Flag (p. 159)
9. Hungary: National Flag, Ensign and Merchant Flag (p. 141)
10. Eire: National Flag (p. 125)
11. Iceland: National and Merchant Flag (p. 124)

Plate 22

FLAGS OF EUROPEAN COUNTRIES

1 Faroe Islands: National Flag (p. 128)

2 Finland: State or Government Flag (p. 127)

3 France: Tricolour, National Flag, Ensign and Merchant Flag
   (p. 130)

4 France: The Lilies (Standard of Charles V) (p. 129)

5 West German Federal Republic: National and Merchant Flag
   (p. 135)

6 West German Federal Republic: Government Authorities
   Flag (p. 136)

7 East German Democratic Republic: State Flag p. (138)

8 Greece: National and Merchant Flag (p. 139)

9 Hungary: National Flag, Ensign and Merchant Flag (p. 144)

10 Eire: National Flag (p. 125)

11 Iceland: National and Merchant Flag (p. 144)

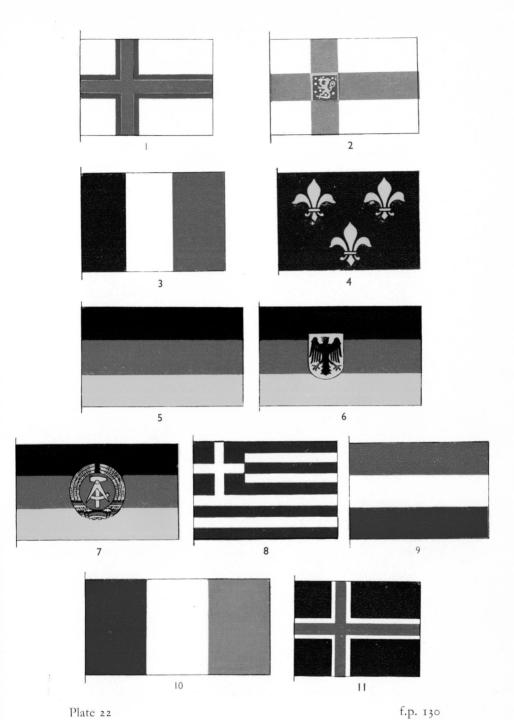

Plate 22   f.p. 130

FLAGS OF EUROPEAN COUNTRIES

that it was in October 1790 that the Constituent Assembly ordered that the flag of France be the tricolour.   Even then it appears that its adoption by the fleet was not immediate; in fact it was first worn by the warships of France as a 'Jack', while they continued with the old ensign until about 1794.   The first tricolour had the red stripe next to the mast, but in 1794 the colours were transposed and the blue was placed at the hoist, where it has remained.   This flag is now used, with a slight variation, as the Ensign for all French ships, whether warships or merchantmen, also as the 'Jack' for warships, the President's Standard and Army flags.   According to Article 2 of the Constitution, dated September 28th 1946, the National Emblem is a square flag with the three stripes of equal width, but it has been found that when used at sea or for display in open places equal stripes do not look equal, but that they can be made to appear to be of the same width if in fact the actual widths are slightly varied.   This was appreciated as long ago as the beginning of the 19th century, when the ship ensign was modified so that the blue next the staff was 30%, the white 33% and the red 37% of the length of the flag.   These proportions are now standard for all the flags in use in France (Plate 22, 3).

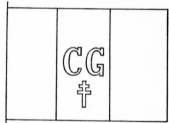

FRANCE:
STANDARD OF
PRESIDENT DE GAULLE

The Standard of the President used to be the National Flag charged with the initials of the President but when General Charles de Gaulle became President he added the Cross of Lorraine which was placed beneath the initials 'C.G.'.   The red Cross of Lorraine was adopted by General de Gaulle in 1940 as the emblem of the Free French Forces.

At the time of writing it is not known what the new President, Georges Pompidou, who was elected in June 1969, will adopt for his standard.

The French word 'Armée' has a slightly different meaning to the English word Army, which is usually taken to refer only to soldiers who fight on the land, whereas the French speak of the Army of the Land, the Army of the Sea, and the Army of the Air. (*Les Armées de*

EMBLEM OF FRENCH
MINISTER OF DEFENCE

terre, mer et l'air.) Thus the French Minister of 'Defence' is known as the 'Ministre des Armées', and his flag is the standard tricolour charged with an emblem in gold consisting of a sword (army), crossed anchors (navy) and wings (air).

As has already been stated the Navy use the tricolour as both Ensign and Jack and merchant ships also wear the national tricolour.

A standard type of Regimental Colour is used by all three services, as in Great Britain it is used as the Colours of regiments of the Army, and it is also used as the Colours of special units of the Navy (e.g. the Nautical College) and for units of the Air Force. These Colours, which date from 1880, consist of a fringed tricolour flag, carrying embroidered in gold the words 'RÉPUBLIQUE FRANÇAIS' on the obverse side, and on the reverse the motto 'HONNEUR ET PATRIE'. A wreath is painted in each corner encircling the number or initial of the unit concerned. The staff, or 'pike', is surmounted by a gilt lance-head, and carries a number of pennants ('Cravates' in French) on which are embroidered in more detail the name of the

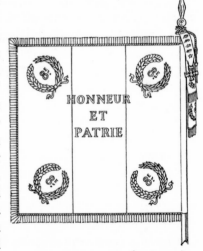

FRENCH COLOURS (REVERSE)

unit, and also the battle honours that it has earned.

The majority of the former colonies of France are now independent, and those that remain attached to France fly the national tricolour. Their Governors and High Commissioners have a dark blue flag with the national tricolour in the canton.

In 1958 General de Gaulle offered French Territories overseas a new form of association with France as self-governing republics, with the option of voting themselves full independence. This association was named the French Community. In May 1960 the former colonies were given the opportunity to become completely independent of France, and the majority chose to take this course, although six states, the Central African Republic, the Republic of Chad, the Republic of the Congo (Brazzaville), the Gaboon Republic, the Malagasy Republic and the Republic of Senegal, decided to remain within the French Community. As the links with France are so very tenuous and as the countries in the French Community have full independence their flags and the flags of the other ex-colonies of France are described under the headings of the continents in which they are situated.

Before there were national flags, ships were distinguished by the flags of their ports, and in the north of Europe these flags, in the course of time, were gradually replaced by the red and white colours of the Hanseatic League, to which so many of them became united. The Hansa was pre-eminently German, and according to Werdenhagen derived its name from Ander-See, 'On the Sea'. As the nations grew, the Hansa naturally decayed.

When in October 1867 the North German Confederation originated, the first German National Flag, a horizontal tricolour of black at the top, white in the centre, and red at the bottom was chosen. The red and white represented the old Hanseatic League, the black and white came from Prussia.

The German States also had their flags: Prussia, black over white; Pomerania, blue over white; Saxony, white over green; Waldeck, black, red and yellow; Württemberg, black over red; Mecklenburg-Schwerin and Mecklenburg-Strelitz, blue, yellow and red; Brunswick, blue over yellow; Hesse, red over white; Baden, red over yellow; Bavaria, white over blue; and Hanover, yellow over white.

With the coming of the German Empire in 1871, the Imperial flags with the well-known black eagle were introduced, but the old flag was retained as the Merchant Flag.

The Ensign under which the German Navy served in World War I was white, and bore thereon a black cross with a narrow black edging. The cross extended to the edges of the flag, and the upright of the cross was nearer to the flagstaff than to the fly.

Superimposed on the centre of the cross was a white disc, with black rim, charged with the crowned black eagle with the sceptre and orb in its talons.   The first quarter was filled with the black, white and red tricolour, charged with the Iron Cross in black, with a narrow white edge.   This was the cross of the old Teutonic Knights.   After that war it became known as the 'Imperial War Flag', and was hoisted at the masthead in German warships once a year on May 31st, in commemoration of the battle of Jutland.

The abdication of the Emperor, combined with the turmoil into which Germany was thrown as a result of her defeat, made drastic changes in her flags inevitable.

By Article 2 of the Weimar Convention, signed at Schwartzburg on August 11th 1919, it was laid down that the Federal colours were to be black, red and gold, while the Commercial Flag was to be the old black, white and red, with the Federal colours in the canton.

These Federal colours—generally known as the 'Weimar Colours'—'Schwarz-Rot-Gold', are said to have their origin in the black coats with red epaulettes and gold buttons worn by members of the irregular force which von Lutzöw raised in 1813 to assist in the struggle against Napoleon I.   This force was largely recruited from the German universities whose students were democratically minded, thus the colours became a symbol of freedom and were adopted for the flag of the German Federation on March 9th 1848, to be superseded, as has been explained on page 133, in October 1867 by the black, white and red horizontal tricolour of the North German Confederation.

In the early months of 1933 the advent into power of Herr Hitler and the Nazi Party brought yet another change in the flags of the Reich.

The parties of the Right had always resented the Weimar colours as being an ever-present reminder of Germany's defeat in the War, and so the red, black and gold were abolished.   On April 22nd a decree was issued regarding the temporary arrangement for the flying of flags.

The National Flags were to be the black, white and red tricolour (black at the top and red at the bottom) and the 'Hakenkreuz'

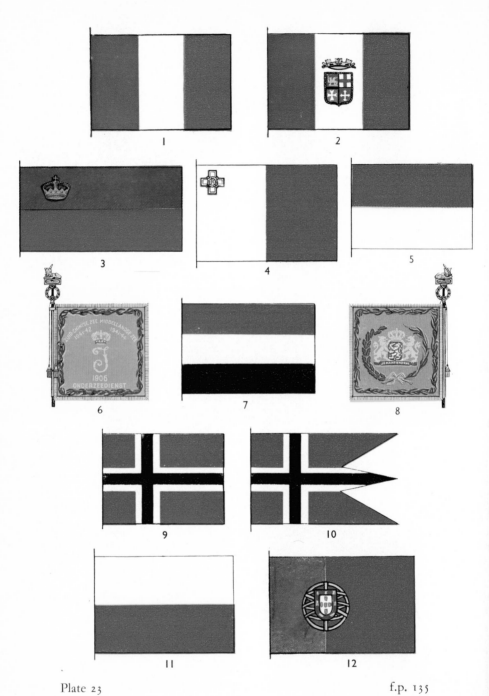

Plate 23

FLAGS OF EUROPEAN COUNTRIES

Plate 23

FLAGS OF EUROPEAN COUNTRIES

Flag, and these two flags were always
to be hoisted together.   The 'Hakenkreuz' Flag, red, charged with a
white disc bearing thereon the emblem
of the Nazi Party—a 'swastika' in
black—also displayed the colours of
the Reich.   It was held that the red and
white was symbolical of the commercial
strength of the nation, while the black

GERMANY: HAKENKREUZ
FLAG

and white represented the armed might on which that prosperity
depended.

All merchant ships were ordered to fly the tricolour at the stern,
and the 'Hakenkreuz' Flag on the signal stay or starboard signal-
yard.

This use of two flags on merchant ships led to an incident which
might have had serious diplomatic consequences. A German
liner was lying in New York harbour when a faction which was
hostile to the Nazi Party hauled down the swastika flag.   The
German authorities, not unnaturally, took exception to this.   It was
pointed out, however, that the insult had been aimed at the 'Party'
Flag, and that the National Flag had not been interfered with.

Thereupon at Nuremburg on September 15th 1935, the Reich-
stag unanimously decided that the Reich and National Flag
was the 'Hakenreuz' Flag, and that this flag was also to be the
Mercantile Flag.   The Reich colours were to be black, white
and red.   The proportions of the flag were to be five by three,
and the white circle with the hakenreuz was to be placed in the
centre of the flag.

With the collapse of Germany after World War II, all swastika
flags and emblems of the Nazi regime disappeared by order of the
occupying powers.

The WEST GERMAN FEDERAL REPUBLIC, the 'Bundesrepublik',
came into being on August 14th 1949, and with it a National Flag
was adopted in accordance with Article 22 of the new Constitution.
This is a horizontal tricolour, proportions five by three, black over
red over gold, the Federal colours of the Weimar Convention of
1919 (Plate 22, 5).   Although this flag was permitted to be

10

used by shipping on rivers and lakes as from the end of the following January, it was not until another twelve months had expired

that it could be worn at sea, and thus it became
the Merchant Flag also.

In June 1950 it was announced that three new
flags had been approved; these were for the
Government Authorities (Plate **22**, 6), the
President and a special one for the Ministry of
Posts and Telecommunications. The President's Flag is a square yellow field with a red
border, and in the centre the same black eagle
as in the flag of the Government Authorities.

WEST GERMANY:
PRESIDENT'S FLAG

For the flag of the Ministry of Posts and Telecommunications the
centre red stripe is a little wider than the stripe in the National Flag
so that it can accommodate a post horn emblem.

This flag is used by the postal
authorities ashore. Afloat a mail
pennant is flown; this is triangular in
shape, with a yellow field and red and
black border, and in the centre a
post horn in black.

The flag of Government Authorities
is used (1) by all non-commissioned
vessels of the Navy, i.e. fleet auxiliaries, and naval establishments; (2)

WEST GERMANY: MAIL PENNANT

the Army; (3) buildings and ships of the various ministries (except
that of Posts and Telecommunications).   A diminutive of this flag
is used as a Jack.

When the Prime Minister, or the Minister of Defence, is embarked in a warship, the national tricolour, having a field *two by one*
and bearing in the centre thereof the eagle badge, is hoisted at the
main masthead.

Vessels of the Coastguard Defence Service wore the Government Authorities flag as an ensign and a diminutive of it as a Jack.
The Masthead Pennant, Commodore's Broad Pennant and the
Flotilla Leader's Pennant had white fields and golden shields
charged with a black eagle having a red beak and claws.

The republic became a free and independent state on May 5th 1955, in accordance with treaties signed by Great Britain, the United States of America and France.

Twelve months later the Coastguard Defence Service was incorporated in the new German navy and a new range of flags was announced; these consist of the Ensign, Jack, Masthead

WEST GERMANY: MASTHEAD PENNANT

Pennant, Squadron Flag and Division Flag. The Ensign is a swallow-tailed edition of the Government Authorities flag. A diminutive of the Ensign does duty as the Jack. The Masthead Pennant, Squadron and Division flags are shown in the accompanying illustrations. Their white fields are charged with the Iron Cross in black with a narrow edging of the same colour.

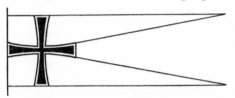 

WEST GERMANY: SQUADRON FLAG   DIVISION FLAG

The Navy, Army and the Air Force all have the same 'Ceremonial Colours', which is the 'Government Flag' (*see* page 136 and Plate **22**, 6), but square in shape and bordered by a red and black lace and a gold fringe. The various units are distinguished by streamers fastened to the head of the flag pike, or staff. These streamers carry the name and badge of the unit, and also are of different colours, blue for the Navy, red for the Army and white for the Air Force.

When the people of the Saar Territory voted for economic union with France on October 11th 1947, their horizontal tricolour, blue (on top), white and black, was superseded by a new flag, in accordance with Article No. 61 of the new Constitution. The field was three by two, divided vertically 'light cobalt' (at the hoist) and 'red vermilion'; the former portion occupied two fifths of the length of the field; overall and centred on the division of these colours, a white cross, the limbs of which were one fifth the hoist in width.   However, on January 1st 1957, this territory became part of Germany, as the State of SAARLAND within the West German Federal Republic, by agreement with France and in accordance with a plebiscite.   A new flag was adopted, consisting of the black, red and gold horizontal tricolour with the Arms of the State.   These arms are quartered thus: (1) Nassau-Saarbrücken—blue, charged with a crowned lion rampant and small crosses (of the type known heraldically as 'botonée fitchée') in white, the tongue of the lion being red; (2) Kur-Trier —white, bearing a red cross; (3) Lothringen—yellow, charged with a red diagonal stripe, bearing three white eaglets; (4) Pfalz-Zweibrücken—black, charged with a yellow lion rampant having a red crown, claws and tongue.

In modern Germany the states have retained their affection for their state flags, and although there have been some changes the majority of states have kept their old flags.

From September 26th 1955 until October 1st 1959 the EAST GERMAN DEMOCRATIC REPUBLIC, the D.D.R. (Deutsche Demokratische Republik) as it is often called, used the same National Flag as the West German Federal Republic, namely a horizontal tricolour, black over red over gold.   In order to make a distinction it was then decided to place the State emblem, in generous proportions, in the centre thereof for the new State Flag.   This emblem consists of a red disc bearing a hammer and a pair of compasses in gold, within a wreath of ears of corn, also in gold, tied with a black, red and gold ribbon (Plate 22, 7).   Merchant ships wear the tricolour with this emblem in the upper hoist. The Ensign worn by naval vessels is red, having three horizontal stripes, black over red over gold, in the centre; overall the State emblem, in this case surrounded by a laurel wreath of gold leaves and red berries on a red background.

The Masthead Pennant is red and has swallow-tails; a small horizontal tricolour, black over red over gold, charged with the State emblem from the Ensign, is positioned at the head.

EAST GERMANY: MERCHANT FLAG   EAST GERMANY: NAVAL ENSIGN

On the 10th August 1966 three new maritime ensigns were introduced for (a) Auxiliary ships of the Navy; (b) the Hydrographic Service; (c) the Salvage and Rescue Service. The Ensign for Auxiliaries is the same design as that for Naval Vessels except that the field is royal blue. The Ensign of the Hydrographic Service is this ensign 'defaced' by an emblem consisting of a yellow lighthouse in the top corner of the fly. The Ensign of the Salvage and Rescue Service has as a badge a yellow diver's helmet in the place of the lighthouse of the Hydrographic Service.

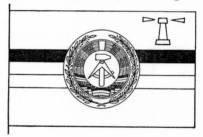

EAST GERMAN
HYDROGRAPHIC ENSIGN

The Minister of Defence flies a blue flag with the State emblem superimposed in the centre thereof. Again this emblem is placed in the centre of the Head of State's flag, the field of which is red, bordered on three sides by a black and red and gold cord.

EAST GERMANY:
HEAD OF STATE

A white triangular flag, edged green, with this emblem in the centre does duty as the Customs Flag, and a similar flag, but with grey edges, is the Fisheries Protection Flag.

GREECE has two National Flags: one is displayed only inside Greece, whereas the other is flown at seaports and outside Greek territory. The former is blue with a white cross, and the latter (perhaps the better known) has nine horizontal stripes, five blue and four white, with a blue canton bearing the white cross; this flag is also the Merchant Flag (Plate **22**, 8).   The stripes are said to stand for the nine syllables in the Greek motto 'Eleutheria a thanatos'—'Liberty or death'.

There seems to be no evidence to substantiate the belief that the first flag of Greece was adopted in 1822 and that its colours were red and white.   In fact it would appear that the colours of Greece have, since the early wars against the Turks, been blue and white, and that these colours were confirmed when Otto of Bavaria (the son of Louis I) became King of Greece in 1833.   It is from this year that the modern flag of Greece dates.   It was, perhaps, providential that the colours of the family of King Otto were also blue and white.   The shade of blue has varied over the years; in 1863 it was dark blue; it has also been a light blue and an azure and now it is royal blue.

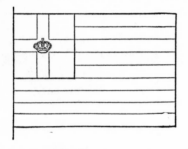

GREECE: ENSIGN

GREECE: JACK

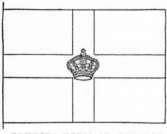

GREECE: FORT OR SERVICE FLAG

The Naval Ensign resembles the National and Merchant Flag, but has a golden crown in the centre of the white cross in the canton. The square Jack is blue and bears the white cross also charged with a crown. The Fort or Service Flag, the Air Force Ensign and the Civil Air Ensign are rectangular flags, all having the same basic design i.e. a royal blue field charged with the white cross, but with the distinguishing marks as shown in the accompanying illustrations.   As to the target on the Air

Force Ensign and the Civil Air Ensign, this is blue, white and blue (*same shade as the field*); and the crowns are in proper colours.   The annulet round the crown on the Air Force Ensign is white.

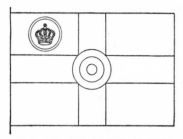
GREECE: AIR FORCE ENSIGN

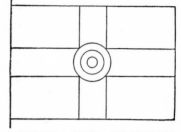
GREECE: CIVIL AIR ENSIGN

Customs vessels fly a pennant, dark blue at the hoist and white at the fly.   The latter bears the letter 'T' in dark blue.   The Masthead Pennant is dark blue, with a small white cross at the hoist.

The Royal Standard has a rectangular blue field with a large white cross superimposed, charged with the Royal Arms (full achievement) which were adopted in 1863.   The shield thereon is blue and bears the white cross.

The King's Personal Standard has a square blue field and also bears the white cross.   On the centre is a shield comprising the

GREECE: ROYAL STANDARD

GREECE: ROYAL ARMS
(FULL ACHIEVEMENT)

Royal Arms, while a golden crown is placed in each of the four squares of blue.   That of the Queen has the same field and white cross, the horizontal limb of which is charged with the Royal Arms on that portion nearest the hoist, and with her own arms on that in the fly.   The Crown Prince's Standard resembles that of the

GREECE: KING'S PERSONAL STANDARD

King, but has only one crown, in the first of the blue squares, while the standard used by other members of the Royal Family has no crowns at all in the squares.

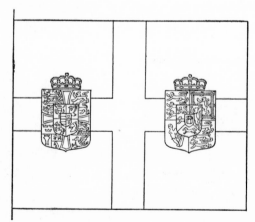

GREECE: QUEEN'S PERSONAL STANDARD

As far as is known, red, white and green made their first appearance as the national colours of HUNGARY at the beginning of the

17th century. It is recorded that at the coronation of King Mathias II in 1608, 'the wooden bridge leading from the Coronation Church of Pozsony to the Franciscan Church had been covered by a carpet in red, white and green colours'; also that three years later the King gave orders for 'sixty flags in red, white and green silk for warfare'.

In 1920, after the downfall of the Dual Empire, Hungary reverted to her old colours of red, white and green. In the old Austro-Hungarian Merchant Flag the right-hand side consisted of the Flag and Arms of Hungary. The 1919–45 National and Merchant Flag was a horizontal tricolour of equal stripes of red at the top, white in the centre, and green at the base. In the centre of the flag was the coat-of arms, but the use of this coat was optional and the plain tricolour was often used. It will be seen that the cross on the top of the crown was bent over; legend has it that thieves once stole the crown and put it into an iron casket which was not deep enough to hold it. The lid of the box was forced down, and this bent the cross.

HUNGARY: OLD ARMS

The Constitution of the new People's Republic of Hungary was approved during August 1949,

HUNGARY: 1949 EMBLEM

and with it the new National Flag and emblem. Details of these were laid down in Decree No. 20, para. 68, of 1949. The old tricolour was adopted and the new emblem placed in the centre of the white stripe, occupying practically the whole depth of it.

The emblem consisted of a light blue field charged with a golden hammer and a golden-yellow ear of corn in saltire, surmounted by a red five-pointed star edged with gold, the rays of which are pendant right across the field, framed by a wreath of golden-yellow corn connected below by a ribbon of the national colours.

This was also the Merchant Flag, but eight years later, in 1957, the old badge was replaced by badge consisting of a shield,

bearing the national colours, and bordered in gold, surrounded by a wreath with an entwined ribbon, and overall a star. In 1965, after another eight years the flag was further simplified and this badge removed, so that the flag is now just the red, white and green tricolour, and it serves as the National Flag, Naval Ensign and Merchant Flag (Plate **22**, 9).

HUNGARY: 1957 BADGE

By the Danish–Icelandic Union Act of November 30th 1918, ICELAND became an independent Kingdom, and by Royal Icelandic Decree of February 12th 1919, King Christian X, King of Denmark and Iceland, approved the flag. The National and Merchant Flag is blue and bears a red cross edged with white (Plate **22**, 11). The Government Flag and Ensign is similar in pattern, but is longer and swallow-tailed.

When Iceland became a Republic on June 17th 1944, these flags were retained, but a new coat of arms and a flag for the President were adopted.

The former consists of a blue shield bearing a red cross with

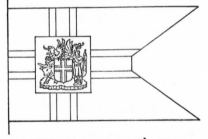

ICELAND: PRESIDENT'S FLAG

a white border, in front of a group comprising a bull, a vulture, a dragon and a giant—the old guardian spirits of the land—on what appears to be a portion of a rocky coastline. The President's Flag is similar to the Government Flag and Ensign, but has a large white square panel containing the arms overall.

A flag similar to the Ensign, but with the addition of distinctive charges, in white,

ICELAND: ARMS

in the first quarter, is used for (*a*) the Post and Telegraph flag and (*b*) the Customs flag. That on the former consists of a post horn and a thunderbolt, whilst that on the latter is the letter 'T'.

The green, white and red tricolour of ITALY was originally the banner of Napoleon's Italian Legion of the 1796 Campaign. It is reputed to have been designed by Napoleon himself. About a half-century later, the King of Sardinia adopted a similar flag and added his arms—namely, those of the House of Savoy: a white cross on a blue-bordered red shield—as a central charge. He was proclaimed Victor Emmanuel, King of Sardinia, King of Italy, in 1861, and this flag became the National Flag. It remained thus until the conclusion of World War II, when Italy became a republic and the Arms of Savoy were removed and the plain green, white and red vertical tricolour became the National Flag (Plate **23**, 1). As this flag is the same as the Merchant Ship Ensign of Mexico (*see* page 95), the Merchant Ship Ensign of Italy has a quartered shield, having as a border a golden rope, positioned in the centre of the white stripe. This shield comprises the arms of the four mediaeval maritime republics of Venice, Genoa, Amalfi and Pisa, thus: first quarter, Venice, is red and charged with the famous winged Lion of St. Mark, supporting an open book in his right paw in gold; second quarter, Genoa, is white with the red Cross of St. George; third quarter, Amalfi, is blue and charged with a Maltese Cross in white; and fourth quarter, Pisa, is also red, and is charged with a white cross known in heraldry as the 'Pisa Cross' because of its distinctive design.

The Naval Ensign (Plate **23**, 2) has a similar shield, but this is surmounted by an unusual but rather handsome crown in gold, of which we shall have more to say later. In regard to this shield, there is a small difference in the first quarter—namely, the winged lion in this case has his *left* paw on a *closed* book and a *sword* in the *right*.

The Jack is square and consists of the four quarters taken from the Naval Ensign, but without the rope border. On Armed Forces Day, November 4th, the Naval Ensign and Jack are half-masted from 11 a.m. until noon.

Yachts of the Yacht Club Italiano and the Naval Yacht Club wear the Naval Ensign.

The Masthead Pennant is divided vertically, green (at the hoist), white and red, the white portion being charged with the shield and crown from the Naval Ensign.

Mention has been made of the unusual type of golden crown which surmounts the shield on the Ensign. This has been referred to officially as a 'towered and rostral' crown, a 'turreted' crown, and also a 'Corona Territa'. It has three towers 'embattled', overall in the centre an anchor, the flukes of which are flanked with what appears to be a representation of the afterpart of a galley (in elevation), which is repeated, in larger proportions, as a projection on each side of the crown. Those responsible for designing it no doubt chose these emblems as being symbolic of naval and coastal defences, and would presumably be justified in calling it a Naval Crown.

GOLDEN CROWN

The Romans invented the Naval Crown, and awarded it for the display of gallantry at sea. Little is known about it except that it was always of gold and was issued in two forms—namely, the Corona Rostrata and the Corona Navalis. One writer suggests that the former was reserved for officers or an officer of high rank who destroyed an enemy's fleet, but states that details of the designs of these two crowns have yet to be brought to light. Others would have it that they consisted of turrets and sails or sterns of ships alternating; however, they may be confusing them with the graded crowns (in which these emblems were varied in size and number according to the number of inhabitants) used by maritime provinces, cities, towns and communes.

These sterns should not be confused with those of our 'wooden walls' used in the design of the British Naval Crown, which, as far as is known at present, first appeared about the middle of the 17th century. This was made up of the sterns of ships and sails alternatively, there being three sterns and two sails. The form of stern was similar to that used in the Royal ships of the period. The sails were just ordinary square ones suitable for any mast except the lower mizzen.

At the time of writing, the Italian President has no distinctive personal flag, but uses the National Flag.

The flag of the Minister of Defence has a dark blue field with a central device, consisting of a conventional grenade with wings and the flukes of an anchor in gold, surrounded by a golden fimbriation which in turn has a deep border the same colour as the field.

ITALY: MINISTER OF DEFENCE

A similar flag, but without the golden fimbriation, is used by the Under Secretary of State for Defence.

The colours of LIECHTENSTEIN are royal blue and red, the flag being divided into two horizontally with the blue half on top (Plate **23**, 3). A princely crown is placed near the hoist on the blue stripe. More often than not this flag is made to be *hung vertically*; in that case the axis of the crown is placed parallel to the line dividing the blue and red stripes. The Royal Flag consists of two horizontal stripes of equal width, yellow over red—the dynastic colours.

The little Grand Duchy of LUXEMBOURG sandwiched between France, Belgium and Germany, flies a tricolour which is almost identical with that of the Netherlands, except that the length of the fly is longer, the proportions of the field being five by three, and the shade of blue somewhat lighter.

LUXEMBOURG: STANDARD
OF GRAND DUKE

The Standard of the Grand Duke is unique in that it shows the Royal Arms on an orange field, but the reverse side consists of the national horizontal tricolour. These arms are quartered, (1) and (4), a lion rampant and five billets, in gold, on a blue field—Nassau; (2) and (3), a red lion rampant on nine horizontal stripes (five white and four blue)—Luxembourg—ensigned with a grand-ducal crown; the supporters are two crowned lions rampant in gold.

Count Roger, the Norman, a cousin of William the Conqueror, is reported to have landed on the island of MALTA in the year 1090, and was welcomed by the Maltese who at that time were subject to an Arab garrison.   His colours are reputed to have been white and red, and these colours have been associated with Malta to the present day, for they form her National Flag, adopted when she attained full independence in 1964.   The history of Malta is long and full of interest, but unfortunately space does not permit more than a brief mention of the more outstanding events, one of the most important of which was the establishment of the Knights Hospitallers in Malta in 1530, after they had been forced by the Turks to leave Rhodes and Cyprus.   The Knights were given the island and became known as the Knights of Malta, and from that time their eight-pointed silver cross, on a black background, came to be known as the 'Maltese Cross'.   Although this was their

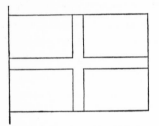

SOVEREIGN ORDER OF MALTA

badge their flag was red with a white cross.   This flag is said to date from the 15th century.   The portrait of Pierre d'Aubusson, the Grand Master, who successfully defended Rhodes against the Turks, under Sultan Mohammed II, in 1480–81, shows the Grand Master wearing a 'surcoat' over his armour which has the device of the flag, red with a white cross upon it.   This portrait dates from about 1676. In the year 1798 Napoleon evicted the Knights from Malta, and as theirs was an international organisation they spread all over the world as the Order of the Knights of St. John of Jerusalem. There is a branch in Britain, a part of which is the well-known Ambulance Brigade of St. John.   However, although it has branches all over the world the Headquarters were established in Rome under the title of the Sovereign Military Order of Malta, and this still flies the old red flag with the white cross.   It is claimed that this flag has been flown continuously for more years than any other.   It is also claimed by some that the Danish and Norwegian flags owe their design to it.

Napoleon was forced to withdraw from Malta in 1800, whereupon the Maltese sought the protection of Great Britain, and to become part of the British Empire. Great Britain agreed and this was finally ratified by the Treaty of Paris in 1814.

At the beginning of the 19th century the Maltese shield and flag had a white field with a red Maltese Cross; but this was superseded, and the Admiralty Flag Books of 1875 and 1889 show the shield divided vertically white and red, with a red and white cross overall. This shield was used to deface the Blue Ensign, which thus became the flag of Malta. Early in the 20th century the cross disappeared from the shield.

During World War II the Island of Malta was awarded the decoration of the 'George Cross' to 'bear witness to the heroism and devotion of its people' during the great siege. In order to perpetuate this award a representation of this cross was included in the Arms of Malta, G.C., which was granted by Royal Warrant, dated December 28th 1943, thus: 'per pale Argent and Gules on a Canton Azure a representation of the George Cross proper' to be borne 'for the greater honour and distinction of Our Island of Malta and its Dependencies upon Seals, Shields, Banners and otherwise according to the laws of Arms'.

Malta became an independent country within the British Commonwealth on September 21st 1964, and adopted a new National Flag and coat of arms. The flag is divided vertically into two equal parts, white to the hoist and red to the fly, bearing the George Cross in silver fimbriated in red in the top corner next to the staff (Plate 23, 4).

The coat of arms has a shield of similar design to that of the National Flag, with as a crest a helmet surmounted by a sally port, and supported by two dolphins, with beneath on a scroll the motto 'VIRTUTE ET CONSTANTIA', 'Courage and Constancy'.

The flag of the Governor General is the usual blue flag (see page 71) charged with a crown and lion and bearing the word 'MALTA'.

MALTA

In November 1965 Malta adopted a Merchant Ensign. The design was approved by the Maltese House of Representatives on

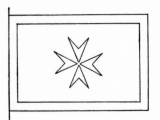

November 3rd 1965, and assented to by the Acting Governor-General eight days later. The design of this flag resembles that of the Grand Masters of the Knights of Malta, and consists of a red field with a white border and charged in the centre with a red Maltese Cross.

MALTA: MERCHANT FLAG

On October 31st 1967 a Personal Flag for the use of Her Majesty Queen Elizabeth when as Queen of Malta she visits the island, was first flown. The flag consists of the National Flag of Malta with superimposed in the centre the same 'device' that is in the other Personal Flags of Her Majesty (Plate 5, 6).

The Principality of MONACO is situated in the South of France, and famous for Monte Carlo. Her colours are simple, halves of red over white (Plate 23, 5). In passing, it is interesting to note that this flag is identical with that of Indonesia (*see* page 221).

The Prince's Standard is white and bears the arms thereon in full colours.

MONACO: ARMS

The NETHERLANDS, under their famous leader William I, Prince of Orange and Count of Nassau, started the war of independence with Spain in 1568. By 1581 the beginning of their independency may be said to have begun, but it was not until 1648 that Spain was forced to recognise officially that it was complete and the Republic of the United Netherlands established. This consisted of seven provinces, of which Holland was one. In choosing a national flag it is not surprising that the colours of the Prince of Orance—orange, white and blue— were adopted. At first there was great latitude of treatment, the number of bars of each colour and their order being variable, but in 1599 it was laid down officially that the flag of the Nether-

Plate 24

FLAGS OF EUROPEAN COUNTRIES

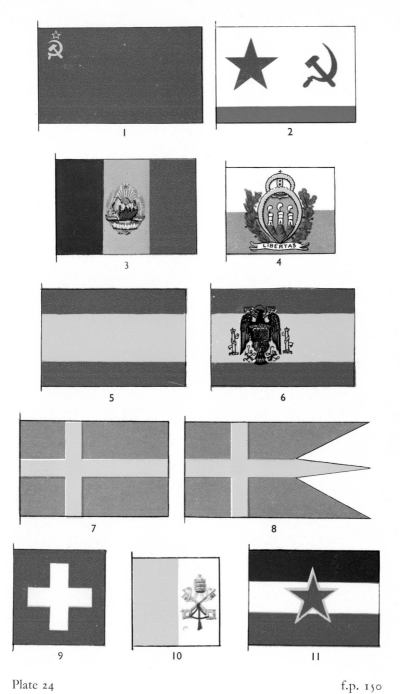

Plate 24   f.p. 150

FLAGS OF EUROPEAN COUNTRIES

lands was to be orange, white and blue, in three horizontal stripes of equal width. The orange was changed to red about fifty years later; it is difficult to be absolutely definite as to the reason. It is possible that the indefiniteness of the orange and its liability to fade in the sea air may have been one of the causes, or it is also possible that the sturdy Netherlanders did not intend to allow the Prince of Orange to have too much power, and so changed the orange to the republican red.

During the French Revolution, when Holland became the Batavian Republic under the French, the Naval Flag had in the upper canton a figure of Liberty on a white field, but the innovation was not popular, as the sailors preferred the old plain tricolour under which the victories of De Ruyter and Maarten Harpetszoon Tromp had been gained, and in 1806—when Louis Bonaparte became King —the figure disappeared.

The horizontal tricolour does duty as the National Flag, Naval Ensign and Merchant Flag (Plate **23**, **7**). On special days, such as Royal anniversaries or days of special rejoicing, public and official buildings fly an orange pennant superior to the National Flag. Many patriotic citizens follow this practice, and display the orange pennant above the National Flag at these times. This pennant is flown continuously from Embassies and Consulates, indicating that they are the representatives of the Sovereign.

Her Majesty the Queen of the Netherlands' Standard was created in accordance with a Royal Decree dated August 27th 1908. The

NETHERLANDS:
ROYAL STANDARD

NETHERLANDS:
STANDARD OF PRINCE BERNHARD

field, which is square, is orange and is charged with a blue cross. In each of the quarters thus formed is a slung 'Nassau' blue bugle-horn, the cords red, each horn garnished with silver. In the centre of the cross is the Royal Shield, 'Azure billety, a lion rampant crowned or, holding in its dexter paw a naked sword and in the other a bundle of arrows'. The shade of blue used for the shield is known as 'Nassau' blue, the tongue and claws of the lion are red, the sword is silver with a golden hilt, and the arrows of which there are seven (symbolising the aforesaid seven provinces), are also silver, with golden points, tied with a golden ribbon. The shield is ensigned with the Royal Crown, and surrounded with the ribbon and badge of the Order of William.

NETHERLANDS: CORONA-
TION BANNER

In addition to the Royal Standard described above there is a Royal Banner which is only used at the ceremony of the Coronation of a Sovereign of the Netherlands.

Prince Bernhard's Standard was created by a Royal Decree dated June 18th 1937. The field, which is six (length) by five, is charged with an orange cross having in the centre a 'Nassau' blue shield charged with the golden lion rampant from the Royal Standard, ensigned with the Royal Crown. The first and fourth quarters are 'Nassau' blue, charged with the same lion; the second and third quarters are white, bearing a red rose, barbed and seeded gold, from the first and fourth quarters of his paternal arms, those of Lippe Biesterfeld. The Standard of H.R.H. Princess Beatrix, Princess

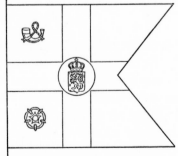

NETHERLANDS: STANDARD
OF PRINCESS BEATRIX

of the Netherlands, was created by Royal Decree dated November 10th 1956; it has an orange field, six by five, with a triangle cut out of the fly; overall a cross, in 'Nassau' blue, charged with an orange disc bearing a crowned shield of the same design as on Prince Bernhard's Standard. The bugle-horn from the Royal Standard is placed in the first quarter while the third quarter is charged with the rose from Prince Bernhard's Standard.

The flag of the Minister of Defence is white with three narrow stripes along the top and bottom; these stripes repeat the national colours, red, white and blue; in the centre are two black anchors in saltire.

All three of the Armed Forces of the Netherlands have ceremonial Colours, which are awarded to the different units, for example the Submarine Service of the Royal Navy, the different regiments etc. All these Colours with one exception follow the same basic pattern. They are orange in colour, with a golden fringe. On the obverse is the cypher of the Monarch who awarded the Colours; this is either 'W' for Wilhelmine I, II or III, or 'J' for Queen Juliana. The initial is surmounted by the Royal Crown. In the base is the name of the unit, and in the corners the citations or honours. On the reverse are the Royal Arms in gold and blue, surrounded by a wreath (Plate 23, 6 and 8).

NETHERLANDS: NAVAL CADET CORPS COLOURS

The exceptional Colour that differs from the others is that of the Naval Cadets. This is the same on both sides and the colour of the field is red.

The Colours are carried on a black staff or colour pike which has a handsome emblem in gold on its summit. In some cases a ribbon hangs from the head of the staff with a special decoration or medal.

In addition to the Colours explained above the different 'Arms' have their distinguishing flags. The Navy, as has already been mentioned flies the National Flag as its Ensign, the Jack is of

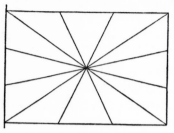

somewhat unusual design; the field is divided into twelve triangles by six diagonal lines, forming what is known heraldically as a 'Gyronny'. The middle triangle at the hoist is white, then moving clockwise the colours are red, blue, white, red, blue white, red, blue, white, red, blue.

NETHERLANDS: JACK

The flags of Flag Officers are the same as the National Flag, but square in shape, with, in the red stripe near the hoist, crossed batons for an Admiral, four white six-pointed stars for a Lieutenant-Admiral (a rank peculiar to the Dutch and Belgian Navies), and two stars for a Rear-Admiral. A Commodore flies a similar flag except that it has a triangle cut out of the fly (i.e. a broad pennant).

NETHERLANDS: NAVAL AIR SERVICE ENSIGN

NETHERLANDS: NAVAL RESERVE ENSIGN

The Ensigns of the Royal Naval Air Service, and for ships commanded by an officer of the Naval Reserve are the national tricolour with the badge of the Naval Air Service, in the former, and the reserve badge, a foul anchor surmounted by a crown, in the latter.

The Army uses the National Flag as a general flag of recognition, while most, but not all regiments have the ceremonial Colours already described. Small red triangular flags with a gold border, and carrying the 'cypher' of the regiment, are awarded to groups for outstanding performances, such as rifle shooting or success in

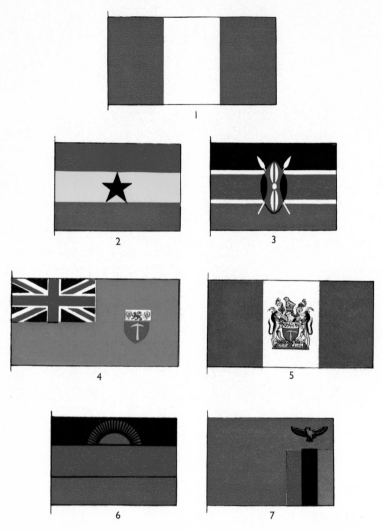

Plate 25

f.p. 155

FLAGS OF AFRICAN COUNTRIES

Plate 25

FLAGS OF AFRICAN COUNTRIES

sporting events. Senior Officers carry distinguishing flags, using stars like the navy to indicate the rank of the officer.

A new Ensign was allocated to the Royal Netherlands Air Force on July 17th 1964. This is similar to the old ensign, light blue in colour with an orange triangle extending from the hoist to the fly. The only thing that has been changed is the badge on the orange triangle.

ROYAL NETHERLANDS
AIR FORCE ENSIGN

And finally two more ensigns that can be seen flying in Dutch waters are the Ensigns of the Royal Netherlands Yacht Club and the Royal Mass Yacht Club, whose members are privileged to wear these ensigns on their yachts. Both ensigns consist of the National Flag with the badge of the club; that of the Royal Nether-

ROYAL NETHERLANDS
YACHT CLUB ENSIGN

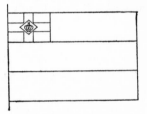

ROYAL MASS YACHT
CLUB ENSIGN

lands is a blue diamond with a gold heraldic 'W' surmounted by a crown, which is placed in the centre of the ensign, while that of the Royal Mass is a red St. George's Cross on a white background with the crown in gold in the centre and is placed in the canton.

The people of the Netherlands take a great interest in flags, and all the provinces, cities and towns down to quite small villages have their own particular flags, of which they are very proud. Perhaps one of the most interesting is that of Friesland. Although there is a province of the Netherlands called West Friesland, Friesland may be said not only to include this province but to embrace the whole

of the north coast of Germany as far as Denmark. The flag of the
Dutch province of West Friesland is not only the flag of that province but is recognised throughout the whole of Friesland. The

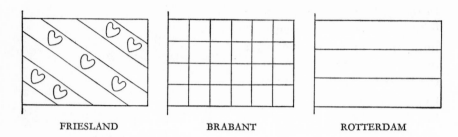

FRIESLAND   BRABANT   ROTTERDAM

flag is blue, with three white diagonal stripes or bends; on these are
seven red hearts (some consider these to be representations of the
'pompe', a water plant), three on the centre stripe and two on the
outer stripes.

It is not possible to show all the local flags of the Netherlands but
the blue and white chequers of Brabant, and the green and white
tricolour of Rotterdam are both well known.

The Netherlands West Indies comprise (1) SURINAM, sometimes
known as Dutch Guiana, situated between British Guiana and
French Guiana in South America, and (2) the NETHERLANDS
ANTILLES, which consist of certain islands in the West Indies—part
of the Lesser Antilles lying off the coast of Venezuela—of which the
chief is Curaçao. They received autonomy in domestic affairs,
as part of the Realm of the Netherlands, on December 29th 1954.

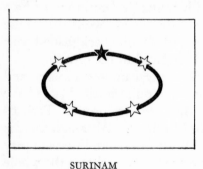

SURINAM

A distinctive design for a flag
for Surinam was approved on
December 8th 1959 (Government Gazette No. 105). It has a
white field bearing a black ellip-
tical ring charged with five five-
pointed stars of different colours.
Starting with the upper one near
the hoist and proceeding clockwise they are white, black,

brown, yellow and red. They are said to represent the different peoples of Surinam—whites, Negroes, half-castes, Chinese and Indians.

The flag of the Netherlands Antilles was approved on December 2nd 1959 (Government Gazette No. 173). It has a white field with a vertical red central stripe and overall a blue horizontal stripe, charged with six five-pointed stars.

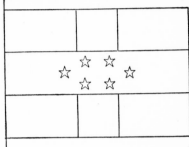

NETHERLANDS ANTILLES

A Royal Proclamation dated 14th March 1966 introduced new flags for the Governors of Surinam and Netherlands Antilles. These are on the same general pattern as the flags for the Minister of Defence i.e. a white flag with three narrow bands of the national colours at the top and bottom, and replicas of the flags of Surinam and the Netherlands Antilles in their centres.

NORWAY and Denmark were united at the end of the 14th century, and both countries used the Danish red flag bearing a white cross—the Dannebrog (*see* page 123). When the dissolution came in 1814, Norway was obliged to enter a union with a stronger country, Sweden, and a change was made in the flag. The golden lion of Norway, wearing the crown of St. Olave and holding in its fore-paw a battle-axe, was placed in the canton. This emblem dates from about the year 1200. Seven years later another change was made. The lion was left out, and a dark blue cross was superimposed upon the white one. Towards the middle of the 19th century a canton of the Union colours was added. The canton was divided saltirewise. The top and bottom triangles were red, while those in the hoist and fly were blue. Overall, and dovetailed into the saltire, was a cross, the upright of which was dark blue with a white edge, and the crossbar was yellow. Thus the top and bottom triangle incorporated the flag of Norway, the other two that of Sweden.

This flag was superseded (except for military purposes) in 1898, when the Dannebrog was re-introduced. However, when the two countries separated in 1905, the Union in the canton was dropped from *all* Norwegian flags. The present National and Merchant Flag, proportions of the field being twenty-two to sixteen, is illustrated on Plate **23**, 9.

NORWAY: ROYAL STANDARD

The Royal Standard is red and bears the lion and axe thereon; that of the Crown Prince is similar but the field is swallow-tailed.

The Jack is a square edition of the National Flag and the Naval Ensign and Government or State Flag resembles the last mentioned, but has three swallow-tails (Plate **23**, 10).

A similar flag, but charged with the crowned lion with axe from the Royal Standard, in white, in the upper red canton at the hoist, does duty as the flag of the Minister of Defence.

Customs vessels and those carrying mails wear the Ensign, with the addition of a white square panel on the centre of the cross and bearing distinctive charges. These are in gold and consist of the crown over the words 'TOLL' and 'POST' respectively.

The Yacht Ensign which may be worn by yachts owned by members of the Royal Norwegian Yacht Club is similar to the above, with the cipher of King Olav in the central panel (*see* Plate **40**, 19).

The Masthead Pennant has a red field with a slit in the fly; overall, a narrow white cross charged with a dark blue cross.

POLAND became an independent republic in 1919, and adopted a very simple design for her National Flag—horizontal halves of white over red (Plate **23**, 11). The arms comprise a red shield charged with an uncrowned white eagle: they are placed in the centre of each of the flags described below (*also see* illustration of the Jack).

When placed in the centre of the white stripe of the National Flag it becomes the Merchant Flag. The Ensign is similar, but in this case the fly is swallow-tailed. A diminutive of the last mentioned is placed in the upper half of the hoist of a blue flag which does duty as the Ensign of Fleet Auxiliaries. Again, the arms are placed in the centre of the Jack, which has a red-bordered white field, the proportions of which are approximately seven to six. In passing, it is interesting to record that its predecessor was of unique design. It consisted of a nearly square version of the National Flag and in the centre thereof a cross pattée counter-changed—that is, a cross of the same type as our Victoria Cross, with the top half red and the bottom white. The centre of this cross was circular and was all red, while on this circle was a human right arm grasping a scimitar. The eagle on a red flag with a red and white ornamental border is the standard of the President of the Republic.

POLAND: JACK

The Flag of the Minister of Defence is similar to the Ensign; however, it has an additional charge, namely, a yellow cannon and

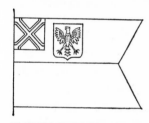

ENSIGN OF YACHT CLUB
OF POLAND

and white anchor in saltire, positioned in the centre of the red stripe. There is a special ensign for yachts whose owners are members of the Yacht Club of Poland; this is similar to the Naval Ensign with, in the upper canton, a white inset fimbriated in red, and charged with a red St. Andrew's Cross fimbriated in blue.

In the days of the Kingdom of PORTUGAL the national colours were blue and white, but with the coming of the republic in 1910 they were changed to red and green placed vertically, the green portion being in the hoist. The red portion is about one-and-a-half times the width of the green.

The old arms have, with only minor modification, been retained by the republic. They appear over the colour division in the flag, and are framed by a yellow armillary sphere (Plate 23, 12). These arms consist of a red shield charged with a smaller white shield. The red shield bears seven golden castles (added by Alfonso III after his marriage in 1252 with the daughter of Alfonso the Wise, King of Castile). The white shield is charged in turn with five blue shields, arranged in the form of a cross, each of these shields bearing five white roundels arranged in a saltire.   The shields commemorate the great victory of Alfonso Henriquez in 1139 over the five Moorish Princes at the battle of Ourique, while the five white roundels symbolise the five wounds of the Saviour in whose strength he defeated the infidels and became the first king of Portugal.   The armillary sphere used to appear on the Braganza Arms of Brazil.

This is the design of the Ensign and Merchant Flag as well as the National Flag.   The Standard of the President is green with the Arms of the monarchy in the centre.   A green bordered square red flag, bearing these arms in the centre thereof, does duty as the Jack, and the Masthead Pennant is green (at the hoist) and red.   Again, a rectangular flag divided vertically, green (at the hoist) and red, bearing five white five-pointed stars arranged in the form of a pentagon, is flown by the Minister of War.

RUMANIA

The National Flag, Ensign and Merchant Ensign of RUMANIA is a vertical tricolour, blue, gold and red, in that order, from the hoist.   In the centre is the National or State Emblem which was established in accordance with the Constitution of 1948.   The Constitution of 1965 introduced a modification to the inscription, but otherwise the device was unchanged. It is a complicated forest and mountain scene, with in the foreground the derrick of an oil well, over this the sun with golden rays is rising, all within a wreath of wheat ears tied with a ribbon of the national colours bearing the words 'Republica ROMANIA Socialista'.   Above is a small red star (Plate 24, 3).

The former white and blue Naval Ensign has been replaced by the National Flag (*see* above).

The Jack, which has also been changed recently is now the same as the national tricolour, but square in shape with two crossed white anchors in place of the national emblem.

A white flag, with the National Flag in the first quarter and a red five-pointed star in the centre of the fly, is flown by the Minister of Defence.

The National Flag of the Republic of SAN MARINO is a very pretty one. It is white over blue, and bears the Arms of San Marino in colour within a wreath of oak and laurel (Plate **24,** 4). In the centre of the arms are three white towers, each having a white ostrich feather on its top; they are said to represent the three castles on the three peaks of Mount Titano. Merchant ships wear this flag without the arms.

Before the Revolution of 1917, RUSSIA had a great variety of flags. Merchant ships wore a horizontal tricolour, white over blue over red. A white ensign charged with a blue diagonal cross was worn by naval vessels; the Jack comprised a red field bearing a white St. George's cross with a blue diagonal cross, edged white, overall.

The Union of Soviet Socialist Republics of Russia possesses a large number of flags. The State Flag has a red field, two by one, and bears in the upper hoist the hammer and sickle emblem of the workers, surmounted by a five-pointed skeleton star, all in gold (Plate **24,** 1).

The Merchant Flag is the same as the State Flag. The field of the Ensign is white, three by two, and has  a light blue border one sixth the depth of the hoist along the bottom edge of the flag. In the white portion are the star and crossed hammer and sickle in red, placed side by side, the star in the hoist and the emblem in the fly (Plate **24,** 2).

U.S.S.R.: JACK

A red flag with a large white five-pointed star, charged with a smaller red star bearing the hammer and sickle emblem in white, serves as a Jack. The proportions of the field are three by two. A diminutive of the Ensign is placed at the hoist of the Masthead Pennant, whose field is red and forked at the fly.

Fleet Auxiliary Vessels wear a dark blue ensign bearing the

U.S.S.R. Ensign in the upper quarter next to the mast.   A similar
flag, with the addition of a black-edged white disc charged
with a lighthouse, in black and white,
positioned in the centre of the fly,
is worn by Hydrographic Vessels and
lightships.

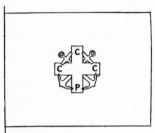

Coast Defence Vessels of the Ministry
of State Security wear a green ensign
with a diminutive of the U.S.S.R. Ensign
in the upper hoist.

U.S.S.R.: SEA RESCUE FLAG   The Sea Rescue Flag of the U.S.S.R.
has a white field, three by two, charged
with two conventional blue anchors in saltire with a red cross
(similar to that on our Red Cross flag) bearing the letters 'C.C.C.P.'
—one on each limb—in gold.   These letters are the Cyrillic
Alphabet—our equivalent being 'S.S.S.R.'—and stand for
Soyuz Sovetskikh Sotsialisticheskikh Republik—Union of Soviet
Socialist Republics.

It would appear that this flag has its origin in that of the Finnish
Sea Saving Society used from 1897 to 1917, which in turn was used
in 1923 as a basis for the design of the Latvian Lifeboat Society's
flag.

Each of the republics which make up the Union has its own flag.
These used to consist of a red field bearing various initials in
cyrillic characters in the upper
hoist, in gold.

Since January 1954, the Russian Socialist Federal Soviet
Republic has used the flag of
the U.S.S.R., with a dark blue
vertical stripe at the hoist; the
field is two by one and the
width of the vertical stripe is
equal to one quarter of the
hoist.

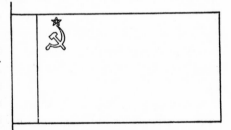

RUSSIAN SOCIALIST FEDERAL SOVIET
REPUBLIC

The design of the flag of the UKRAINIAN S.S.R. was changed on
November 21st 1949, in accordance with Article 125 of the

Plate 26

FLAGS OF AFRICAN COUNTRIES

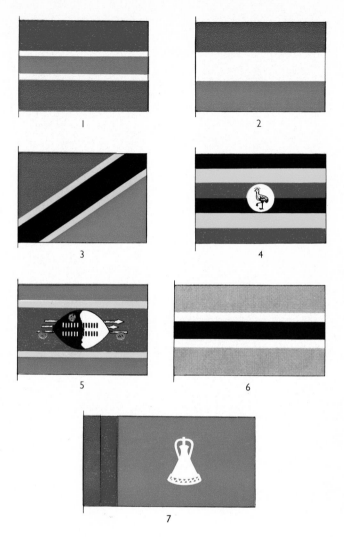

Plate 26

FLAGS OF AFRICAN COUNTRIES

amended Constitution, thus: the field is two by one, divided horizontally red over light blue, the width of the former being twice that of the latter; in the red portion, the hammer and sickle in gold surmounted by a red five-pointed star edged with gold. It would appear that the light blue was taken from the old Ukrainian national colours, yellow and light blue.

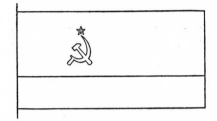

UKRAINIAN S.S.R.   BYELORUSSIAN S.S.R.

The BYELORUSSIAN S.S.R. adopted a new flag, called the National State Flag, on December 31st 1951. Like that of the Ukrainian S.S.R., it has the U.S.S.R. Flag with a horizontal stripe beneath and occupying one third of the hoist. However, this stripe is light green in colour, and there is, in addition, a very distinctive red strip at the hoist. This has a width equal to one quarter of the hoist, and bears what appears to be a woven carpet or inlaid linoleum pattern, in white.

The remainder of this new series of flags followed during 1953–54. In each case, the hammer and sickle emblem is in gold, and the red five-pointed star is edged in gold.

Here, then, is a brief description and an illustration of each flag, the colours reading from the upper edge of the field.

UZBEK S.S.R.—Red, white, light blue, white, red.

KAZAKH S.S.R.—Red, light blue, red.

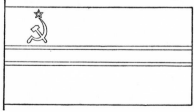

UZBEK S.S.R.   KAZAKH S.S.R.

GEORGIA S.S.R.—Red, light blue, red; with a light blue canton having red rays.

AZERBAIDJAN S.S.R.—Red, dark blue.

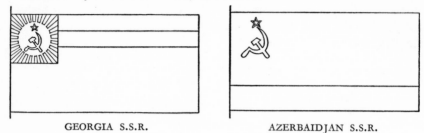

GEORGIA S.S.R.   AZERBAIDJAN S.S.R.

MOLDAVIA S.S.R.—Red, Green, red.

KIRGHIZ S.S.R.—Red, dark blue, white, dark blue, red.

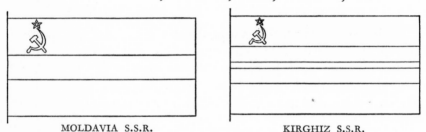

MOLDAVIA S.S.R.   KIRGHIZ S.S.R.

TADJIK S.S.R.—Red, white, green, red.

ARMENIAN S.S.R.—Red, dark blue, red.

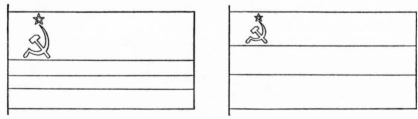

TADJIK S.S.R.   ARMENIAN S.S.R.

TURKMEN S.S.R.—Red, light blue, red, light blue, red.

KARELO-FINNISH S.S.R.—Red, light blue, green.

The Karelo-Finnish S.S.R. flag is now obsolete, the republic having been incorporated in the R.S.F.S.R. (*see* page 162) on June 16th 1956.

TURKMEN S.S.R.   KARELO-FINNISH S.S.R. (1953–1956)

When independent ESTONIA, LATVIA and LITHUANIA had their own National Flags, that of Estonia was a horizontal tricolour, bright blue at the top, then black, then white.   Latvia's had a dark crimson field with a white horizontal stripe, and her Ensign was

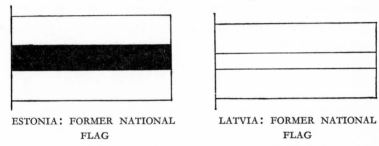

ESTONIA: FORMER NATIONAL   LATVIA: FORMER NATIONAL
         FLAG   FLAG

white with a white St. George's Cross fimbriated in dark crimson. The flag of Lithuania was another horizontal tricolour, yellow at the top, then green, and finally gold.

When they became part of the U.S.S.R. they adopted flags similar in design to those of the other Soviet Republics i.e. the Soviet State Flag, defaced in the case of Estonia by a horizontal blue stripe, invected (five points), and charged with two narrow white stripes.   Latvia's has four wavy stripes, two white and two blue, across

LITHUANIA: FORMER
NATIONAL FLAG

the lower part of the field, and at the bottom of the flag for Lithuania are two stripes, the upper and narrower white, and the lower, on the edge of the flag, green.

One of the best-known flags in the world was that of

Royal SPAIN, which comprised the colours of Aragon—red and yellow.

After the revolution of 1931, the republic added another colour—namely, purple. The Merchant Flag became a horizontal tricolour of red on top, yellow and purple at the bottom. The National Flag and Naval Ensign were similar, but with the national arms placed in the centre of the yellow stripe.

However, General Franco reverted to the old colours, and the Merchant Flag now consists of three horizontal stripes, red, yellow and red, the width of the yellow stripe being equal to that of the two red stripes combined (Plate 24, 5). The National Flag and the Ensign are similar, but have the new national arms, which are more elaborate than the previous coat, superimposed slightly nearer the hoist than the fly. These comprise an eagle supporting a quartered shield (1) and (4) the Arms of Castile quartered with those of Leon; (2) and (3) the Arms of Aragon impaled —placed side by side—with those of Navarre, whilst in the base there is a triangular inset, heraldically described as 'enté-en-point', in which appears the pomegranate of Grenada in full colours, on a white background. Behind the eagle's head, a golden halo and also a red scroll bearing the motto 'UNA GRANDE LIBRE'. Two pillars (the Pillars of Hercules) in silver, having a red scroll with the motto 'PLUS ULTRA'—'More Beyond'—in golden lettering, serve as supporters (Plate 24, 6).

SPAIN: JACK

The Jack is square, and is quartered thus: (1) red, bearing the yellow castle of Castile; (2) white, charged with the red lion rampant with golden crown of Leon; (3) gold, with four vertical red stripes superimposed, of Aragon; (4) red, bearing the golden chains of Navarre.

The Ensign and the Jack are worn at half-mast on Holy Thursday and Good Friday, also on Remembrance Day, November 20th. The Masthead Pennant is striped horizontally, red over yellow over red.

The Air Force Ensign consists of the Merchant Flag bearing the

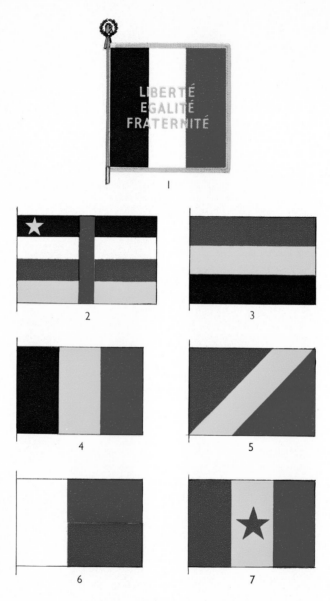

LIBERTÉ
EGALITÉ
FRATERNITÉ

1

2   3

4   5

6   7

Plate 27   f.p. 167

FLAGS OF THE FRENCH COMMUNITY
IN AFRICA

Plate 27

FLAGS OF THE FRENCH COMMUNITY IN AFRICA

national arms over the inscription AVIACION in the centre of the yellow stripe and a winged emblem above on the red stripe, as shown in the accompanying illustration. The silver wings are charged with the black eagle on a red disc ensigned with a naval crown.

Again, ships of the Naval Reserve wear the Merchant Flag charged with the national arms on the centre of the yellow stripe; large block letters 'R' and 'N' in silver are placed on either

SPAIN: AIR FORCE ENSIGN

side of the arms.   Two other ensigns are similar, namely, those of the Fishery Protection and Customs vessels.   In the case of the former, the large block letters are 'V' and 'P' and in the latter, 'N' and 'H', each of the last mentioned being surmounted by a Naval Crown.

The Standard of the Head of State is a very striking one.   It has

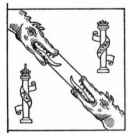

SPAIN: STANDARD OF
THE HEAD OF STATE

a square red (of a very deep shade) field bearing the Pillars of Hercules, one in the base at the hoist and the other in the upper portion of the fly; on a bend (a diagonal stripe extending from the top of the hoist to the bottom of the fly) the heads of two 'dragantes lobos' (wolf-dragons)—one each end and facing each other—all gold, except the tongues which are red, as shown in the accompanying illustration.

Light blue, thereon a golden yellow cross, the upright of which is placed one third the length of the flag from the staff, is the design of the National and Merchant Flag of SWEDEN (Plate 24, 7). This flag has been flown since Gustavus Vasa became King of Sweden in 1523.   When Sweden and Norway were united, the first quarter of the flag was occupied by the Union device (*see* page 157), but this went with the separation in 1905.   The Ensign is the National Flag with a swallow-tail, but the horizontal bar of the cross is prolonged into a point, so as to give the flag three tails.   It is used by all establishments and vessels of the armed

12

services and also as the Jack in naval vessels (Plate **24**, 8). The Masthead Pennant is divided horizontally, light blue over yellow. Naval Reserve officers in command of merchant ships fly a light blue broad pennant charged with an anchor and three cornets in gold: the latter are positioned as follows—one above and one on either side of the anchor.

The Royal Standard consists of the Ensign with the addition of a large square white panel placed over the centre of the cross. This is charged with the Royal Arms and Supporters upon a pavilion ensigned with the Royal Crown, and known as the 'Great Coat of Arms'.

SWEDEN: ROYAL ARMS

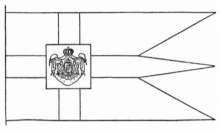

SWEDEN: ROYAL STANDARD

When His Majesty the King is embarked, the Royal Standard—with the Royal Pennant superior—is worn at the main masthead. However, if H.M. the Queen only is on board, the Royal Standard is worn without the Royal Pennant.

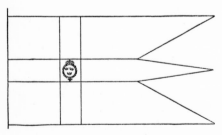

SWEDEN: FLAG FOR MEMBERS
OF ROYAL FAMILY

This long, narrow, swallow-tailed pennant of light blue over yellow has a small white square charged with the Great Coat of Arms at its head.

Other members of the Royal Family fly a similar flag, but the centre of the cross is formed of a small white square, which bears a blue oval shield, charged with the three golden crowns, two and one, of Sweden. The oval is surrounded with the collar and pennant of the Order of the Seraphim and is ensigned with the Crown. In order to distinguish this charge from the previous one, it is designated the 'Small Coat of Arms'.

When the Crown Prince is embarked his standard may be recognised by the addition of the Royal Pennant, worn superior.

The distinguishing flag of the Minister of Defence is the Ensign with two white batons in saltire in the upper canton at the hoist. A square flag divided horizontally, light blue over yellow, with the three golden crowns of Sweden on the former and two blue batons in saltire on the latter, is used by the Supreme Commander of the Armed Forces.

Each of the Royal Swedish Air Force Wings has its own Colour. The rectangular light medium blue field is charged with stylised wings and propeller ensigned with the Royal Crown, in gold, with a distinguishing emblem, depending on the county in which the Wing is located, in the top of the hoist.

ROYAL SWEDISH AIR FORCE

The Colour illustrated belongs to *Kungl Östgöta flygflottilj* (fighter) at Linköping, the emblem consisting of a winged lion between four roses, in gold.

The flag of the Ministry of Shipping consists of a light blue burgee bearing a yellow five-pointed star, with rays, over a foul anchor. Vessels carrying mails fly a light blue pennant charged with the Crown over a post horn in yellow. A similar pennant, but bearing the Crown over the letter 'T', in yellow, is used by Customs vessels.

Again, a light blue pennant with a yellow border and charged with the Crown over a winged wheel, also in yellow, does duty as the Railway Ferry flag. Another flag, which is sometimes seen, is a triangular one displayed by vessels employed in fisheries protection duties: it is similar to the one flown by our North Sea Fisheries protection vessels.

The Swiss, being in want of a flag, chose the simple white

cross of the Crusaders, and Gautier tells us why. 'The first time it is mentioned is in the chronicle of Justinger the Béarnois. He says, after giving an enumeration of the Swiss forces leaving Berne to march against the coalition of nobles in 1339, "And all were distinguished by the sign of the Holy Cross, a white cross on a red shield, for the reason that the freeing of the nation was for them a cause as sacred as the deliverance of the Holy Places!"'

Thus the National Flag of SWITZERLAND is red, square in shape, with the white cross (Plate **24**, 9); ships registered at Basle wear the Merchant Flag. This is the same as the National Flag but has a field three by two. Each canton has its own colours. Aargau has black beside blue; Appenzell, white over black; Basel, white over black; Berne, red over black; Freiburg, black over white; St. Gallen, white over green; Geneva, yellow beside red; Glarus, red over black; Lucerne, blue beside white; Neuchatel, green, white and red vertical; Shaffhausen, green beside black; Solothurn, red over white; Thurgau, white and green diagonal;

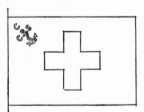

FLAG OF CRUISING CLUB
OF SWITZERLAND

Schwyz, red; Unterwalden, red over white; Uri, yellow over black; Valais, white beside red; Zurich, white and blue diagonal; Zug, white, blue and white horizontal, and so on for all the cantons. Yachts of the Cruising Club of Switzerland wear the National Flag; in the upper corner next the hoist is a small foul anchor with the letters 'C.C.S.', all in gold, round the top.

The flag of the FREE PORT OF TRIESTE has a red field, one hundred by seventy centimetres, bearing a spear-like halberd in white: it occupies about one half of the hoist.

The rapprochement between the Church and State in Italy and the creation of the VATICAN STATE or PAPAL STATE brought out the ancient yellow and white flag of the Papal States again, but with a slightly altered design of the crossed keys and triple

FREE PORT OF TRIESTE

crown (Plate **24**, 10). Yellow and white were the colours of the
banner of Godfrey of Jerusalem, and the gold and silver of the Keys
of Saint Peter are supposed to be the origin.

YUGOSLAVIA, the Kingdom of the Serbs, Croats and Slovenes,
dated from 1918, when Serbia, Montenegro, Bosnia, Herzegovina
and other provinces were united with Croatia and Slavonia. Red,
blue and white were the colours of the old flags of Serbia and Montenegro, and the tricolour of Yugoslavia retained them, with the
blue on top, the white in the middle, and the red at the bottom—the
exact reverse of the Dutch tricolour.

After World War II, the Federal People's Republic was formed,
in accordance with the new Constitution which was adopted on
January 31st 1946.

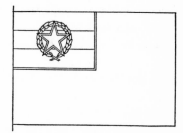

YUGOSLAVIA: JACK AND FORTRESS FLAG

YUGOSLAVIA: ENSIGN

Although the new National Flag, and also the Merchant Flag,
comprise the old tricolour with the addition in the centre of a large
red five-pointed star outlined in gold (Plate **24**, 11), the field of
the former flag is, strangely enough, two by one, whereas that of
the latter is three by two—the reverse of what one would have
expected.

The field of the Ensign is red, three by two, with a canton,
fimbriated white, containing the National Flag having an additional small charge—namely, a golden wreath encircling the star.
The Masthead Pennant is red with the canton from the Ensign in
the head; a white fimbriation separates it from the field.

The Jack and Fortress Flag have a red square field charged with
the State emblem.

The President flies the National Flag, bearing the State emblem in the centre thereof, having a narrow border composed of blue, white and red triangles alternated.   The State emblem comprises

five flaming torches, in red, flanked by a wreath of golden corn ears, tied with a blue ribbon, bearing the inscription '29 XI 1943', surmounted by a gold-edged red five-pointed star.

The Federal People's Republic of Yugo-slavia consists of the People's Republic of Serbia (January 17th 1947), Croatia (January 18th 1947), Slovenia and Herze-govina (December 31st 1946), Macedonia (December 31st 1946), and Montenegro

YUGOSLAVIA: PRESIDENT

(December 31st 1946), the dates indicating when each new Constitution was proclaimed.

The Federal Flag has a rectangular white field, fourteen by nine; in the centre thereof the State emblem occupying approximately nine tenths the depth of the field.

In each of the aforementioned new Constitutions provision is made for a State Flag.

Serbia and Montenegro have the same design as the National Flag of Yugoslavia, except that the colours of the tricolour are trans-posed: red on top, blue in the centre and white at the bottom.   In the case of Croatia the flag is similar, but the order of the colours is red over white over blue, whereas for Slovenia they are white over blue over red.   The Flag of Bosnia and Herzegovina has a red field, the first quarter bearing the National Flag of Yugoslavia with a white fimbriation.   In the case of Macedonia the field is also red, but there is a gold-edged red five-pointed star in the upper hoist.

Chapter Seven

AFRICA

It was not so many years ago that the only fully independent sovereign states in Africa were Ethiopia and Liberia; today the only states under foreign rule are the Portuguese colonies of Angola, Mozambique, Portuguese Guinea and the small colony of French Somalia. Twelve of the former colonies of Great Britain which have attained independence have elected to remain within the British Commonwealth. South Africa has become a republic and severed its official connection with Great Britain. Similarly six of the former French colonies on becoming independent have elected to remain in the French Community; the remainder have no official ties with France.

In the course of one life-span most of Africa has emerged from a state of servitude to independence.

The twelve states in the British Commonwealth are Gambia, Ghana, Kenya, Malawi, Nigeria, Uganda, Sierra Leone, Tanzania, Zambia, Botswana, Lesotho and Swaziland.

GAMBIA became independent on February 18th 1965. Her old badge was an elephant standing in front of a palm-tree, but her new flag consists of three broad horizontal stripes divided by thin white stripes; the broad stripes are coloured red at the top, then blue with dark green at the bottom (Plate **26**, 1). Gambia acknowledges the Queen of Great Britain as the Head of State and the Governor-General uses the standard pattern of Governor-General flags described on page 54.

The Gold Coast became the self-governing dominion of GHANA on March 6th 1957, and an independent republic within the British Commonwealth of Nations on July 6th, when it adopted as its National Flag a simple horizontal tricolour, proportions three by two, red over yellow over green, with a large five-pointed black

star on the centre stripe.   In 1964 the colour of the centre stripe
was changed to white.   The new military government which dis-

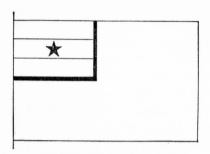

placed that led by President
Nkrumah announced in June
1966 that they would revert to the
flag with the yellow stripe (Plate
25, 2).   The red field of the Ensign for merchant ships has the
usual proportions of eight by five;
the National Flag is in the upper
canton and is separated from the
field by a narrow, black border.

GHANA: MERCHANT FLAG

As a colony KENYA had as a
badge a very poor specimen of a lion rampant guardant in red.
However, on becoming independent on December 12th 1963, she
made amends by adopting a new National Flag of striking design.
This has a field of three by two and has three equal horizontal
stripes, black over red over green; these stripes are divided by thin
white stripes.   In the centre is an African shield of
generous proportions placed vertically.   This shield
is coloured red, white and black; beneath the shield
are two crossed native spears, or assegais, in white
(Plate 25, 3).

In 1953 the Federation of Southern and Northern
Rhodesia and Nyasaland was formed.   The badge
of the Federation comprised a shield from the arms
granted by the Royal Warrant, July 1954.   This
Federation was dissolved at midnight on December

FEDERATION OF
RHODESIA AND
NYASALAND

31st 1963 and the three partners went their
own way: Nyasaland became an independent
country in the Commonwealth on July 6th
1964, assuming the name of Malawi;
Northern Rhodesia on October 23rd 1964
became Zambia and Southern Rhodesia
became Rhodesia.

FORMER ARMS OF
SOUTHERN RHODESIA

On November 11th 1965 RHODESIA declared herself 'independent' and adopted as

her flag what can best be described as a pale blue British Ensign defaced with the shield from the Arms of the old Southern Rhodesia (Plate 25, 4). On November 11th 1968 this was superseded by a new National Flag, which has not been officially recognised. The proportions are two by one with three equal vertical stripes, green, white and green. In the centre of the white stripe is the full achievement of the Arms of Rhodesia (Plate 25, 5).

With independence MALAWI adopted a new National Flag, a horizontal tricolour black over red over green, with a rising sun super- imposed on the centre of the black stripe (Plate 25, 6). Malawi has also adopted a Standard for her President which consists of a flag with a red field with, in the centre, a golden lion with black claws and tongue and under- neath on a scroll the word 'MALAWI'.

MALAWI: PRESIDENT'S FLAG

The National Flag of ZAMBIA is of of an unusual design: the field is green, proportions three by two, and in the upper part of the fly an eagle coloured orange and in the lower corner three vertical stripes, red towards the hoist, then orange and black nearest the fly (Plate 25, 7).

NIGERIA, the largest British Colonial territory, comprising the Northern, Eastern and Western Regions and the Federal Capital of Lagos, became the Federation of Nigeria on October 1st 1954, an independent country in the British Commonwealth of Nations on October 1st 1960, and, finally, a republic in the British Common- wealth on October 1st 1963, when the Governor-General, who had used the standard Governor-General flag (*see* page 54), was replaced by a President. On becoming independent Nigeria adopted a distinctive National Flag. The field, which is two by one, is divided into three vertical stripes, green, white, green (Plate 25,1). This replaced the former Blue Ensign defaced by the old badge of Nigeria, and has been retained now that Nigeria has become a republic. The National Flag is also the Jack and the Ensign for merchant ships. The Ensign worn by naval units is similar to the

White Ensign except that a diminutive of the National Flag takes the place of the Union Flag in the upper canton next to the hoist. The Masthead Pennant is green with the red cross of St. George at the head. The flag of the Nigerian Naval Board is green, charged with a large, conventional, yellow foul anchor lying along the horizontal line with its stock towards the hoist.

The flag of the Nigerian Ports Authority is green, proportions two by one, with a white disc in the centre, occupying one third of the hoist; this disc is charged with a green dolphin, similar to the supporters in the Arms of the Authority, but is ensigned with a naval crown in gold. Around the neck of the dolphin is a gold chain, beneath which are two interlaced triangles, also in gold.

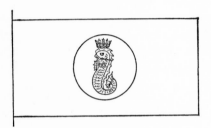

FLAG OF NIGERIAN PORTS
AUTHORITY

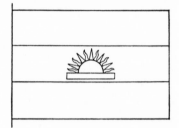

BIAFRA

At the time of writing a civil war is raging in Nigeria in which the eastern part of the country, which calls itself BIAFRA is endeavouring to break away from the rest of Nigeria. Biafra has adopted a flag which has three equal horizontal stripes, red at the top, then black and green at the bottom. In the centre is a rising sun with eleven rays. This flag cannot as yet be taken as official.

FORMER BADGE
OF SIERRA LEONE

After being a British colony for 153 years SIERRA LEONE attained independence within the British Commonwealth on April 27th 1961, and adopted as her National Flag a horizontal tricolour, proportions three by two, of green over white over cobalt blue (Plate 26, 2). The badge on the Union Flag and Blue Ensign, which this flag supersedes, comprised a Union Flag as it was before 1801. The lower part was divided into halves: a liberated slave seated on the seashore with a ship, reputed to be H.M. brig *Miro*, in the offing; and a palm-tree on a golden ground. Beneath was a motto 'AUSPICE BRITANNIA LIBER' ('Free under Britain's protection').

In May 1961 approval was given to the design for the Queen's Personal Flag for Sierra Leone (*see* page 26). This consisted of the Arms of Sierra Leone, as granted by Royal Warrant dated December 1st 1960, with the Queen's device of the crowned 'E' upon a royal blue ground surrounded by a chaplet of gold roses placed in the centre. This flag was depicted and used as a long flag, in the proportions three by two, but there was no particular reason for this and a square banner would have been equally correct (Plate 5, 5).

UGANDA, together with Buganda, became an independent country in the Commonwealth on October 9th 1962, and a republic a year later. Prior to independence the badge of Uganda was a bird, the African Balearic crested crane, and this badge was placed in the centre of her new National Flag which has six horizontal stripes of equal width, black at the top, then gold, red, black, gold and red (Plate 26, 4).

Tanganyika, a former German Colony, was placed under British trusteeship in 1919. Its badge was the head of a giraffe in natural colours. Tanganyika became an independent republic within the Commonwealth on December 9th 1961, and her new flag was hoisted for the first time. This had a field of three by two and consisted of three horizontal stripes of equal width, bright

TANGANYIKA

green over black over bright green; these colours were separated by narrow golden yellow stripes one sixteenth of the hoist in width.

The National Flag of Zanzibar used to be a plain red flag, and her badge, which was placed in the centre of the Union Flag of the British Resident, showed a native dhow. Zanzibar became independent in 1963 and adopted a handsome red flag with a green disc, on which were displayed two golden cloves. The first government was overthrown and on January 12th 1964 a new flag was adopted, but this did not last very long for on April 24th 1964 Zanzibar merged with Tanganyika and the two countries became the United Republic of Tanganyika and Zanzibar which shortly afterwards became the Republic of TANZANIA. The National Flag of this new republic has proportions three by two with a broad black stripe bordered by gold running diagonally from the bottom corner of the hoist to the upper corner of the fly. The top half of the flag is green and the lower blue (Plate **26**, *3*).

BOTSWANA: PRESIDENT'S FLAG

Bechuanaland, Basutoland and Swaziland were formerly known as the High Commissioners' Territories and of these Basutoland was the only one who had a badge. These three countries are now independent. Bechuanaland became the Republic of BOTSWANA on September 30th 1966, remaining within the British Commonwealth. The proportions of the new flag are three by two. There are five horizontal stripes, the upper and lower blue, divided by thin white stripes from the narrow central black stripe (Plate **26**, *6*). The Standard of the President of Botswana has an azure blue field with the Arms of Botswana in the centre. These arms are within a white circle with a black outline.

Basutoland became the Kingdom of LESOTHO on October 4th 1966 and adopted a quaint flag, the field of which is blue with two narrow vertical stripes next to the hoist, coloured red and green. In the centre of the blue field is a white Basuto hat (Plate **26**, *7*). The Royal Standard of Lesotho is the same as the State Flag with the addition of the Arms of Lesotho.

ARMS OF LESOTHO

The third, SWAZILAND, became independent on September 6th 1968 and adopted a new flag, the field of which is red with horizontal blue stripes at top and bottom, divided from the red by thin white stripes. In the centre is a native oxhide shield with two spears and a Zulu fighting stick (Plate **26**, 5). The Royal Standard is the same as the National Flag but with a gold lion in the centre of the top stripe.

As has been stated, six former French colonies have retained their connection with France. They are the Central African Republic, the Republics of Gabon, Chad, Congo (Brazzaville), Malagasy and Senegal, and form the French Community whose banner flag is the French tricolour bearing the inscription 'Liberté, Egalité, Fraternité' in gold, with a golden fringe on three sides of the field. The banner is square, and is carried on a staff surmounted by a device of clasped hands surrounded by laurel and oak leaves—all in metallic blue (Plate **27**, 1). The Ensign of the Community is the tricolour which is flown from buildings and is the Ensign for merchant ships.

In addition each member state has its own distinctive flag as described below:

On attaining independence French Equatorial Africa divided into two countries: Ubanghi-Shari becoming the CENTRAL AFRICAN REPUBLIC and Gabon the REPUBLIC OF GABON. The National Flag of the Central African Republic has a field five by three, and consists of four horizontal stripes of equal width, blue (at the top), white, emerald green and yellow, overall in the centre a vertical red stripe; a five-pointed star is positioned at the hoist on the blue stripe (Plate **27**, 2). The National Flag of Gabon, field three by two, is a horizontal tricolour, green at the top, golden yellow, and royal blue (Plate **27**, 3).

CHAD's National Flag, adopted on November 6th 1959, is a vertical tricolour, proportions eleven by seven, blue at the hoist, yellow and red (Plate **27**, 4).

The REPUBLIC OF CONGO (Brazzaville) has a distinctive National Flag, field three by two, with a broad, yellow diagonal stripe running from the tack (the lower corner of the hoist) to the upper corner of the fly; the upper triangle so formed is green and the lower red (Plate **27**, 5).

Madagascar became the REPUBLIC OF MALAGASY and its new National Flag, three by two, is divided horizontally, red over emerald green, with a broad white stripe at the hoist (Plate **27**, 6).

The flag of the REPUBLIC OF SENEGAL, on the north-west coast of Africa, just south of Mauritania, is a vertical tricolour, green at the hoist, yellow and red, with a five-pointed green star on the centre stripe (Plate **27**, 7).

The remaining African countries are completely independent and have no ties with other countries.

ALGERIA, the northern part of which was once part of Metro-politan France, became an independent republic on July 3rd 1962, and adopted as its National Flag the flag displayed by the revolu-tionaries in 1959. This flag is divided vertically, green (at the hoist) and white, in the centre thereof a five-pointed star between the horns of a crescent, both in red (Plate **28**, 1).

The former Belgium trust territory of Ruanda-Urundi achieved independence on July 1st 1962, and divided into two countries: the Kingdom of Burundi and the Republic of Rwanda. The Kingdom of BURUNDI has now become a republic and after several variations from its original flag has now finally adopted one which is similar to the flag of the Kingdom in that it has four quarters, red top and bottom and green to hoist and fly, which are divided by a white saltire, but the ancient device in the centre has been replaced by three green-bordered red six-pointed stars (Plate **28**, 2).

The flag of the REPUBLIC OF RWANDA is a vertical tricolour, red, yellow and green, with a large letter 'R' in black in the centre (Plate **28**, 3).

The former trust territory of the French Cameroons, part of the old German colony of Kamerun, became the CAMEROUN REPUBLIC on January 1st 1960. The flag consists of a vertical tricolour, green (at the hoist), red and yellow, with two yellow stars in the upper corner of the green stripe (Plate **28**, 4).

The former Belgian Congo, now the CONGOLESE REPUBLIC (Kinshasa), adopted a new National Flag in 1963. This consists of a blue field with a diagonal red stripe running from the bottom corner next the hoist to the upper corner of the fly; this red stripe is bordered or fimbriated by two thin yellow stripes. In the

top corner next the hoist is a large yellow five-pointed star
(Plate 28, 5).

DAHOMEY, another former French colony, adopted a new flag of
simple design on November 16th 1959; it consists of a green stripe
at the hoist with horizontal stripes, yellow over red, in the fly
(Plate 28, 6).

The horizontal tricolour, green over yellow over red, of
ETHIOPIA (Abyssinia) does not seem to have come into existence
before 1894, and even then it took the form of three pennants of the
aforementioned colours, one above the other.   These pennants are
said to have been used as distinguishing colours for different bodies
of troops.

In 1898 the first Abyssinian mission which came to France hoisted
these colours as the National Flag.   After World War II the yellow
stripe was charged with a crowned lion, in natural colours, supporting a cross-staff bearing a green, red and yellow pennon,
known as the 'Lion of Judah'.   It should be noted that the lion
is depicted as walking away from the hoist.   Although this is the
National Flag and Merchant Ship Ensign, the plain tricolour is
sometimes used as an alternative (Plate 28, 7).

Several reasons are given for the adoption of these colours, namely:

They represent the three parts of Ethiopia: Tigre, red; Amhara,
yellow; and Choa (our form of which is Shoa), green.

The colours are those of the rainbow, frequently seen in
Ethiopia.

The emblem of the Trinity: yellow for the Father; red for the
Son; and green for the Holy Ghost.

They represent the three Christian virtues: Faith, red; Hope,
green; and Charity, yellow.

The Naval Ensign has a blue field with a diminutive of the
National Flag in the first quarter.   Blue is also used for the Masthead Pennant, the head of which bears the same diminutive.

When Emperor Haile Selassie returned in January 1941, after
nearly five years in exile, he hoisted the green, yellow and red
standard bearing the brown Lion of Judah with the Amharic
inscription 'Lion of Judah.   King of the Kings of Ethiopia'.

The accompanying illustrations show the standard which has

ETHIOPIA:
EMPEROR'S STANDARD, OBVERSE

been in use since 1949. The field is ninety-five by fifty-five and comprises the national tricolour charged with the Grand Cordon of the Seal of Solomon with seal pendant. Above is an inscription, which translated means 'Conquering Lion of the Tribe of Judah.' Within the Grand Cordon is the Lion of Judah bearing the national colours.

The seal is also placed at each of the four corners of the flag; these charges are in gold.

The reverse side of the standard is similar, but the Lion of Judah gives place to a representation of St. George and the Dragon. The horse is white and St. George wears a purple suit and cap, red plume and cape, and green stockings; the green dragon has purple wings and a red tongue. The meaning of the inscription over the charge is 'Strong Star of Honour'.

ETHIOPIA:
EMPEROR'S STANDARD, REVERSE

The standard has a golden fringe on three sides.

Great Britain took over the administration of ERITREA, a former colony of Italy, from the end of World War II until September 11th 1952, when it was federated with Ethiopia. The flag of Eritrea was sky blue, bearing in the centre an olive twig with six branches, flanked by two olive branches, each having fourteen leaves, in green. This flag was abandoned on December 23rd 1958, and the Ethiopian flag used in its place.

The former colony of Spanish Guinea and the Island of Fernando Póo became the independent REPUBLIC OF EQUATORIAL GUINEA on October 12th 1968. The new State Flag is a horizontal tricolour,

Plate 28

FLAGS OF AFRICAN COUNTRIES

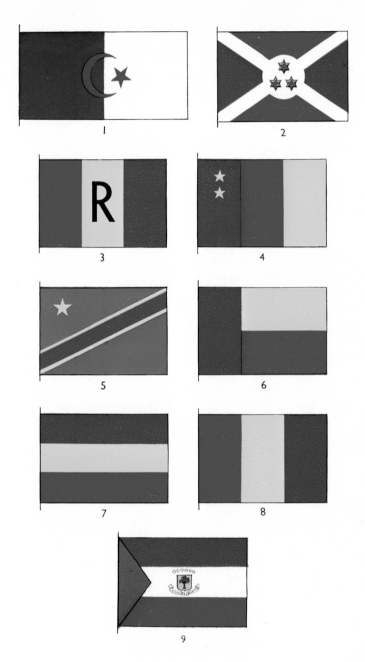

Plate 28   f.p. 182

FLAGS OF AFRICAN COUNTRIES

green at the top then white and red at the bottom with a blue triangle in the hoist and the national coat of arms in the centre of the white stripe. The arms have a golden shield which bears a God-tree (brown trunk, green foliage); above are six six-pointed silver stars with black centres and below the motto 'UNIDAD PAZ JUSTICIA' in black upon a silver scroll (Plate 28, 9).

REPUBLIC OF GUINEA (formerly French Guinea) has a flag consisting of three vertical stripes of equal width, red (at the hoist), yellow and emerald green (Plate 28, 8).

The IVORY COAST REPUBLIC, Ghana's western neighbour, has as her National Flag a vertical tricolour, field eleven by seven, which is the reverse of the National Flag of Eire, i.e. orange at the hoist, then white and emerald green (Plate 29, 1).

LIBERIA was founded about 1821 by the American Colonisation Society as an experiment in the colonisation of Africa by Africans. The Society bought land and settled upon it freed slaves from America. In 1847 it became an independent Negro republic and in 1857 absorbed the African Maryland, which had been started as a colony in a similar way. The National Flag, Naval and Merchant Ship Ensigns frankly declare their origin, but there are only eleven stripes instead of thirteen, and only one white five-pointed star in the dark blue upper canton (Plate 29, 2). This star is on a dark blue panel at the head of the Masthead Pennant, whose field is divided vertically red and white.

After World War II Great Britain and France undertook, on behalf of the United Nations, the administration of LIBYA, which had been a pre-war colony of Italy. Under a United Nations Resolution an independent State of Libya, comprising Tripolitania, Cyrenaica and Fezzen, had to be set up by January 1st 1952. Provision for a National Flag was made in the Constitution of Libya, which was drawn up by the Libyan National Assembly and promulgated on October 7th 1951. Libya achieved full independence on December 24th 1951. The field of her National Flag is two by one, and consists of three horizontal stripes, red over black over green, with a white crescent and five-pointed star in the centre of the middle stripe. The width of this stripe is equal to that of the red and green stripes combined (Plate 29, 3). The black stripe and

13

its charges were taken from the black flag which the King had adopted when he was proclaimed Amir of Cyrenaica in 1947; the red stripe represents Fezzen, and the green Tripolitania.

The black flag of the Amir mentioned above, with the addition of the white crown in the upper hoist, became the Royal Standard of the Amir when he became King of the United Kingdom of Libya.

LIBYA: ROYAL STANDARD

MALI, a former French possession, is named after one of the great Negro Emperors of the Middle Ages. Its flag, field three by two, is a vertical tricolour, emerald green (at the hoist), yellow and red. The symbolic representation of a Negro dancer which was formerly on the middle stripe has been deleted, and the flag is now a simple tricolour (Plate 29, 4).

In accordance with the decree signed on April 1st 1959, the ISLAMIC REPUBLIC OF MAURITANIA (formerly French West Africa) adopted an emerald-green flag, three by two, bearing a crescent and five-pointed star, in gold, in its centre (Plate 29, 5).

The KINGDOM OF MOROCCO came into being on March 2nd 1956, when the former French Protectorate attained its independence and Sultan Mohammed V adopted the style of King. The old National Flag was retained. This had a red field, three by two, charged with a pentagram in green; this flag is also the Merchant Ship Ensign (Plate 29, 6). Formerly, this flag had a small French tricolour in the upper canton. At the time of writing the King uses the National Flag. As Sultan, he used to fly a red triangular flag, with a yellow border on the upper and lower edges, charged with a green-bordered yellow 'Solomon's Seal'.

On April 7th 1957, after some forty-five years, Spanish Morocco declared its independence and became part of the new Kingdom of Morocco. Previously the Caliph flew a green flag bearing the Solomon's Seal emblem in yellow in its centre, and the merchant ships wore a Red Ensign, the first quarter of which was green, fimbriated white, and charged with the same emblem.

NIGER, on attaining independence, adopted a flag having three horizontal stripes of equal width, orange over white over emerald green, with an orange disc in the middle of the central stripe (Plate 29, 7).

The REPUBLIC OF SOUTH AFRICA has a most interesting history, which is complemented by many unique and interesting flags.

The first Europeans to land in South Africa were the Portuguese in 1488, but their settlements were further north in what is now Mozambique. Thus the first flag seen in South Africa was probably that of Portugal; whether it was flown ashore or only on the visiting ships is unknown. However, in the early part of the 17th century the English and the Dutch started using the Cape as a revictualling station. In April 1652 Jan van Riebeeck, a ship's surgeon of the Dutch East India Company, founded the first European settlement at the Cape, a settlement that was to become Cape Town. Although there are no records, it seems likely that the first flag flown in South Africa was the old National Flag of the Netherlands the so-called Prinsevlag, a horizontal tricolour, orange, white and pale blue; this flag was, of course, soon changed to the red, white and blue tricolour of Holland (*see* page 151). In 1795 Great Britain agreed to occupy Cape Town in order to assist in its defence against the French, and the Union Jack (1606 pattern) was hoisted at the Castle of Good Hope, which had been built on the site of the old Dutch fort.

One of the outstanding events in South African history was the Great Trek of the Cape frontiersmen, undertaken during the years 1835 to 1848. To seek security and independence they 'trekked' away to form new settlements and became known as the Voortrekkers. A number of settlements or republics were founded, all with their own distinctive flags.

Most of these flags remained in use until the Treaty of 1902 with Great Britain was signed and the Union Flag of Great Britain superseded the flags of the republics which became incorporated in South Africa. Although the majority of the flags of the old republics have gone out of use, two have been retained and are now incorporated in the design of the National Flag of South Africa. These two flags are those of the Orange Free State and the Transvaal.

In 1854 the Orange Free State asked King William III of the Netherlands to present the new republic with a flag that would illustrate the mutual relationship between the two countries.   On February 28th 1856 the Volksraad adopted the design received from the King.   This design typified the close bonds between the House of Orange and the new Free State.   It consists of seven horizontal stripes, four white and three orange, with in the canton, occupying the first three stripes, the tricolour, the flag of the Netherlands.

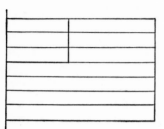

ORANGE FREE STATE FLAG

The flag of the Transvaal is known as the Vierkleur, and is the flag of the Netherlands, a horizontal tricolour red, white and blue, with the addition of a green 'pale' or narrow stripe next to the hoist.

The National Flag of South Africa was introduced at the instance of General Hertzog after the Imperial Conference had given the Dominions equal status with the mother country.   It is described in detail in the Union of Nationality and Flag Act No. 40 of 1927. This flag is the old Prinsevlag, already mentioned, with a device in the centre of the white stripe.   This device is composed of three flags, hanging vertically the old Orange Free State Flag, with the Union Jack spread horizontally towards the hoist and the old Transvaal Vierkleur spread towards the fly.   The proportions of the flag are two by three (Plate 30, 1).

From 1927 to 1957 the British Union Flag and the Flag of South Africa, both of equal size, were flown on public buildings side by side, each on its own staff, but since 1957 only the Flag of South Africa has been flown.

On May 31st 1961 South Africa withdrew from the British Commonwealth of Nations and became the Republic of South Africa, retaining as her National Flag the design that had been adopted in 1927.

It is interesting to note that while all the other former colonies which have newly become independent have, in spite of remaining within the British Commonwealth, adopted national flags which

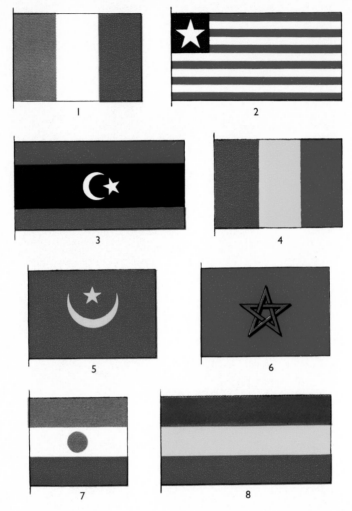

Plate 29

FLAGS OF AFRICAN COUNTRIES

Plate 29

FLAGS OF AFRICAN COUNTRIES

have no connection with the flags of Britain, South Africa, on the other hand, although out of the Commonwealth has retained a representation (albeit small) of the Union Flag. However, an announcement has been made that a new National Flag is now under consideration.

The flag of the President of the republic is royal blue with in the centre the full achievement of the arms of the republic ensigned with the letters 'S' and 'P', (State President) in gold. The shield or 'arms' is quartered, the horizontal dividing line being wavy. In the first quarter on a red ground a woman leaning on a rock, representing the Cape of

SOUTH AFRICA: PRESIDENT'S FLAG

Good Hope; in the second two black wildebeeste for Natal; the third an orange tree for the Orange Free State; the second and third have gold fields and the fourth has a green field with a white trek-wagon representing the Transvaal.

Merchant ships registered in South Africa wear the National Flag as an ensign; formerly they wore a Red Ensign defaced by the badge of the Union, the 'arms' described above.

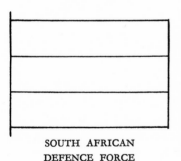

SOUTH AFRICAN
DEFENCE FORCE

The flag of the South African Defence Force is a horizontal tricolour, light blue over red and dark blue. The flag of the Minister of Defence is the National Flag with a miniature of the same flag in the canton, but in this miniature the device of the three flags in the centre is replaced by the red lion from the crest of the Arms of South Africa (*see* above). A vertical orange anchor is superimposed on the lower part of the fly.

Until September 1946 ships of the South African Navy wore the British White Ensign. Several different designs were then tried, until March 1952, when the pattern, which is basically the present Ensign, was adopted. This has a white field on which is super-imposed a dark green cross with the centre limb off-set towards the hoist; the National Flag is placed in the canton. The National Flag is also used as the Jack. The Masthead Pennant is white with the dark green cross in the hoist.

The Flag of the Chief of the Naval Staff is similar to the Ensign, except that it is a broad pennant i.e. it has a swallow-tailed fly, and also the device in the centre of the miniature in the canton is the red lion from the crest of the Arms of South Africa.

With the formation of the Republic of South Africa in 1961 the National Flag in the canton of the Ensign, and the miniature tri-colour in the flag of the Chief of the Naval Staff were separated from the cross by a white fimbriation, or narrow stripe (Plate 30, 2).

The Flag of the Army is orange-red with the National Flag in the canton, and in the fly the head of a springbok.

The Ensign of the South African Air Force has a field of Air

SOUTH AFRICAN ARMY FLAG

S.A.A.F. EMBLEM

Force blue with the National Flag in the canton. Formerly it was defaced by a circular dark blue badge with a white centre on which there was a leaping springbok, coloured orange. In 1958 this badge was replaced by one shaped like the plan of the old fort at Cape Town, dark blue in colour with a white fimbriation and in the centre the same leaping springbok.

The Republic of South Africa is establishing a certain number of 'native states', or 'Bantu Homelands'. The first of these, and so far the only one, is Transkei. These states are to be responsible for their own internal administration, and have the right to use their own language, anthem and flag. This latter is flown from all Transkei government buildings, but only in conjunction with and in an inferior position to the Flag of South Africa, which retains the overall responsibility for the government and foreign affairs of Transkei. The flag of Transkei is a horizontal tricolour, the top stripe ochre-red, then white and green at the bottom. The proportions are three by two (Plate 30, 3).

The SUDAN was proclaimed an independent Republic at Khartoum on January 1st 1956. The new National Flag, which consists of three horizontal stripes of equal width, imperial blue over yellow over emerald green, was hoisted at the ceremony (Plate 29, 8). Blue symbolises the Nile, yellow the desert, and green agriculture. Previous to independence the Sudan was administered by an Anglo-Egyptian Condominium Agreement of 1899 and the Treaty of 1936, during which time the British and Egyptian flags were flown equally on all

SUDAN: CUSTOMS SERVICE

official buildings. Two white equilateral triangles, each charged with a similar red triangle, are placed in the centre of the blue flag of the Customs Service.

TOGO, a former French trustee territory, was originally the western zone of the old German colony of Togoland. It was granted self-government in 1956 and in accordance with Law No. 56-1, Article 1, adopted a distinctive flag. This had an emerald-green field, charged with two yellow stars positioned on the diagonal running from the lower corner of the hoist to the upper corner of the fly; a small canton in the upper hoist contained the French tricolour. Complete independence was attained on April 27th 1960, and it became the Republic of Togo and a new flag was designed, the field of which consisted of five horizontal stripes of equal width, three emerald green and two yellow; in a large red canton in the upper hoist is a white five-pointed star (Plate 30, 5). It is said that green is for agriculture, yellow for mineral resources, red to commemorate the blood of the strugglers for independence, and the white star is the 'Star of Hope'.

TUNISIA, a French Protectorate since 1881, formally proclaimed itself a republic on July 25th 1957. The National Flag and Merchant Ship Ensign has a red field, proportions three by two, bearing in the centre a white disc charged with a crescent and five-pointed star in red (Plate 30, 6). At the time of writing the President flies the same flag.

It is interesting that previous to independence H.H. the Bey flew a very striking standard consisting of nine horizontal stripes; commencing from the top they are: yellow, red, yellow, red, green, red, yellow, red and yellow. The green stripe is twice the width of the others and is charged with a white two-edged sword, the hilt and pommel of which are laminated yellow, red, green and white. The remaining stripes are charged with rowels (stars with a central perforation) and crescents, positioned in five vertical rows. The yellow stripes have red rowels with green centres, and blue crescents on red; the red stripes have yellow rowels with blue centres and green crescents on yellow.

H.H. THE BEY'S STANDARD

On the formation of the UNITED ARAB REPUBLIC, consisting of Egypt and Syria, on February 1st 1958, a distinctive flag was adopted, and although Syria dropped out of the republic, Egypt continued to style herself the United Arab Republic and to use the new flag as her National Flag and Ensign for her merchant ships. This flag consists of three horizontal stripes of equal width, red over white over black, with two green five-pointed stars on the white stripe (Plate 30, 7). With the addition of two

UNITED ARAB REPUBLIC: NAVAL ENSIGN

white conventional foul anchors in saltire this flag becomes the Naval Ensign and also the Jack. The Masthead Pennant, red over white over black, has the two green stars from the National Flag on the centre of the white stripe next the hoist.

The Air Force Ensign has a sky-blue field with a diminutive of the National Flag in the upper hoist. A 'target' consisting of black (centre) white and red is positioned in the lower fly; the white is charged with two small five-pointed stars.

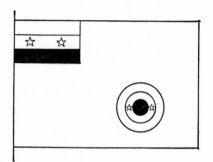

UNITED ARAB REPUBLIC: AIR FORCE ENSIGN

Prior to becoming a part of the United Arab Republic, Egypt had a number of flags. Under Turkish rule her flag was red and bore three crescents, each with a five-pointed star within its horns, all in white. On becoming an independent kingdom in 1922 she changed her flag to green with one white crescent in the place of three, but the three white stars were kept. This was the National Flag and the Ensign for merchant ships.

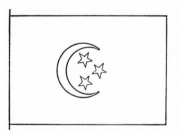

OLD EGYPTIAN FLAG

King Farouk at the time of his abdication on July 27th 1952, had no less than four Royal Standards; the one for use ashore resembled the National Flag, but had a crown in colour in the upper left-hand corner. The standard for use afloat was dark blue, bearing in the centre the Royal Arms enclosed in a mantle ensigned with the Royal Crown. This achievement was encircled with the collar and badge of the order of Mohammed Ali. Each corner had a small Royal Crown.

The third standard, known as the Royal Standard (Air), was white with three broad green horizontal stripes, one in the middle and one each at the top and bottom edges, with two narrower green stripes between. In the upper corner of the hoist was a small crown in proper colours. When this crown appeared on the Ensign of the Royal Egyptian Air Force it became the standard flown on the King's aeroplane.

The UNITED SOMALI REPUBLIC was formed by the amalgamation of the former British Protectorate of Somaliland and the former colony of Italian Somaliland. As a British Protectorate Somaliland used the Blue and Red Ensigns defaced by a badge on a white disc in the fly. On attaining independence the new republic adopted a light blue flag, field three by two, bearing a large white five-pointed star in the centre (Plate 30, 4).

The REPUBLIC OF UPPER VOLTA, a former French Colony, became independent on August 5th 1960, and adopted as its National Flag a horizontal tricolour, black over white over red (Plate 30, 8).

Chapter Eight

THE MIDDLE EAST

The State or Island Flag of BAHRAIN is scarlet, having a vertical white stripe, the width of which is one fifth the hoist, at the mast.

The dividing line between these colours may be straight or serrated; in the latter case it consists of eight white points (Plate 31, 7). The Personal Standard of the Sheik is white, with a scarlet inset in the fly; the serrated edge has eight white points.

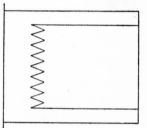

BAHRAIN: SHEIK'S PERSONAL STANDARD

When World War I broke out the Hejaz —a slip of territory along the northern part of the Arabian coast of the Red Sea, in which lie Mecca and Medina, the Holy Places of Islam—was under the domination of the Turks. During the Arab revolt of 1916, the Emir, Sherif Hussein Ibn of Mecca, with British assistance, threw off the Ottoman control and established a kingdom. He became King Hussein of the Hejaz. His old banner became the new Royal Standard and National Flag; it consisted of three horizontal stripes of equal width, black over green over white, with a red triangle in the hoist. These four colours are sometimes referred to as the Pan-Arabian colours. There are several interpretations of the meaning of them, including the following: red is for the blood of the Arab enemies; green the fertility of Arab lands; black the fate in store for the Arab enemies; and white represents Arab nobility and chivalry.

King Hussein's second son, Abdullah Ibn, became Emir of Transjordan in 1921 and adopted an amended version of his father's banner. He added a white seven-pointed star in the centre of the red triangle and transposed the green and white stripes.

When Jordan's title was changed to the HASHEMITE KINGDOM OF THE JORDAN in 1950, this flag became the National Flag (Plate 31, 6).

JORDAN: ROYAL FLAG

A new Royal Flag or Standard has now been adopted; this has in its centre a representation of the National Flag, but with a crown, in place of the star, in the red triangle, at the hoist. This is surrounded by what is known heraldically as a 'gyronny of twelve pieces'—in other words radial stripes, alternately white, red, white, black, white and green, repeating these colours to make twelve stripes.

In 1921 the third son of King Hussein of the Hejaz was elected King Feisal of IRAQ (formerly Mesopotamia). In accordance with the Treaty of Lausanne, Iraq was placed under the protection of Britain, and seven years late became completely independent. The Royal Standard consisted of the Jordan flag described on page 193, but the red triangle at the hoist was charged with a large golden crown instead of the white star; that of the Crown Prince was similar, but was swallow-tailed, the tails being cut off square, while his coronet appeared in the red triangle. The National Flag had a red trapezoid in the hoist, bearing two white seven-pointed stars, in place of the red triangle.

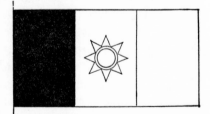

IRAQ: OLD NATIONAL FLAG

The Royal Family was assassinated in Baghdad and a republic declared in July 1958. Twelve months later a new National Flag was adopted. This was a vertical tricolour, black (at the hoist), white and green; the white stripe bore a large red eight-pointed star charged with a white-bordered yellow disc. This star recalls the revolution of July 14th 1958, and its eight points represent the Arab nations. The yellow disc is said to have been

Plate 30

FLAGS OF AFRICAN COUNTRIES

1 South Africa, Republic of: National Flag, Merchant Flag and Jack (p. 186)

2 South Africa, Republic of: Naval Ensign (p. 188)

3 Transkei: National Flag (p. 189)

4 United Somali Republic: National Flag (p. 192)

5 Togo: National Flag (p. 189)

6 Tunisia: President's Flag, National and Merchant Flag (p. 190)

7 United Arab Republic: National and Merchant Flag (p. 190)

8 Upper Volta, Republic of: National Flag (p. 192)

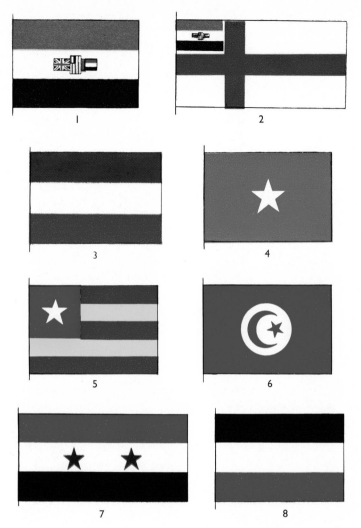

Plate 30   f.p. 194

FLAGS OF AFRICAN COUNTRIES

taken from the flag of Salahuddin Al-Ayubi and expressed the co-operation between Arabs and Kurds.

The government formed in 1958 under Kassem was overthrown in February 1963, and a new government under Marshal Abdul Salam Mohammed Arif was formed. On August 23rd 1963, this government adopted a new National Flag, which was a horizontal tricolour, proportions three by two, with stripes of equal width, red at the top, white and black, with three green five-pointed stars placed on the white stripe (Plate 31, 1). Although there has been another change of government since, the National Flag has not been changed.

Ibn Saud became Sultan of the Nejd in 1921, and five years later conquered the Hejaz and became King Saud of the Hejaz and Nejd and its Dependencies. The name of this kingdom was changed to SAUDI ARABIA in 1932.

The National Flag is green and bears the great Arabic inscription 'LA ILLAHA ILLA ALLAH WA MUHAMMAD UR-RUSUL ULLAH' ('There is no God but God, Mohammed is the Prophet of God'). The inscription, in accordance with Arab custom, reads from right to left. In order that it shall appear correctly on the reverse side of the flag it is necessary to print it in duplicate and sew the two back to back before fixing the canvas 'heading'. Under the inscription, which is in white, there used to be two swords in saltire. Now the Saudi Arabian flag has only one white sword. The National Flag is 150 by 100 centimetres—two by one (Plate 31, 2).

The Royal Standard and the ensign for warships are the same as the National Flag, except for the size of their fields (*see* below), and the ensign has an additional charge in the form of a white anchor in the upper corner of the fly. The Army and Air Force use the National Flag.

The Royal Standard is 250 by 230 centimetres, and the Warship Ensign 150 centimetres square. The Ensign for merchant ships is unique in that it is triangular (each side being 140 centimetres); the two white swords in saltire are in the centre of the flag and a small white anchor is in the upper hoist.

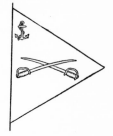

SAUDI ARABIA:
MERCHANT FLAG

Sometimes the Saudi-Arabian flags have only one white sword instead of the two in saltire.

After thirty years of mandated control by Great Britain, Palestine became the independent State of ISRAEL on May 14th 1948.

The National Flag is white with a blue horizontal stripe near the upper and lower edges of the field, and between them in the centre

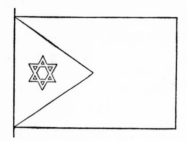

ISRAEL: ENSIGN

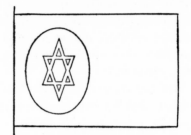

ISRAEL: MERCHANT FLAG

of the flag the 'Magen David' (Shield of David, sometimes erroneously referred to as the 'Star of David'), also in blue. This is composed of two interlaced equilateral triangles, whose bases are horizontal (Plate **31, 5**). This flag was apparently based on the design of the flag adopted by the Zionist movement, which dated back to 1891. The choice of colours is said to have been inspired by the 'tallith'—the traditional Jewish prayer shawl.

The Naval and Merchant Ships Ensigns both have blue fields. The former has a white triangle at the hoist, bearing the Magen David device in blue, and the latter has a white oval panel near the hoist, charged with the same emblem. The Air Force Ensign has two dark blue horizontal stripes, one each near the top and bottom

ISRAEL: AIR FORCE ENSIGN

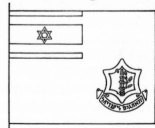

ISRAEL: DEFENCE FORCE

edges, followed inwards by narrow white stripes, which in turn have narrow dark blue borders. In the centre of the field is a dark blue-bordered white disc, bearing a dark blue six-pointed star.

The Defence Force Flag has a sky-blue field with a white canton bearing two horizontal stripes and the Magen David emblem in sky blue; in the lower fly is a device in gold.

The President's Standard has a dark blue square field with a white border. In the centre is the Great Menorah—a seven-branched candlestick—between two olive branches, with the word Israel beneath in white. The Great Menorah is said to be a symbol of light and inspiration for the Jews.

ISRAEL: PRESI-
DENT'S STANDARD

The Sheikdom of Kuwait or Koweit became the independent State of KUWAIT on June 19th 1961. The new National Flag adopted in accordance with decree No. 26 1961 was published in the official Government gazette on September 10th 1961. It is a horizontal tricolour, green over white over red, with a black trapezoid at the hoist (Plate 31, 3). Prior to independence the Sheikdom had four National Flags; two of these were rectangular and two were triangular. All four flags had a scarlet field, with a

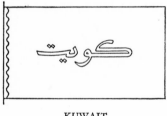

KUWAIT

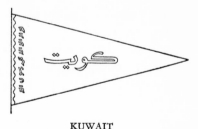

KUWAIT

narrow white stripe at the hoist, the scarlet edge of the stripe being wavy, and all had the word 'Kuwait' in Arabic, also in white, along the centre of the field. One of each of the pairs was charged with the Arabic inscription 'There is no god but God', in white, positioned along the aforesaid wavy edge. As far as can be ascertained any one of the four could be flown, there being no official ruling on the matter, but it appeared that the triangular pattern was the one more commonly used.

While LEBANON was under French Mandate she used the French tricolour with a representation of a cedar-tree of the Lebanon in the centre of the white stripe. At the end of World War II she became an independent republic, and adopted a new National Flag. This has a field of three by two, and is composed of three horizontal stripes, red at the top, then white, then red, the width of the red stripes being half that of the white stripe; in the centre of the latter and occupying nearly its whole width is a green cedar-tree with a brown trunk (Plate 31, 4). With the addition of a white vertical stripe charged with a red anchor at the hoist and fly, it becomes the Jack. The Masthead Pennant is divided vertically red, white, red.

MUSCAT and OMAN use a plain red flag, proportions three by two, as their National Flag (Plate 32, 3).

The National Flag of QATAR has a maroon field, three by two, with a white stripe at the hoist; the dividing line between the colours has a serrated edge of nine points. Sometimes the field is more of the colour of chocolate than maroon (Plate 32, 9).

When the Federation of South Arabia became independent on November 30th 1967 it was re-named the PEOPLE's REPUBLIC OF SOUTH YEMEN. The former Federation of South Arabia was originally the South Arabian Protectorate which consisted of the British colony of Aden and nineteen states. Although these states were under the protection of Great Britain they were all governed by their own rulers, sheiks or sultans etc. Most of these had their own flags which in many cases were of striking design, such as the

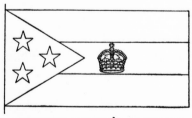

KATHIRI: SULTAN'S STANDARD

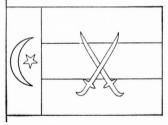

WAHIDI SULTANATE

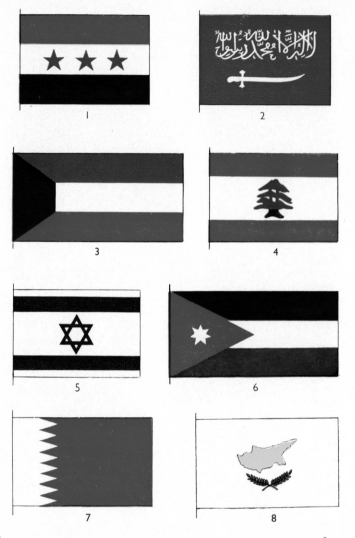

Plate 31

FLAGS OF MIDDLE EAST COUNTRIES

Plate 31

FLAGS OF MIDDLE EAST COUNTRIES

flag of the Sultan of Kathiri, with its yellow, green and yellow stripes (page 198); the State Flag was similar but without the crown.   The flag of Wahidi was green, yellow and blue horizontal stripes with crossed daggers and crescent and star.   However, these flags are now only of historical interest as the states have lost their identities and have been merged into the new People's Republic of South Yemen, the flag of which consists of three equal horizontal stripes, red at the top, then white, and black at the bottom; in the hoist there is a pale blue triangle with a red star placed slightly askew (Plate 32, 1).

SYRIA was freed from Turkish domination by British, French and Arab troops in 1918, and with Lebanon was placed under French mandate.   In 1930 Syria and Lebanon were established as a republic and adopted a flag composed of the so-called Pan-Arabian colours, black, white, red and green.   It was a horizontal tricolour, green over white over black with three red stars.   During World War II Syria and Lebanon separated (see Lebanon on page 198), but Syria retained the flag which had been adopted in 1930.   For a short period until April 1963 there was a provisional agreement for Syria to merge in a federal State with Egypt, to be called the United Arab Republic and have one flag, the black, white and red tricolour of the old United Arab Republic (Egypt), but with three stars instead of two; this arrangement has not been ratified. In 1966 in view of her closer ties with the United Arab Republic she changed her old flag to one very similar to that of the United Arab Republic, namely a horizontal tricolour, red over white over black, but with three green stars.   This flag is in fact the same as that of Iraq, from which it is distinguished by its proportions, for the dimensions of Iraq's flag are three by two and Syria's two by one (Plate 32, 5).

The TRUCIAL STATES comprise seven independent sheikdoms. They have treaty relations with the British Government, which is responsible for their external affairs.   Six of these states are at the southern end of the Persian Gulf, namely: (a) Abu Dhabi; (b) Umm el Qawain; (c) Ajman; (d) Dubai; (e) Sharjah; and (f) Ras al Khaimah; the seventh (g) Fujairah, is on the Gulf of Oman.   Details of the various flags are as follows:

14

(*a*) Red field with a white canton; (*b*) red field with white crescent and five-pointed star with vertical white stripe at the hoist (Plate **32**, 7 and 8); (*c*) and (*d*) a similar flag, but without the crescent and star; (*e*) and (*f*) white field, with a small red square in the centre; (*g*) plain rectangular red field, the same as Muscat and Oman.

The National Flag of TURKEY is red charged with a white crescent and five-pointed star. This star is placed at a slight angle to the vertical, inclined towards the hoist (Plate **32**, 6). Turkey was the first of the Mohammedan or Ottoman countries to adopt the star and crescent as a national emblem. How this device came to be the emblem of these countries is described in Chapter One, page 16.

The National Flag is also the Ensign for both warships and merchantmen. The Masthead Pennant is red and bears the white crescent and star in the hoist. Customs vessels fly a white-bordered version of the National Flag.

The Standard of the President is similar to the National Flag, but is square in shape and bears in the top corner of the hoist a golden petal-shaped flower device surrounded by a ring of sixteen golden five-pointed stars.

Since September 1962 the YEMEN has been in the throes of a civil war. Rebel forces, with the assistance of the United Arab Republic, have been endeavouring to overthrow the old Moutawakilite Kingdom of the Yemen and establish a republic. On November 5th 1964 it was announced that a cease-fire had been arranged between the opposing forces prior to talks. The flag of the Moutawakilite Kingdom is a simple red flag, with certain charges symbolic of Moslem and Yemenite virtues. Although this has been in use for many centuries the present National Flag, Naval and Merchant Ship Ensigns date only from 1927. They are all of the same simple design (Plate **32**, 4), a red field with a white scimitar and five white five-pointed stars. Each star is said to represent one of the five divisions into which the Yemen is divided, and also the five dogmas of Islam; the scimitar is the traditional Arab symbol. The forces which have been seeking to establish a republic are said to have adopted as their flag a horizontal tricolour of three equal stripes, red on top, white and black, with a single green star in the centre of the white stripe. This flag is the same as that of the United Arab Republic (Plate **32**, 2), except that it has only one star instead of two. What will eventually be the government and flag of the Yemen remains to be seen.

During its long history CYPRUS has had many masters, Roman, Venetian, Turkish and finally the British, but eventually on August 1st 1960 Cyprus became an independent republic and the Union Flag of Great Britain was replaced by a white flag bearing a map of the island with two sprigs of green leaves beneath (Plate **31**, 8).

Previously the badge of Cyprus which defaced the Union Flag and Ensign was two lions, one above the other, in fact similar to what is believed to have been the first Standard of King Richard I.

Although Cyprus has become a republic she has remained a member of the British Commonwealth.

Chapter Nine

ASIA

With one or two very minor exceptions, all the countries of Asia are now fully independent. The former British Dominions, apart from Burma, have remained within the British Commonwealth. Although the number of countries so affected is much fewer than in the case of Africa, the size and population of these individual countries are much greater.

There are seven British Commonwealth countries, Ceylon, India and Pakistan, the Maldive Islands, Mauritius, Malaysia and Singapore.

CEYLON, on obtaining 'self-constitution' in 1946 adopted as her National Flag the old Sinhalese Royal Flag (the Sinhala rajakiva dajaya) the Standard of the last King of Kandy. It had a dark red field with a golden border and in each corner an ancient Sinhalese spire or pinnacle. In the centre was a golden lion 'passant' holding a golden sword in his right paw.

The 'Lion Flag', as it is called, was first hoisted, together with the Union Flag, on Government Offices on February 7th 1948 at 7.30 a.m. the day that Ceylon became a self-governing Dominion of the British Commonwealth. The early hour fixed for the ceremony was chosen by local astrologers as being the most propitious for the future of the new Dominion.

This flag was not altogether popular and in March 1948 a National Flag Committee was appointed. After many meetings it recommended in February 1950 that the Lion Flag should be retained but that it should be modified by the addition of two vertical stripes in the hoist, one green and one saffron, the width of these stripes to be one seventh of the length of the flag within the gold border. The proportions of this flag are approximately thirty-five by eighteen centimetres. This is now the official National Flag of Ceylon (Plate 33, 6).

It was officially announced in Colombo on October 30th 1953 that the Union Flag would no longer be flown side by side with the flag of Ceylon, and from that day the latter has been the only flag to fly from public buildings and at official functions.

A new Ensign was approved by H.M. the Queen on September 1st 1955 for the use of the Royal Ceylon Navy, which up to that time had worn the British White Ensign. This new ensign is similar to the former but has the National Flag of Ceylon in place of the Union Jack in the canton.

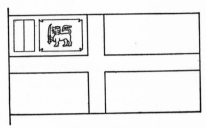

CEYLON: ENSIGN

Command Flags are similar to those of the Royal Navy, except that where appropriate the red discs are replaced by discs bearing the Royal Lion in yellow. The Jack is a miniature National Flag.

CEYLON:
ENSIGN OF GOVERNMENT VESSELS

Four other ensigns were introduced in December 1954: a plain blue for Naval Auxiliaries; the Blue Ensign defaced with special distinguishing badges for the Government vessels and the Customs Service; and a Red Ensign for Merchant Ships. All these ensigns are similar to their British counterparts except that they have the National Flag of Ceylon in the canton. The badge of the Government vessels has two golden anchors in saltire entwined with a cable,

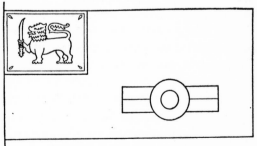

CEYLON: AIR FORCE ENSIGN

while that of the Customs consists of the national arms. It is surmounted by the gold crown of the last King of Ceylon.

CEYLON:
BADGE ON
CUSTOMS
ENSIGN

The Ensign of the Ceylon Air Force has an air force blue field with in the canton the original Lion Flag (*see* page 202). The device in the fly is a red disc with a gold centre over two horizontal stripes, saffron over gold.

When INDIA and PAKISTAN became separate Dominions on August 15th 1947, each adopted a distinctive National Flag.

INDIA chose a field, three by two, consisting of three horizontal stripes of equal width, deep saffron (on top), white and bottle-green; in the centre of the white stripe, a representation of the 'Chakra' of Asoka, the Buddhist ruler of the 3rd century B.C., in dark blue (Plate 33, 4).

Of this new flag it has been said that the dark saffron colour symbolises the spirit of renunciation, humility and disinterestedness; the white denotes a path of light, truth and simplicity; and the bottle-green represents the relation with the soil. The 'Chakra' of Asoka is the wheel of the Law of Dharma denoting motion and virtue and represents the dynamism of a peaceful change.

The flag of her first and only Governor-General, Earl Mountbatten, has already been described on page 54.

Each of the Governors of the ten provinces (Bombay, Madras, West Bengal, Bihar, Orissa, United Provinces, Assam, East Punjab, Central Provinces, and Central Provinces and Berar) had a special flag, whose field was dark saffron, proportions two by one. This was charged with the Royal Crown in natural colours, with the name of the province in white block letters, on a slight curve.

When India became a republic within the British Commonwealth of Nations on January 26th 1950, it was decided to adopt the National Flag of the former Dominion. This flag thus became the first of a new range of official flags, all of which have the proportions of three by two, except those of the Air Force Ensign, which are two by one.

The flag of the President is quarterly, blue and red, with the charges in gold line: first, the Asoka lions; second, an elephant; third, a pair of scales; fourth, a lotus bowl (Plate 33, 3). The lions came from the Asoka column capital, and are said to represent unity. Patience and strength are supposed to be embodied in the lively-looking, 5th century A.D. elephant, taken from the Ajanta frescoes. The scales, a 17th century A.D. Moslem design, came from the Red Fort, Delhi, and symbolise justice and economy; and the lotus bowl, from Sarnath, *circa* 1st century B.C., stands for prosperity and plenty.

The Asoka lions charge in the first quarter of the flag was adopted as the State Emblem and Seal of the Government of India, and with the other three, represent certain epochs in her political and cultural history.

STATE EMBLEM
OF INDIA

The Royal Crown on the former flags of Governors of provinces was superseded by the State Emblem, and the names of the provinces were changed into Devanagri script, which is said to be less understood by many than the English on the old ones!

Units of the Indian Navy wear a white Ensign similar to ours, except that the Union in the first quarter has now given place to the National Flag of India. Some surprise has been expressed at the retention of the red St. George's Cross on this ensign; however, it is regarded as a symbol of the Indian Navy's association with the other navies within the British Commonwealth. The same may be said regarding the Naval Reserve Ensign—a dark blue field with the National Flag in the first quarter.

The Jack is a diminutive of the National Flag, but the Masthead or Commission Pennant, Admirals' Flags and Commodores' Broad Pennants, also Senior Officers' Pennants, of the Royal Navy continued in use, as heretofore, until April 22nd 1958. Since then, the dark blue 'Chakra' has been superimposed on the centre of the red cross of St. George on these pennants and flags.

Government vessels (including vessels on Charter), other than ships of war, wear a Blue Ensign with the National Flag in the upper canton and a plain yellow Admiralty anchor in the fly. This Blue Ensign charged with two yellow conventional anchors in saltire and a star, and positioned in the lower corner of the fly is worn by vessels belonging to the Bombay Harbour Trust.   It is also flown on shore over its administrative buildings.

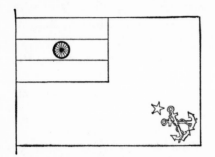

FLAG OF BOMBAY HARBOUR
TRUST

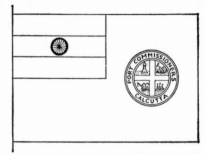

CALCUTTA: PORT COMMISSIONERS'
FLAG

The Commissioners of the Port of Calcutta use the Blue Ensign bearing their badge in the centre of the fly.   It comprises an amulet in gold, edged white and thereon the name in white lettering.   The centre of the badge has a cross in gold; each of the quarters so formed is white and charged with a seascape, as in the accompanying illustration.

Again the Blue Ensign of the Port of Cochin has two conventional anchors in gold in the upper and lower corners of the fly.

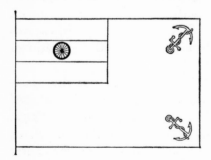

ENSIGN OF PORT OF COCHIN

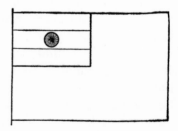

INDIAN MERCHANT FLAG

Indian merchant ships wear a Red Ensign, with the National Flag in the first quarter.

The regiments of the old Indian Army when under British Command bore Colours similar to those of British regiments; that is (although there were some exceptions) regiments had a Sovereign's Colour and a Regimental Colour. When India became the Independent Republic of India the Sovereign's Colours were ceremonially laid up on November 23rd 1950, but the regiments retained, for the time being, their old Regimental Colours; these are being replaced as opportunity offers by new Colours of a design more

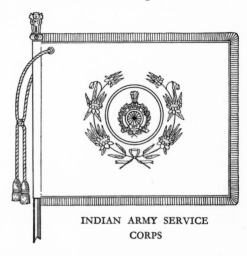

INDIAN ARMY SERVICE
CORPS

appropriate to the new status of India. An illustration of the new Regimental Colours of the Indian Army Service Corps is shown.

INDIAN ARMY FLAG

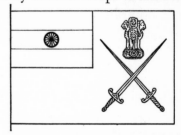

FLAG OF COMMANDER-IN-CHIEF

A new Army Flag has also been adopted; this, like that of the British Army is red with two swords in saltire, but in the centre is the State Emblem of India, the Asoka lions. The flag of the Commander-in-Chief of the Army is similar to the Merchant Ensign, with in the fly two swords in saltire beneath the State Emblem, all in gold.

The field of the Air Force Ensign is air force blue in colour, containing the National Flag in the first quarter, and a target in the

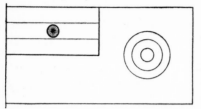

fly similar to that of the Royal Air Force, but composed of the national colours, i.e. saffron, white and green, the last being in the centre.

It is understood that the flag of JAMMU AND KASHMIR is no longer used. It had a red field bearing a representation of a native plough, also three vertical bars in white at the hoist (Plate 35, 9).

INDIAN AIR FORCE ENSIGN

The National Flag of the Dominion of PAKISTAN consisted of a bottle-green field, three by two, having a white vertical stripe at the hoist occupying one fourth the length of the flag; the green portion bore a white crescent and five-pointed star positioned on an imaginary diagonal line running from the top of the fly. It also did duty as the Jack and the Merchant Flag. Vessels of the Royal Pakistan Navy continued to wear the White Ensign and Masthead Pennant, as in the days of the Royal Indian Navy.

Governors of the four provinces, Sind, East Bengal, West Punjab and North-West Frontier Province, had flags similar to those of their opposite numbers in India before the republic was inaugurated; however, in this case the field was green, of the same shade as that on the National Flag.

The Islamic Republic of Pakistan was formally declared a republic within the British Commonwealth of Nations on March 23rd 1956. It was decided to retain the old National Flag (Plate 33, 2), and also use it as the Ensign for naval vessels; however, in the latter case the field should be two by one instead of three by two. The shade of green used in all flags was changed to tartan green (*see*

PAKISTAN: JACK

British Colour Council's Colour Card). The Masthead Pennant is white (at the mast) and tartan green; the Jack has a tartan green field, three by two, bearing in the centre thereof a five-pointed star within a crescent (horns pointing upwards) and a representation of a foul anchor, in white, in each of the lower corners. At the same time a distinctive Merchant Flag was adopted. It had a royal blue field, three by two, with a white canton bearing a crescent and five-pointed star in tartan green. However, in accordance with the Ministry of Commerce Government of Pakistan, notification No. 365 116 54-Sh, dated October 22nd 1958, this was superseded by one having a red field, also three by two, with the National Flag in the first quarter next to the mast.

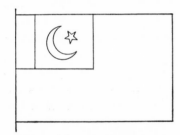

PAKISTAN: MERCHANT FLAG

PAKISTAN: REAR-ADMIRAL

It should be noted that merchant ships of other countries wishing to fly a 'courtesy flag' at the foremast when visiting Pakistan now use the National Flag of that country for this purpose (*also see* page 18).

The President's Flag has a royal blue field, nine feet by six feet six inches; superimposed in the centre thereof, in gold, the crescent and star emblem between two olive branches with the word 'PAKISTAN', in Pakistani script, below (Plate 33, 1).

Admirals' Flags and Commodores' Broad Pennants are royal blue, the principal charge on each consisting of a white foul anchor surmounted by the white crescent and small five-pointed star emblem.

The addition of larger white five-pointed stars is used to denote
rank, thus—five for an Admiral-of-the-Fleet, four for an Admiral,
three for a Vice-Admiral, two for a Rear-Admiral and one for a
Commodore.   A Senior Officer's Pennant is similar to that of a
Commodore but bears no larger five-pointed star.

The Pakistani Army is largely modelled on the British Army, and
there is the same system of Regimental and National (in place of the
Sovereign's) Colours.

The proportions of the Ensign of the Pakistan Air Force are
the same as those of the National Flag; it has an air force blue field

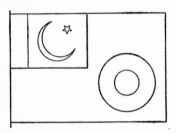

with the National Flag in the first
quarter.   Situated in the centre of an
imaginary diagonal line running from
the middle of the upper edge of the
flag to the bottom corner of the fly, is
a green-and-white target, the former
colour being outside and the latter in
the centre.

PAKISTAN: AIR FORCE
ENSIGN

Although it is not strictly speaking a
Pakistani flag, it is appropriate to
mention here the flag of the Aga Khan, the spiritual leader of the
Ismaili Moslems.   It has a dark emerald green field with a diagonal
crimson stripe running from the top of the hoist to the bottom of
the fly.   The width of this stripe is approximately one quarter the
hoist (or breadth) of the flag, the proportions of which are two by
one.

Four hundred miles to the south-west of Ceylon lie the MALDIVE
ISLANDS.   They became an independent republic within the British
Commonwealth on January 1st 1953.   Fourteen months later they
reverted to being a sultanate, as they had been for more than 800
years.   The National and Merchant Flag has a white crescent on a
green field, with a broad red border (Plate 33, 9).   Formerly there
was a narrow 'pale', or vertical stripe, at the hoist, formed of white
and black diagonal stripes.

The old federated and unfederated Malay States and two settlements were united in the new Federation of Malaya which came into
being in May 1950, and which became independent within the

British Commonwealth of Nations on August 1st 1957. The
Federation of Malaya consisted of the Malay States of Johore,
Kedah, Kelantan, Negri Sembilan, Pahang, Perlis, Perak, Selangor
and Trengganu, together with the two British Straits Settlements of
Malacca and Penang.

On September 16th 1963 MALAYSIA was formed by amalgamating
the Federation of Malaya with the State of Singapore and the
Colonies of Sarawak and North Borneo, which assumed the name of
Sabah.   However, difference arose between the State of Singapore
and the Federation, and on August 9th 1965 Singapore parted from
Malaysia and became a Sovereign Independent State.

The National Flag of the old Federation consisted of eleven horizontal stripes of equal width, six red and five white, and in a royal
blue canton occupying half the length of the flag and of a depth
equalling the width of seven stripes was a crescent and an eleven-
pointed star of generous proportions in gold.   The new National
Flag of Malaysia, which superseded the flag of the Federation, is
very similar in design.   Its proportions are still two by one, but the
number of stripes has been increased to fourteen and the number of
points on the star is now also fourteen, one for each of the member
states of Malaysia (Plate **33**, 8).   This flag was not changed when
Singapore parted from Malaysia in 1965.

The Royal Standard of the
Head of State, the Yang Di-
Pertuan Agong, is a golden
banner with in the centre the
Arms of Malaysia, in full
colours and surrounded by a
wreath.

MALAYSIA: ROYAL STANDARD

Units of the Royal Malayan
Navy used to wear the White
Ensign, Blue Masthead Pen-
nant, and as a Jack a square Blue Ensign defaced by the badge of
Singapore in the fly.   These were replaced by the Federation Naval
Ensign, Masthead Pennant and Jack in June 1958.   The Naval
Ensign was similar to the White Ensign, except that the Union Flag
in the upper canton was replaced by the Federation Flag.   The

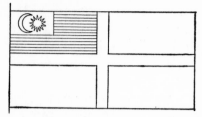

MALAYSIA: NAVAL ENSIGN

Masthead Pennant is blue and has a crescent and star in gold at the head; the Jack is a diminutive Federation flag. With the formation of Malaysia in September 1963, the Naval Ensign and Jack were again modified; the new ensign now has the National Flag of Malaysia in the upper canton, and similarly the Jack is a miniature of the National Flag.

All the states which form Malaysia have their own flags, which are as follows:

The State Flag of JOHORE is dark blue, having a red canton (of rather unusual proportions—half the length of the flag and two thirds the hoist) with a crescent moon and a five-pointed star in white.

That of KEDAH is red, having a yellow shield over a green crescent moon turned upwards, all within a yellow wreath of coconut leaves, in the upper hoist.

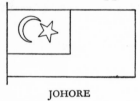

JOHORE

KEDAH

The State Flag of KELANTAN is also red, bearing in the centre thereof a complicated design in white.

KELANTAN

NEGRI SEMBILAN

NEGRI SEMBILAN, on the other hand, has a yellow flag with a canton (occupying one quarter of the field) divided diagonally, from the upper hoist to the lower fly, red over black.

The State Flag of PAHANG is halved horizontally, white over black.

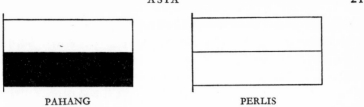

PAHANG   PERLIS

Equal halves of yellow over dark blue form the State Flag of PERLIS.

That of PERAK consists of three horizontal stripes of equal width, white over yellow over black.

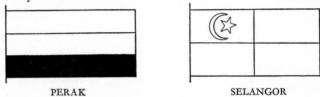

PERAK   SELANGOR

The State Flag of SELANGOR is quartered, first and fourth red and second and third yellow; in the first quarter a crescent moon and five-pointed star in white.

TRENGGANU possesses a white-bordered black flag with a white crescent moon and five-pointed star superimposed in the centre of the field.

The State Flag of MALACCA consists of two horizontal stripes of equal width, red over white, having a dark blue canton,

TRENGGANU

charged with a yellow crescent and five-pointed star, in the upper half of the hoist.

The original badge of Malacca was a representation of the Santiago Gate of Malacca town taken from the arms granted by

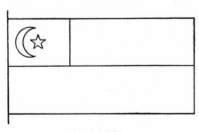

MALACCA   MALACCA

Royal Warrant dated August 14th 1951. This badge and coat of arms has been replaced by one consisting of a shield supported by two deer. The upper portion of the shield is blue with five golden daggers, or krises; the lower part is divided into three, the right-hand section yellow and the left red; in the centre is a tree in full foliage on a greensward. Above is a horizontal crescent and five-pointed star, and below on a blue scroll is inscribed in roman and native script 'BERSATU TEGOH—MELAKA' ('Unity is strength—Malacca').

PENANG

The State Flag of PENANG is a vertical tricolour, azure blue (at the hoist), white and golden yellow; the charge on the white stripe comprises a representation of a Pinang or Areca-nut Palm, in proper colours, on a green mount, from the crest of the arms.

The badge of Penang comprises the shield from the Arms granted by Royal Warrant on September 11th 1949. The eight wavy bars are blue and white—the uppermost being blue; in chief, the three white feathers from the badge of the Prince of Wales. The blue ribbon bearing the words ICH DIEN has now been replaced by the motto 'BERSATU DAN SETIA' ('United and loyal'). Above the shield is the Pinang Palm.

PENANG

The flag of SARAWAK is taken from its old badge, which in turn was taken from the colours of the former Rajah, Sir Charles Vyner Brooke. It has a golden field on which there is a St. George's Cross divided vertically black and red (black to the hoist), and in the centre an antique crown in gold.

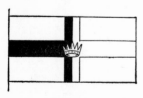

SARAWAK

SABAH has modified the old badge she had when she was North Borneo. Instead of one of the supporting arms being that of a native of Borneo and the other that of a

Plate 32

FLAGS OF MIDDLE EAST COUNTRIES

1 People's Republic of South Yemen: National Flag (p. 199)

2 Yemen: Flag of the 'Republic' (p. 200)

3 Muscat and Oman: National Flag (p. 198)

4 Yemen: National Flag, Ensign and Merchant Flag (p. 200)

5 Syria: National Flag (p. 199)

6 Turkey: National Flag, Ensign and Merchant Flag (p. 200)

7 Trucial States, Abu Dhabi: Flag (p. 200)

8 Trucial States, Umm el Qawain: Flag (p. 200)

9 Qatar: National Flag (p. 198)

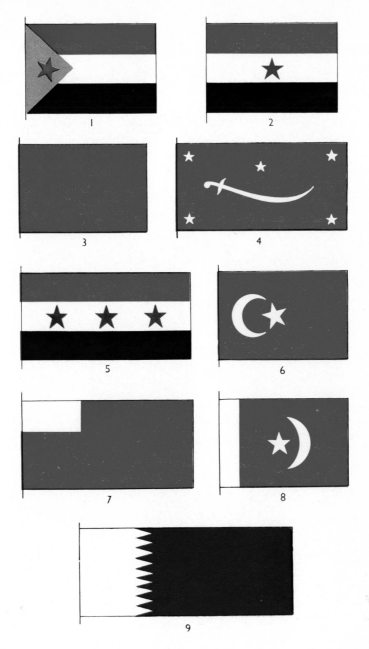

Plate 32   f.p. 214

FLAGS OF MIDDLE EAST COUNTRIES

white man they are now both arms of a native, and the flag they now support is Sabah's new flag, which consists of four horizontal stripes of equal width, red on top, then white, yellow and blue, with, in the upper hoist, a green canton on which is displayed a brown mountain, Kinabalu, taken from the Coat of Arms of Sabah.

SABAH

SABAH

When SINGAPORE became a self-governing state in the British Commonwealth she adopted a new State Flag which was approved by the Legislative Assembly in November 1959. This flag has been retained by Singapore while part of Malaysia and also since August 1965, when she severed her connections with Malaysia and again became an independent state. The proportions of this flag are three by two, and it is equally divided horizontally, the upper half red and the lower white. In the upper corner of the hoist there is a crescent and five stars, all in white, arranged as shown in Plate 33, 5. The red is said to stand for the universal brotherhood and equality of man, and the white for purity and virtue. The crescent stands for a young country and the stars for its ideals, democracy, peace, progress, justice and equality.

Government vessels of the State of Singapore wear a Blue Ensign with, in a red canton, the white crescent and five stars of the State Flag. In the bottom of the flag is a device variously described as a star or a mariner's compass in red and white. The flag of the Yang di-Pertuan Negara (re-styled President in 1965) is the same as the canton in the Ensign for Government vessels.

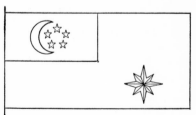

SINGAPORE: ENSIGN FOR
GOVERNMENT VESSELS

15

Mauritius became an independent country within the British Commonwealth on March 12th 1968 and on becoming independent adopted as a National Flag a design which has four equal horizontal stripes, red at the top, then navy blue, yellow and green (Plate **33**, **7**).

Independent Mauritius has retained the arms that were used when

MAURITIUS

it was a colony. These arms were granted by King Edward VII on August 25th 1906. The shield is quartered: in the first there is an ancient galley in gold on a blue field, in the second three palm-trees on gold, in the third a red key on gold and in the fourth a reversed pile and five-pointed star in white on blue. The supporters are a sambur deer and a dodo, that quaint extinct bird, both embattled. On a scroll beneath is the motto 'Stella Clavisque Maris Indici' which freely translated means 'the sign is a star and the key of the sea'. These arms were formerly used on the Blue Ensign and the Union Flag of the Governor. The Governor-General now flies the usual blue flag (*see* page 54).

We now come to those Asian countries which are not part of the British Commonwealth of Countries.

Afghanistan gained independence in August 1919, and for a while the old black flag continued in use. However, when Nadir Khan became King in 1929, a new flag was adopted, a vertical tricolour, black (at the hoist), red and green with an emblem in white overall (Plate **35**, 10). The design of the latter consists of an open mosque, the entrance of which is flanked by two flags, symbols of the Mohammedan religion, between two sprays of wheat linked with a scroll inscribed 'Afghanistan' and above the date '1348' (Mohammedan calendar—equivalent to 1929 in ours) in Persian.

The State Flag of Bhutan has a field of the approximate proportions of five by four, divided diagonally from the top of the fly to the bottom of the hoist—orange-yellow over crimson. In the centre thereof, a dragon in white, of the type known heraldically as the 'Chinese Dragon'; this is similar to the dragon of the West, except that it has no wings. It will be seen from the illustration that this particular one appears to be holding an egg in the claws of the right fore foot whilst trampling on the shell of another with the left fore foot (Plate 35, 6).

The Blue Ensign defaced with the Burmese Peacock was superseded by the National Flag of the REPUBLIC OF BURMA, in accordance with Paragraph 215 of the Constitution of the Union of the Republic of Burma, dated September 24th 1947. It has a red field with a blue canton charged with a large white five-pointed star surrounded with five similar, but smaller, ones (Plate 35, 5).

The design has its origin in the flag of the Anti-Fascist Resistance Movement of World War II, which had a red field with a large white five-pointed star in the upper hoist. This star has been retained to commemorate the Resistance Movement of the whole of Burma, and the five smaller ones symbolise the unity of all the races of Burma—namely, Burmans, Karens, Shans, Kachins and Chins; the Burmans embrace Mons and Arkanese and the remainder of their respective minorities.

As to the significance of the colours of the new flag, the red field is said to denote courage, solidarity and tenacity of purpose; the dark blue canton symbolises the profound depths of the night sky out of which the stars shine forth, and is considered aesthetically the most satisfying colour on a red background; the white colour of the stars is for purity, truth and steadfastness.

The flag of the President is of orange-gold with the 'Burmese Peacock in his pride' in the centre. This emblem was taken from the design which appeared on the silver coinage of King Mindon, dated 1852.

BURMA: PRESIDENT'S FLAG

In choosing the Naval Ensign, it was decided to retain the White Ensign of the British Navy, but replace the Union Flag in the upper quarter with the blue canton from the new National Flag. It is half-masted on Martyr's Day, July 19th.

Government vessels, other than ships of war, wear a dark blue

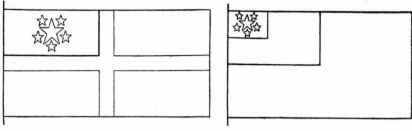

BURMA: ENSIGN

BURMA: ENSIGN OF
SHIPS IN GOVERNMENT SERVICE

Ensign with the National Flag in the upper quarter next to the mast.

The field of the Merchant Flag is divided horizontally, dark blue over red, the upper stripe being charged with the white stars from the National Flag at the hoist. The Board of Management of the Port of Rangoon uses this flag with the addition of its badge in the fly of the red stripe.

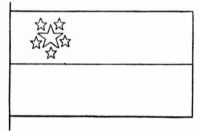

BURMA: MERCHANT FLAG

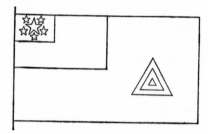

BURMA: AIR FORCE ENSIGN

Of unique design, the Burma Air Force Ensign is sky blue with the National Flag in the upper hoist; in the fly is the distinguishing mark of the Burma Air Force—an equilateral triangle in dark blue, charged with a smaller triangle in white which in turn bears yet a smaller triangle in gold.

The Chief of the Air Staff flies a sky-blue burgee with the same charge in the centre thereof, and the G.O.C. of the Army a burgee, horizontally red over blue over red, with a large white star on the centre stripe.

A new design for the National Flag of CAMBODIA was approved

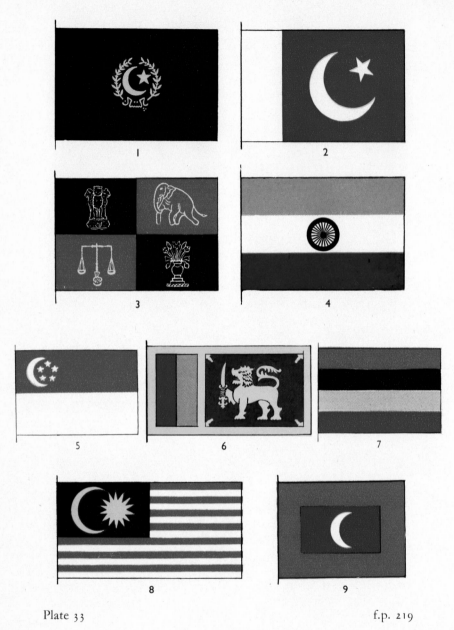

Plate 33

FLAGS OF ASIAN COUNTRIES

Plate 33

FLAGS OF ASIAN COUNTRIES

1 Pakistan: President's Flag (p. 209)

2 Pakistan: National Flag (p. 208)

3 India: President's Flag (p. 205)

4 India: National Flag (p. 204)

5 Singapore: National Flag (p. 215)

6 Ceylon: National Flag (p. 202)

7 Mauritius: National Flag (p. 216)

8 Malaysia: National Flag (p. 211)

9 Maldive Islands: National and Merchant Flag (former version) (p. 210)

by the late King in October 1948.   It consists of three horizontal stripes, blue over red over blue, the red portion being twice the width of one of the blue stripes; in the centre of the red stripe, a conventional representation of a pagoda, the 'Anger-Watt' surmounted by three towers, in white (Plate 35, 3).

This flag also does duty as the Naval Ensign and the Merchant Flag.   A diminutive of it is placed in the first quarter of a white swallow-tailed field to form the flag of the Chief of Naval Staff. The Masthead Pennant is divided vertically, blue (at the mast) and red.

The Royal Standard consists of a red-bordered square blue field with the charges in gold outlined red, as shown in the accompanying illustration.

On special occasions a similar standard, but bearing the very ornate and elaborate Royal Arms in the centre thereof, is displayed.

CAMBODIA: ROYAL
STANDARD

After the Geneva Conference of 1954 Cambodia became finally economically independent not only of France but also of Vietnam and Laos.

As described in Chapter One, it is probable that CHINA was the first country to use flags and banners, and so in her long history she has had a large number of different flags, many of them very beautiful.   Many more are ascribed to her incorrectly, and are purely imaginary.

In the old Imperial days the colour was yellow, the one dominant feature being the dragon.   The dragon on the Emperor's Standard had five claws on each foot, and it was said that, by a standing law of the Empire, no mandarin or nobleman, on pain of death, should show more than four claws to each foot.

The first Republican flag was a Jack of five equal horizontal stripes of red, yellow, blue, white and black, one for each of the four provinces and the fifth for the Mohammedan members of the republic.

When the Nationalist Party (Kuomintang) set up the Nanking

Government in 1928, the National Flag, shown on Plate 34, 1, was adopted. This is red, with a dark blue canton on which is a white twelve-rayed sun. The red symbolises sacrifice, the white justice, and the blue purity. This flag is also the Naval Ensign. The Merchant Flag is similar, but has, in addition, four rows of zigzag yellow stripes running across the red portion of the field; the blue canton with the white star serves as the Jack.

A diminutive of the Jack is placed in the head of the red Masthead Pennant.

A red rectangular flag, bordered yellow, bearing on the centre of the field a dark blue disc charged with the white twelve-rayed sun, does duty as that of the President. The Vice-President uses a similar one, but this has a yellow border on the upper and lower edges only.

NATIONALIST CHINA:
MERCHANT FLAG

NATIONALIST CHINA:
MINISTER OF DEFENCE

The Minister of Defence, and the Chief of General Staff, both fly white flags as shown in the accompanying illustration; in the case of the former the anchor and crossed rifles emblem is in red and the latter dark blue.

A flag similar to the Merchant flag, but having the four zigzag stripes in green, is used by the Customs Authority.

The PEOPLE's REPUBLIC OF CHINA was proclaimed by Mao Tse-tung in Peking on September 21st 1949. The National and Merchant Flag is red, with a large golden five-pointed star and four similar, but smaller stars arranged in an arc slightly nearer the fly, in the upper hoist (Plate 34, 2). The large star is said to represent the 'Common Programme' of the People's Political Consultative Committee which adopted the new

Constitution, and four smaller ones the four classes of the People's Republic—workers, peasants, petty bourgeoisie and 'patriotic' capitalists, who, it had been repeatedly stressed, were indispensable for Chinese recovery.

With the addition of a special charge, in gold, in the lower corner of the fly, this flag becomes the Customs Flag. This charge consists of a key in saltire with a caduceus—the staff of Mercury, consisting of a ball-headed rod, winged and entwined by two serpents.

PEOPLE'S REPUBLIC OF
CHINA: LIBERATION ARMY

The flag of the Liberation Army is also red; it has charges in gold as shown in the accompanying illustration.

TIBET is now an Autonomous Region of China and uses as her National Flag that of the People's Republic of China. Before 1950 Tibet had a flag which almost defies description. It represented a snowy mountain behind which was a rising sun. The red and blue rays were merely used to fill up the space and had no meaning. On the mountain was the device of the 'Kilin lions' fighting for the pearl, and above them a flaming gem (Plate 35, 8).

Formerly the Netherlands East Indies, the new REPUBLIC OF THE UNITED STATES OF INDONESIA came into being in accordance with an Act which was signed by H.M. Queen Juliana of the Netherlands on December 27th 1949. It is laid down in the Constitution that the National Flag shall consist of two horizontal stripes of equal width, red over white (Plate 34, 11). This flag is said to have been used during various periods between the end of the 13th century until just before the beginning of the 19th century, the colours being regarded by some as representing freedom and justice. It is not surprising, therefore, that this flag was much in evidence during the Indonesian National Movement of 1929. Readers will note that this flag is identical with that of the Principality of Monaco in the South of France (*see* page 150).

INDONESIA:
PRESIDENT'S STANDARD

The President's Standard has a canary-yellow square field with a golden-yellow fringe on three sides. In the centre there is a large five-pointed star surrounded by a wreath of rice and cotton blades, also in golden-yellow.

The Naval Ensign and the Ensign for merchant ships are the same as the National Flag.

The ceremonial flags of the three armed forces have golden fringes on three sides and are really banners used in similar circumstances to our Queen's Colours. That of the Navy is royal blue, the Army emerald green, the Air Force sky blue, the field in each case being three by two.

INDONESIA:
NAVAL CEREMONIAL FLAG

INDONESIA:
ARMY CEREMONIAL FLAG

INDONESIA:
AIR FORCE CEREMONIAL FLAG

REVERSE SIDE OF ALL THREE

The distinctive device of each service, in golden-yellow, is placed in the centre of the *obverse* side of the appropriate field.

In regard to the Naval Ensign, the small quartered shield borne by the Garuda bird surmounting the anchor is in full colours, as described below. The small shield on the Army Flag is divided diagonally, red over white, while that on the Air Force Ensign is golden-yellow and bears a map of the Indonesian islands in black.

Here follow the mottoes on the *obverse* sides of the flags:

Navy. JALEṢVEVA JAYÂMAHE—'On the Seas We are Glorious'.

Army. KARTIKA EKI PAKṢI—'Strength, Unity and Loyalty'.

Air Force. SWA BHUWANA PAKṢA—'The Wings of the Father-land'.

All mottoes are written in the old Indonesian language (Kawi) in black lettering.

The Indonesian Arms, in full colours, are superimposed on the *reverse* side of all three flags. They comprise a representation of the Garuda—the sacred bird of Hindu epics, in golden-yellow, and thereon a quartered shield (1) red, charged with a buffalo head in black; (2) white, bearing a bayan tree in green; (3) white with rice and cotton sprigs; and (4) red, charged with a yellow chain; overall a small black shield bearing a yellow five-pointed star. The motto BHINNEKA TUNGGAL IKA—'Unity through Diversity'— in black lettering is inscribed on the white scroll.

The Jack worn by naval vessels consists of nine horizontal stripes of equal width, five red and four white, the field being also three by two.

The Royal Standard of JAPAN is red, charged with the State 'Mon' (*see* page 6) of Japan (Kiku-non-hana-mon), a convention-alised golden chrysanthemum of sixteen rays (Plate 34, 3).

Japan is the land of the rising sun, and the sun as a plain red ball on a white field is the National, Merchant Flag and Jack (Plate 34, 4). If rays are added to the plain ball of the sun the design can be treated to admit of a wide variety, and noteworthy advantage has been taken of this. The Naval Ensign has the ball (placed on the centre horizontal line of the field and one third the length of it from the hoist) putting forth sixteen rays to the edges of the flag, five to the top, five to the bottom and three to each of the sides (Plate **34, 5**). The Masthead Pennant is white with an eight-rayed sun at the hoist.

Ships of the Coastal Defence Force, which superseded the former Coastal Safety Force in June **1954** wear the Naval Ensign (*see* above and Plate **34, 5**).

The RYUKYU ISLANDS, an archipelago extending from Japan to Formosa, have since the end of World War II been adminis-tratively controlled by the United States. Nevertheless the inhabitants have remained loyal to Japan, and in order to satisfy this feeling it has been agreed that the flag of Japan can be flown

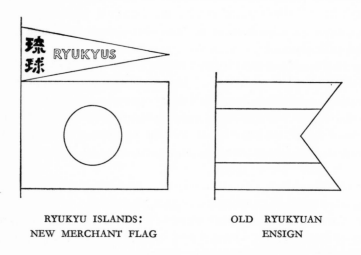

RYUKYU ISLANDS:
NEW MERCHANT FLAG

OLD   RYUKYUAN
ENSIGN

on special holidays alongside that of the United States from public buildings etc. Also it was agreed that there should be a special Ryukyuan Ensign for merchant ships registered in the Ryukyus. This ensign is unusual in that it consists of two flags: the lower is the flag of Japan (*see* above and Plate **34, 4**), and immediately above a white pennant with inscribed in red letters and Japanese characters is the word 'RYUKYUS'.

This ensign came into force on July 1st 1967, replacing the special ensign introduced after the war, which was Flag 'D' of the International Code with a triangle cut out of the fly.

As yet the Ryukyu Islands have no National Flag, but the old Standard of the Sho kings, which was used in the islands before the war, is occasionally seen. This had a white field charged with three 'commas' or clockwise waves, a Japanese heraldic character called a 'mon' (*see* page 6). These 'commas' are yellow (centre), red (upper) and blue (lower).

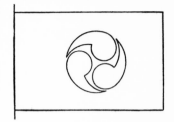

RYUKYU ISLANDS

Korea was under Japanese control for the forty years ending 1945, when Japan surrendered to the Allies. The Armies of Occupation of the United States of America and the U.S.S.R. moved into the Southern and Northern Zones respectively, the famous 38th Parallel being an arbitrary boundary dividing them.

Within three years—to be precise, on August 15th 1948—SOUTHERN KOREA was granted independence and a republic was inaugurated. Some eight months previously, General MacArthur had established a new flag which eventually became the new National Flag (Plate 34, 7). It is a variation of the old design of pre-World War II years. With its charges (described below), which are rich in symbolism, it is one of the most beautiful flags in the world.

The field is white, and in the centre thereof is a circular device, which is to be found in the writings of the ancient Chinese philosopher, Chu-Hsi, the two components of which are called 'Yang' and 'Yin', representing the opposites in Nature—male and female, summer and winter, fire and water, heaven and earth etc. It is similar to the Japanese badge of triumph and honour called the 'Tomoye', which dates from about the 12th century, and is said to have been adopted from the Chinese cosmogony. The shapes formed by the S-like boundary line are red on top and blue below, being variously described as 'streptocones', 'pines' or 'commas'.

In each of the corners of the field are parallel bars, broken and unbroken, in black, called 'trigrams': these also symbolise opposites such as father and mother, boy and girl, positive and negative etc.

KOREAN ENSIGN

The Naval Ensign and Jack worn by naval vessels have a blue field with a white canton bearing two black conventional anchors in saltire with the 'Yang' and 'Yin' device, from the National Flag, superimposed.

Coastguard vessels wear a similar ensign, but the emblem in the white canton is as shown in the illustration; the circle round it, and also the eagle, are white, but the anchors are yellow. A plain blue flag with the same device is flown ashore. Naval command flags are blue. They bear five-pointed stars to denote rank; Vice-Admiral three, in the form of a triangle; Rear-Admiral two, one above the other; and a Commodore one in the centre.

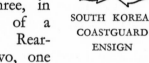

SOUTH KOREA: COASTGUARD ENSIGN

SOUTH KOREA: PRESIDENT'S FLAG

The President's Flag has a unique device in white on a rectangular blue field.

In Northern Korea the DEMOCRATIC KOREAN PEOPLE'S REPUBLIC adopted a red flag with blue stripes along the upper and lower edges of the field, each being separated from the latter by a white fimbriation. In the centre of the red field is a large red five-pointed star on a white disc, positioned on the horizontal centre-line, slightly nearer the hoist than the fly (Plate 34, 8).

According to the Constitution of the Kingdom of LAOS, adopted on September 14th 1949, the National Flag is a red flag, three by two, with the Laotian National Emblem, a white three-headed elephant surmounted by a conventional parasol also in white, in the centre (Plate 35, 2).

Before World War II the National Flag of Outer Mongolia was red with the State emblem, in blue, in the centre thereof and occupy-

Plate 34

FLAGS OF ASIAN COUNTRIES

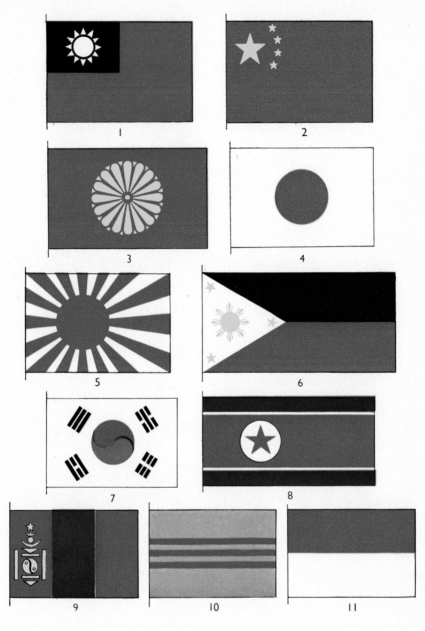

Plate 34

f.p. 226

FLAGS OF ASIAN COUNTRIES

ing approximately half the hoist; the Merchant Flag was yellow with a red saltire having the same emblem overall, also in blue. This emblem, an ideogram called the soyonbo, comprised mystical symbols, which included a flame, the sun and moon, a triangle and and the 'Yang and Yin' symbol found in the writings of the ancient Chinese philosopher Chu-Hsi, and which is dealt with in detail on on page 225 in the description of the flag of Southern Korea.

Outer Mongolia finally broke away from China's sovereignty when the newly formed MONGOLIAN PEOPLE'S REPUBLIC was recognised by the Sino-Soviet treaty, which was formally confirmed on January 5th 1946.

The flag adopted consists of three vertical stripes of equal width, red, blue and red; the red stripe at the hoist is charged with the soyonbo used on the earlier Mongolian flags, mentioned above but surmounted by a five-pointed star, in gold (Plate 34, 9).

We now come to NEPAL, that mountainous country that lies between northern India and Tibet. The famous Gurkha regiments were recruited from here. The flag is not too easy to describe, consisting as it does of a very distorted edition of the shape of a broad pennant of a Commodore in the British Navy. In regard to its colours, the field is crimson, bordered with blue and the charges are in white. These consist of a representation of the crescent moon (in the upper portion of the field) and the sun (Plate 35, 7).

The Royal Standard is also red with white charges, but the border in this case is an orange-gold shade (*see* page 228).

The flag of the Commander-in-Chief of the Armed Forces has a red field with a white canton containing the National Flag. In regard to the last mentioned, it should be noted that, in this instance, the crescent moon is white but the sun yellow. The charges in the fly are as follows: the crescent, crossed swords and kukri are white and the remainder yellow. The upper and lower edges of the flag have a narrow white border and there is a narrow yellow vertical stripe at the hoist as shown in the illustration on page 228.

Formerly the many 'suns' in the flags of Nepal were embellished

NEPAL: ROYAL STAN-
DARD (FORMER
VERSION)

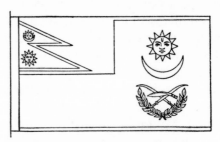

NEPAL: COMMANDER-IN-CHIEF
ARMED FORCES (FORMER
VERSION)

by having the features of a human face upon them; these faces have now been removed and the suns are plain discs.

PERSIA

PERSIA or IRAN has had many flags since Kawah's blacksmith's apron, until it arrived at its present horizontal tricolour of green, white and red. For many years her colours were a tricolour of apple-green on top, white in the centre and pink at the base.

In 1933, however, some drastic and official alterations were made. The National and Merchant Flag was to be a tricolour of grass-green at the top, white in the middle and red at the bottom. Its length was to be three times the hoist (Plate 35, 11). Charged with the badge of the lion and the sun (which is inset) in yellow, this flag does duty both as Naval Ensign and as a military flag. Take away the crown and the wreath and it becomes the flag flown over Government offices etc.

The Masthead Pennant is divided horizontally, green over white over red and bears the lion and sun badge in full at the hoist.

All the Imperial Standards are light blue and are square in shape. The Imperial Standard itself bears the Imperial Crown in the centre in yellow, while in the small canton in the upper hoist is a square tricolour of the national colours charged with the badge in yellow.

The Standard of the Crown Prince is similar, but has no badge on
the tricolour in the canton; while those flown by the other Princes
of the Blood have no canton at all.

Bright green square flags, charged in the centre with the lion and
sun (without the wreath or crown) in yellow, denote Ministers,
that flown by the Minister for War and Marine having a large
yellow anchor in each corner, placed so that the ring is in the corner,
while the rest points diagonally to the centre.

Out of the huge number of other Persian national flags, the
equivalent of our Geneva Red Cross flag must be mentioned, the
lion and the sun in red upon white (Plate 37, 4).

The National Flag, Naval Ensign and Merchant Flag of the
PHILIPPINES is illustrated on Plate 34, 6. As the scale is so

small, it must be mentioned
that each of the eight rays
of the yellow sun is itself composed of three rays, as is shown
in the same emblem on the
flag of the President.

The design was first adopted in
the early months of 1898 by the
'Junta Patriotico', the council
of exiled Filipino leaders in Hong
Kong, and incorporates features
of the earlier revolutionary flags.

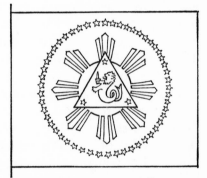

PHILIPPINES: PRESIDENT'S FLAG

A certain Mrs. Marcela Marino Agoncillo was responsible for
making the first flag, and General Emilo Aguinaldo took it to
the Philippines on May 19th of the same year and carried it to
victory in the closing stages of the war of independence against
Spain. On June 12th it was adopted as the official flag of the
ephemeral Philippine Republic. Then followed the war with
America which ended in the defeat and capture of General
Aguinaldo on March 23rd 1901.

With the agreement of the United States, it was adopted as the
National Flag on March 26th 1920, with the proviso that when
other flags were flown, the Stars and Stripes should take precedence,
with the Filipino flag next. This flag was retained when the

Philippines were granted Commonwealth status on November 15th 1935, and it continued as the National Flag of the Philippine Republic when independence was attained on July 4th 1946; from that date the Stars and Stripes has no longer taken precedence. It now takes its place among those of other members of the United Nations.

Originally the President had a dark blue flag charged with an emblem consisting of the yellow eight-rayed sun, and overall a red equilateral triangle having a small yellow five-pointed star in each corner: in the centre of the triangle a yellow sea-lion holding a dagger. There were four large yellow five-pointed stars, one in each corner of the field. Subsequently these were deleted, and at the same time the colour of the field was changed to sky blue, the centre being surrounded with fifty-two white five-pointed stars.

The design of the Vice-President's Flag is identical to the President's original flag, but the colours are as follows: field—white, sun—blue, triangle—red, sea-lion and three small stars—white.

The Jack is dark blue bearing a yellow twenty-four-rayed sun in the centre thereof, and three large yellow five-pointed stars positioned one each at the upper and lower hoist, and at the centre of the free edge of the field, respectively. The Masthead Pennant is divided horizontally, blue over red and is swallow-tailed; at the hoist there are three yellow five-pointed stars on a white background.

The State of SIKKIM has adopted a simplified version of the very ornate old flag. It comprises a white field with a red border. An ornamental emblem in yellow and red is superimposed in the centre of the field (Plate 35, 12).

THAILAND, the Land of the Free, formerly known as SIAM, is sometimes referred to as the country of the White Elephant and has many flags. The legend of the white elephant is that before Zacca, the founder of the nation, was born, his mother dreamt that she brought forth a white elephant, and the learned affirm that Zacca, after a metempsychosis of eighty thousand changes, concluded his very varied experiences as this white elephant, and thence was received into the company of the gods. The white

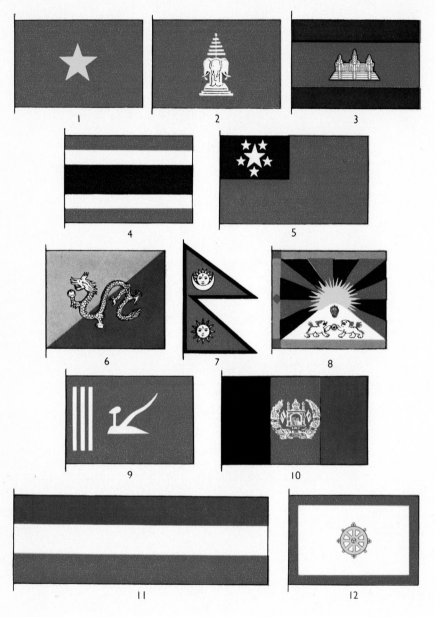

Plate 35

FLAGS OF ASIAN COUNTRIES

Plate 35

FLAGS OF ASIAN COUNTRIES

Plate 41

FLAGS OF ASIAN COUNTRIES

elephant thus stands in the same relation to Thailand as a patron saint.

The National Flag was originally plain red, but in December 1899 this was changed to red with a white elephant in the centre. Just over a quarter of a century later, the flag was again changed to a horizontal pattern of red with two white stripes, each of the latter being one sixth of the depth of the flag and being placed one sixth of the depth from the top and bottom of the flag respectively. A year later, however, King Rama VI decided to introduce blue into the design (blue being the colour of the Siamese Navy flags and having been used in the ancient service flags of Siam), and so the broad central stripe of red was changed to blue. This is the National and Merchant Flag, and is known as the 'Trairanga Flag' (Plate 35, 4). The Naval Ensign is similar, but bears in the centre the device of an elephant on a red circle.

THAILAND: NAVAL ENSIGN   THAILAND: ROYAL STANDARD

The design of the Royal Standard was also changed by King Rama VI. The King now flies a square standard of yellow, which is charged with the 'Garuda' in red. According to the Brahman religion the Garuda was the bird upon which the god Vishnu rode, and Rama was one of the forms of incarnation of the latter.

The Queen's Standard is similar, but has the fly forked. That of the Crown Prince is square like the King's, but has a deep dark blue border. That of the Crown Princess also has the dark blue border, but the fly is forked. The other Royal Princes fly

16

square dark blue standards, in the centre of which are yellow discs, each charged with the red Garuda. The Royal Princesses fly standards of a similar pattern, but the fly is forked.

The flag used by the Diplomatic and Consular Services is also the Trairanga, which bears the white elephant in the centre of the blue stripe, but here it is placed on blue circles, and for the Diplomatic Service it is caparisoned, while for the Consular Service it is not caparisoned.

The Jack is again the Trairanga, charged in the centre with the device in yellow of an anchor, a jagged-edged wheel and the crown of Siam. The flag of the Minister of Defence is white and bears

THAILAND: JACK

THAILAND: FLAG OF
MINISTER OF DEFENCE

the same device as the Jack, but has, in addition, a pair of green wings incorporated. It should be noted, however, that in this case the crown is yellow, the jagged-edged wheel red and the anchor blue.

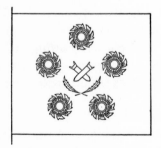

THAILAND: FLAG OF
ADMIRAL-OF-THE-FLEET

THAILAND: AIR FORCE ENSIGN

Admiral's flags have a dark blue field with white jagged-edged wheels, the number varying according to the rank held.   An Admiral-of-the-Fleet has five white wheels, set in the form of a pentagon, and a white device in the centre, as shown in the illustration on page 232.   The flag of an Admiral has four white wheels (one in each corner), a Vice-Admiral three (one above two), a Rear-Admiral two (side by side) and a Commodore one (in the centre).

The Masthead Pennant is red at the hoist and blue in the fly, and the Air Force Ensign comprises the Trairanga bearing an emblem in gold, as shown in the illustration on page 232.

Soon after the conclusion of World War II, French Indo-China was divided into three independent states of Vietnam, Laos (*see* page 226) and Cambodia (*see* page 218), associated with France within the French Union.   Great Britain and the United States of America announced recognition of them as such on February 7th 1950.

The National Flag of Vietnam (Plate **34**, 10) was adopted by H.M. Bao Dai (the former Emperor of Annam) in May 1948 when the French granted Vietnam her independence.   It had in fact been designed and adopted in 1944, when Tongking, Annam, Cochin China and Cambodia were amalgamated into a 'free state' by the Japanese-sponsored separatist régime and re-named Vietnam.   The flag has a deep yellow or orange field, three by two, with three narrow horizontal stripes, in crimson, in the middle, separated by two similar stripes of the field, all of equal size i.e. one fifteenth of the hoist.

In May 1949 the French National Assembly agreed to end the colonial status, and in the following month Bao Dai was officially invested as head of the new State of Vietnam, comprising Tongking, Annam and Cochin China.

In accordance with the Geneva Conference of 1954, Vietnam was divided into two zones.

The Southern zone became the new REPUBLIC OF VIETNAM during the year that followed, with Ngo dinh Diem as its first President. It was decided that the National Flag of Southern Vietnam should be the old flag of Vietnam described above, and also that a

TIẾT TRỰC TÂM HU'

VIETNAM: PRESIDENT'S FLAG

distinctive flag should be adopted for the President. This has a golden-yellow field bearing in the centre a representation of a bamboo tree in green, and underneath an inscription in red, which may be freely translated as 'Duty and Sacrifice', as shown in the accompanying illustration. It will be noted that this flag has a golden fringe.

The Northern Zone was designated the DEMOCRATIC REPUBLIC OF VIETNAM, with Ho Chi Minh as its President. The latter signed a decree, No. 249-SL, on November 30th 1955, adopting a red flag, proportions three by two, bearing a large yellow five-pointed star in the centre thereof, as the National Flag (Plate 35, 1).

The 'Vietcong' or National Liberation Front of Vietnam have adopted a flag which bears a resemblance to that of North Vietnam. It has in the centre the same large

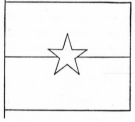

VIETCONG

yellow five-pointed star, but the field instead of being plain red is divided horizontally, red over blue.

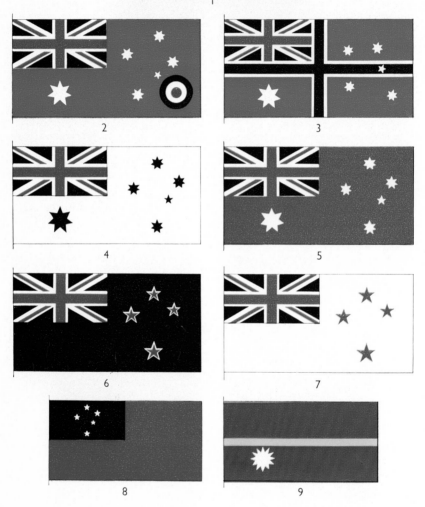

Plate 36

f.p. 235

FLAGS OF OCEANIA

Plate 36

FLAGS OF OCEANIA

Chapter Ten

OCEANIA

Oceania embraces the whole of the South Pacific Ocean, and although this vast area has a multitude of islands they are all with very few exceptions either under the protection of, or are dependencies of, one or other of the great powers, the majority being under the control of the U.S.A. The two major countries are the British Commonwealth Dominions of Australia and New Zealand.

When AUSTRALIA adopted her distinctive Blue Ensign in 1901 no official steps were taken to determine the circumstances of its use. However, during the reign of Edward VII, the draft of a Bill, whereby it should become the National Flag, was prepared. The King agreed with its contents, but it was not proceeded with immediately; however, during the course of time, this flag came to be accepted and used as such. It was not until the passing of the Flags Act, 1953, that legislative effect was given to this custom. When the Bill was being drafted, the question of the shade of the blue colour was raised. After due consideration, it was decided to adopt the shade of royal blue. Australians are indeed very proud of the fact that H.M. Queen Elizabeth II gave her personal assent to the Act on February 15th 1954, during her visit to Canberra, the Federal Capital. This was an historic occasion of some importance in that it was the first Australian legislation to which a reigning sovereign had ever assented in Australia.

The Act also proclaims that the flag which is declared by Section 406 of the Navigation Act, 1912–1953, to be the proper colours for merchant ships registered in Australia shall be known as the Australian Red Ensign. It further preserves the right or privilege of a citizen to fly the Union Flag, as had been the custom heretofore.

Thus the National Flag (Plate **36**, 1) comprises the British Blue Ensign defaced with a large seven-pointed white star beneath the Union, and a representation of the Southern Cross, consisting of four similar stars and a still smaller five-pointed star. The Merchant Flag is the plain Red Ensign defaced in a similar

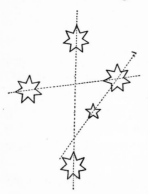

manner (Plate **36**, 5). Although there is no legal requirement for ships entering Australian ports to fly a courtesy flag, British merchant ships (irrespective of whether they are sailing under the Red or Blue Ensigns) may display the Australian Red (*not Blue*) Ensign at the fore for this purpose (*see also* page 18 of text).

The inset diagram shows how the stars are placed in their true position, and it will be seen how freely they have to be treated to get them into the shape of a cross as they appear on the flag. The big star under the Union is the 'Commonwealth Star' and, of course, has nothing to do with the Southern Cross. It represents the six states, and the Territories of Australia. Of the stars in the actual cross, the top one is 'Gamma Crucis', the left-hand one 'Beta Crucis', the one to the extreme right 'Delta Crucis', the small five-pointed 'Epsilon Crucis' and the star in the base is 'Alpha Crucis'.

On September 20th 1962 Royal approval was given to the design for the Queen's Personal Flag for Australia. This consisted of the Arms of the Commonwealth of Australia, as granted by Royal Warrant dated September 10th 1912, with the Queen's device of a crowned 'E' upon a royal-blue ground, surrounded by a chaplet of gold roses, super-imposed upon the gold seven-

GOVERNOR-GENERAL OF THE
COMMONWEALTH OF AUSTRALIA

pointed star from the crest of the arms of Australia, and the whole placed in the centre. In this case a banner of more heraldically conventional shape was approved, although in practice a longer shape was used (Plate 5, 3).

The Governor-General flies the usual blue flag.

A special flag has been adopted for the use of the Australian Prime Minister to display on his cars, aircraft etc. when on official visits as a personal standard. This consists of the Australian National Flag with the achievement of the Arms of Australia in full colour placed in the centre of the lower half of the flag between the Commonwealth Star and the Southern Cross.

Ships and Naval Establishments of the Royal Australian Navy used to wear the White Ensign of the Royal Navy; however, in 1967 Australia adopted her own distinctive Ensign for her Navy. This is a plain white ensign with a Union in the canton and the same arrangement of stars as in the National Blue except in this case the stars are blue (Plate 36, 4). The Royal Australian Navy continues to use the miniature of its Blue Ensign as a Jack. Command and senior officers' flags are the same as those of the Royal Navy. When dressing ship, the Royal Australian Navy uses the new ensign as a masthead flag.

The Australian Army uses flags very similar to those of the British Army, the regiments having a Queen's and Regimental Colour of similar design to those of British regiments.

The Royal Australian Air Force uses an adaptation of the Australian Blue Ensign with two important differences, namely, the field is air force blue in colour, and the Southern Cross constellation is turned slightly in a clockwise direction in order to make room for the R.A.F. target in the lower corner of the fly (Plate 36, 2). Those responsible for this design overlooked the fact that the target will soon suffer damage in use.

The Australian Civil Air Ensign is similar to that of the United Kingdom, but has the large seven-pointed Commonwealth Star and the Southern Cross constellation added. When first adopted in 1935, these stars were yellow; however the colour was changed to white in 1948 (Plate 36, 3).

Each of the states has its own badge, the design of which is, in each case, modelled upon the coat of arms of the individual state. These badges are inserted in the fly of the plain Blue Ensign and flown on State Government Buildings: they are also displayed, encircled with the usual garland, on the Union Flag flown by their respective Governors.

NEW SOUTH WALES   QUEENSLAND

The badge of NEW SOUTH WALES is white, thereon the red Cross of St. George.   In the centre of the cross is a lion, and on each arm is an eight-pointed star, all in yellow.

QUEENSLAND also has a circular white background, thereon being a blue Maltese Cross, charged with a Royal Crown in full colour in the centre.

SOUTH AUSTRALIA is known by its white-backed piping shrike on a yellow ground.

SOUTH AUSTRALIA   TASMANIA

WESTERN AUSTRALIA   VICTORIA

A red lion on a white ground distinguishes TASMANIA, and a black swan on yellow stands for WESTERN AUSTRALIA.   It should be

noted that this swan was depicted as swimming towards the
sinister until 1953.

VICTORIA has a blue background on which, in white, are the
stars of the Southern Cross, surmounted by the Royal Crown in
full colour.

Vessels belonging to the Melbourne Harbour Trust Commissioners wear the Blue Ensign
bearing two conventional anchors
in saltire, in white, in the centre
of the fly, as shown in the accompanying illustration.   So far
as can be ascertained, no records
are extant as to the date of origin,
but it is believed that it was taken
over by the Trust on January 1st

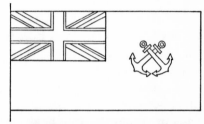

MELBOURNE HARBOUR TRUST

1877 from the State Government Department which preceded it,
which explains the absence of an Admiralty warrant.

The Government of Australia is responsible for the administration of the Territories of PAPUA and NEW GUINEA.   The Australian
National Flag (the Blue Ensign with the Southern Cross in the fly)
is flown on Government offices and by private citizens.   Government vessels wear the same flag but merchant ships wear the
Australian Red Ensign.

The small Pacific island of NAURU became independent on
January 31st 1968, having been annexed by Germany in 1888 and
subsequently, with the exception of the years 1942–45 when she
was under Japan, administered by Australia.

With independence, Nauru has chosen her own National Flag.
This has a field of royal blue with a narrow gold stripe horizontally
across the middle and in the lower corner towards the hoist a
twelve-pointed white star; the proportions of the flag are two by
one (Plate 36, 9).

The flag of the Governor-General of NEW ZEALAND is the standard flag of Governor-Generals as described on page 54.   Her ensigns bear a representation of the Southern Cross, consisting of four
five-pointed stars, in the fly.   The sizes of these stars vary slightly;
that nearest the fly is the smallest and that in the base the largest, the

other two being identical.   On the Blue Ensign the stars are red, edged with white (Plate **36**, 6).   On the Merchant Flag, the Red Ensign, the stars have to be white.   Theoretically the Union should be the National Flag of New Zealand, but almost everywhere in that country the Blue Ensign described above is in fact used, and it can be taken that for practical purposes the blue New Zealand Ensign is the National Flag.

On August 25th 1962, Royal approval was given to the design for the Queen's Personal Flag for New Zealand.   This consisted of the Arms of New Zealand, as granted by Royal Warrant dated August 26th 1911, with the Queen's device placed in the centre (*see* page 26).   In this case a banner almost square, and of more heraldically conventional shape, was approved, although in practice flags of somewhat longer shape were used (Plate **5**, 4).

The Royal New Zealand Navy, like the Royal Australian Navy, has recently adopted its own White Ensign to replace the White Ensign of the Royal Navy which it formerly used.   This, like the Australian Ensign, has a plain white field but it has the same arrangement of four red stars as is in the New Zealand National Flag (Plate **36**, 7).

The Command flags and senior officers' flags are the same as those of the Royal Navy and when dressing ship the Royal New Zealand Navy uses its own ensigns in place of the White Ensign.   The miniature of the national blue is used as a Jack.

The flag of the New Zealand Navy Board bears the British Admiralty's yellow anchor and cable on a field bisected vertically red and blue, the red portion being nearer the hoist.

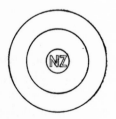

R.N.Z.A.F.

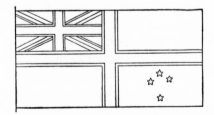

N.Z. CIVIL AIR ENSIGN

The Royal New Zealand Air Force Ensign can be distinguished from that of the R.A.F. by the addition of the letters 'NZ' superimposed in white upon the red centre disc of the target.

In regard to the Civil Air Ensign, this is the same as ours, but the fourth canton—i.e. the lower quarter in the fly— is charged with the Southern Cross of four five-pointed stars coloured red.

The Trust Territory of Samoa had a rather pretty badge, three coconut palms growing on sandy base.

SAMOA

The people of Samoa obtained permission from the Government of New Zealand, on May 26th 1948, to fly a red flag, proportions of the field two by one, with a blue canton containing four white stars, each having five points, *on land*, equally with the Blue Ensign of New Zealand. On February 24th of the following year, a smaller five-pointed white star was added. Samoa became independent on January

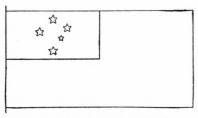

SAMOA (ON LAND)

1st 1962, and this flag became the National and Merchant ship Ensign (Plate 36, 8).

Chapter Eleven

FLAGS OF INTERNATIONAL
ORGANISATIONS

It was at Geneva, in 1863, that the International Conference was
held to consider how far the horrors of war could be mitigated by
aid to the sick and wounded. This Conference proposed that in
time of war the neutrality should be fully admitted of field and
stationary hospitals, and also recognised in the most complete
manner by the belligerent powers in the case of all officials employed
in sanitary work, volunteer nurses, the inhabitants of the country
who shall assist the wounded, and the wounded themselves; and
that an identical, distinctive sign should be used for the medical
corps of all armies, and an identical flag for all hospitals and
ambulances, and for all houses containing wounded men. The
distinctive mark of all such refugees where Christian armies were
engaged was to be a white flag with a red cross upon it, the flag of
Switzerland reversed in colouring (Plate 37, 2). Thus the design of
the RED CROSS FLAG originated in, and as a compliment to,
Switzerland; and like her flag is 'for a cause as sacred as the
deliverance of the Holy Places'. It was not to be expected that
Mohammedan troops would agree to the use of the Cross, so their
flag is white with a red crescent, while that used in Persia is white,
with the lion and sun thereon in red (Plate 37, 3 and 4).

All medical stores, ambulances, and the like are to bear one of the
devices of mercy, and doctors, nurses and stretcher-bearers are to
wear white armlets charged with the sign in red.

No flags fly over a nobler work of mankind; none has been more
disregarded and abused by unscrupulous combatants.

We now pass on to the UNITED NATIONS' FLAG. The United
Nations Organisation came into official being on October 24th

Plate 37

FLAGS OF INTERNATIONAL ORGANISATIONS AND OF THE INTERNATIONAL CODE SIGNALS

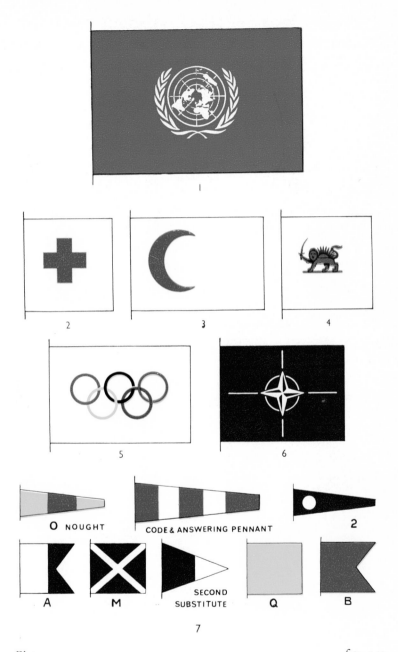

Plate 37   f.p. 242

FLAGS OF INTERNATIONAL ORGANISATIONS
AND OF THE INTERNATIONAL
CODE SIGNALS

1945. In accordance with the General Assembly's resolution of October 20th 1947 the flag has a United Nations blue (a shade midway between light and smoke blue) field, and in the centre thereof the official emblem in white. This consists of a conventional map of the world showing the continents centred round the North Pole on the Greenwich Meridian, flanked by two olive branches; it is also the Official Seal. The flag was hoisted for the first time at noon on October 21st 1947, over the interim headquarters at Lake Success, New York (Plate 37, 1).

At the same time, a code was adopted regulating the use of the flag and protecting its dignity. Those responsible for drafting it would appear to have done their work very thoroughly, having provided as they did for almost every foreseeable eventuality. The Flag Code has twelve sections. Space will not permit the inclusion of more than their headings; they are: (1) Design of Flag; (2) Dignity of Flag; (3) Flag Protocol; (4) Use of the Flag by the United Nations; (5) Use of the Flag by Specialised Agencies; (6) Use of the Flag by Individual Members of the United Nations; (7) Use of the Flag Generally; (8) Prohibition; (9) Mourning; (10) Manufacture of the Flag; (11) Violation, and (12) Regulations.

For those interested, the full details are to be found in a booklet published under the title of *The United Nations Flag Code*.

The flag of N.A.T.O. (the North Atlantic Treaty Organisation) is a very distinctive one (Plate 37, 6). It has a dark blue field (shade No. 218 of the British Colour Council) of the proportions four by three. This is charged with a thin white circle and thereon a four-pointed star—the compass rose. The star, of the type known heraldically as 'gyronny', is white and blue, the latter being fimbriated white, the fimbriation tapering towards the points of the star. Beyond these points, and radiating towards, but just short of the edges of the field, are four thin white lines. White and blue are the colours of the organisation. The circle is the symbol of unity, the compass rose suggests the common direction towards peace taken by the fourteen Member Nations of the Atlantic Alliance, and the dark blue background represents the Atlantic Ocean. This flag was flown for the first time on October 28th 1953.

At its twenty-third sitting on September 25th 1953, the

CONSULTATIVE ASSEMBLY OF THE COUNCIL OF EUROPE adopted a distinctive flag in accordance with Recommendation No. 56. It comprised fifteen stars—one for each of the nations represented in the Assembly—in gold on a sky-blue field. In accordance with Recommendation No. 88 of October 25th 1955, the number of stars was reduced to twelve.

The field of this flag is three by two and the stars are arranged in a circle, the diameter of which is equal to two thirds the hoist, each star being contained within an imaginary circle, the diameter of which is equal to one tenth the hoist.

COUNCIL OF EUROPE FLAG

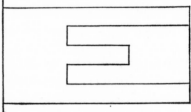

UNITED EUROPE FLAG

The flag of the 'Mouvement Européen', known as the UNITED EUROPE FLAG, has a white field bearing the letter 'E' in green occupying exactly two thirds the area of the field. Mr. Duncan Sandys is reputed to have been largely responsible for the design of this flag. It was flown for the first time at the meeting of the Council at The Hague, April–June 1948.

In 1951 S.H.A.P.E.—the Supreme Headquarters Allied Powers Europe—adopted a very distinctive flag; the field is green, two by one, and centred thereon its insignia in proper colours. The last mentioned consists of a green shield, edged silver, charged with two golden swords, unsheathed, a golden scroll bearing the inscription 'VIGILIA PRETIUM LIBERTA-

S.H.A.P.E. FLAG

TIS' ('Vigilance is the price of Liberty'). At the base of the scroll are two sprays of olive leaves in gold; within the scroll and behind the swords are twelve silver fronds issuing from the base. This emblem occupies approximately two thirds the depth of the hoist.

The two sprays of olive leaves are said to indicate the dedication of the North Atlantic Treaty Organisation (N.A.T.O.) powers to peace, the swords the necessity of armed strength in order to preserve peace, the twelve silver fronds represent the original signatories of N.A.T.O. and produce, by their position, rays of hope, and the position of the swords forms a letter 'A'—symbolising the Allied Powers. The colour green is said to signify the peaceful woods and fields of Europe. This flag was flown for the first time on October 5th 1951, over General Eisenhower's Headquarters at Marly near Paris.

A flag for the WESTERN UNION Commanders-in-Chief, the Headquarters of which is at Fontainebleau and whose first Chairman was Field-Marshal Viscount Montgomery of Alamein, was adopted in January 1949. It has a dark blue field bearing five links forming an unbroken chain, in gold. The field has a multi-coloured border: red (outside), gold, black and white, as shown in the accompanying illustration. These colours were taken from the National Flags of the member countries, namely, Great Britain, France, Belgium, Holland and Luxembourg, each of these countries being represented by one of the links mentioned above.

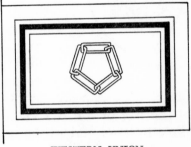

WESTERN UNION

An unusual flag is used by the EUROPEAN COAL AND STEEL COMMUNITY. It has a field, proportions three by two, divided horizontally ultramarine blue over black, charged with six yellow five-pointed stars as shown in the accompanying illustration. Each star represents one of the six member nations, namely,

EUROPEAN COAL
AND STEEL COMMUNITY

Belgium, the West German Federal Republic, France, Italy, Luxembourg and the Netherlands; the black stripe is said to symbolise coal and the blue one steel. This flag was hoisted for the first time in 1958, at the Brussels World Exhibition.

The SOUTH-EAST ASIA TREATY ORGANISATION (S.E.A.T.O.) has a very appropriate emblem which, incidentally, was displayed for the first time on February 19th 1959. It consists of a white shield, the symbol of defence; thereon a representation of the globe outlined in light ultramarine blue and overall an olive branch in gold.

The latter forms the vertical axis of the globe, which also has a horizontal axis and four curved lines of latitude and four of longitude; the lower right-hand quadrant of the globe is coloured the same shade of blue with the lines of latitude and longitude in white. As to the charges, the globe illustrates the world-wide nature of the organisation membership and the blue quadrant is indicative of the area afforded protection by the South-East Asia Collective Defence Treaty. Lastly, the olive branch denotes peace and the benefits which flow therefrom.

S.E.A.T.O.

The flag of S.E.A.T.O. is light ultramarine blue, proportions three by two, and in the centre thereof the emblem; the latter occupies two thirds of the hoist. It should be noted that the blue quadrant is on the right hand of the observer on *both* the obverse and reverse sides of the flag.

The OLYMPIC flag, which flies in the main stadium and all other venues of the Olympic Games, is white with five interlaced rings in the centre. These are blue, yellow, black, green and red, with the blue ring nearest the hoist (Plate **37**, 5). These rings represent the five continents joined in the Olympic Movement.

This flag was created in 1913 at the suggestion of Baron de Coubertin and was used for the first time at the Olympic Games in 1920 at Antwerp.

There are official flags for both the Olympic Games and the Winter Olympic Games, and they are preserved from one Olympiad to the next.

Plate 38

NELSON'S FAMOUS SIGNAL

(*See page 248*)

England:	253
Expects:	269
That:	863
Every:	261
Man:	471
Will:	958
Do:	220
His:	370
D:	4
U:	21
T:	19
Y:	24

Engage the
Enemy more } 16
Closely

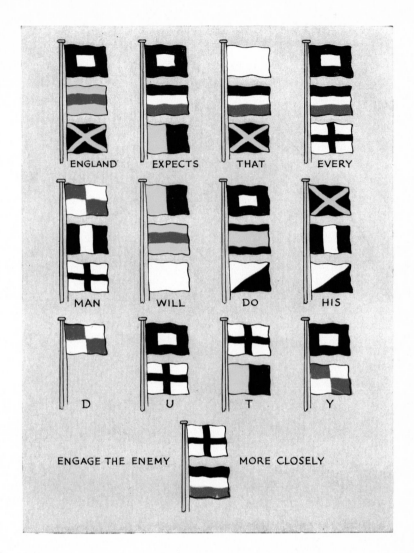

Plate 38

f.p. 246

NELSON'S FAMOUS SIGNAL

Chapter Twelve

SIGNAL FLAGS; THE INTERNATIONAL CODE

It is said that the idea of signalling by flags can be dated back to the 13th century, if not earlier, and it may be recalled that on page 2 mention was made of Themistocles hoisting his red cloak in the rigging as a signal to the Greeks to attack the galleys of Xerxes. All the references, however, are obscure, and it was not until after the establishment of a Royal Navy that we come across anything definite.

In *Fighting Instructions*, 1530–1816, so ably edited by Mr. Julian Corbett for the Navy Records Society, we not only have a most interesting book, but are, for the first time, provided with the means of noting when the flags were introduced and the use that was made of them.

It is evident that up to the 17th century, flag signals were of an elementary character, and that from then onwards properly organised codes of naval signals were gradually evolved and adopted.

Various codes were tried out, and by the end of the 18th century the numerary method was well established. Lord Howe produced his first and second signal books in 1782 and 1790 respectively. From then onwards many alterations, improvements, and additions were made; also Sir Home Popham drew up his *Telegraphic Signals*, or *Marine Vocabulary*—the word 'Telegraphic' being used in the literal sense of writing at a distance, for it was not until some thirty years later that the electric telegraph was invented. Popham's method was to use a short dictionary and interpret the words in it by numeral groups of flags.

This Vocabulary was used by the Fleet as a companion volume to Howe's 1799 *Signal Book for Ships of War*.

In order to make it perfectly clear that the signal hoisted was to be deciphered by the Vocabulary Code, Popham designed a special 'Telegraph or Preparative' flag. This had to be hoisted in a conspicuous position prior to making the signal. It could remain in this position throughout the period of the message, and then be hauled down to indicate that it had been completed, or, alternatively, be hauled down before actually commencing to make the signal. In the latter case, provision was made for hoisting another special flag, called the 'Message finished' flag. However, as far as is known, the last mentioned was never used.

The field of these two flags was divided diagonally from the top of the fly to the bottom of the hoist. These flags are described in the text of Popham's Vocabulary thus:

Instructions for the Flags used with this Vocabulary only.

Preparative. Preparatory to any message a diagonal red and white flag.

Message finished. It is denoted by a diagonal blue and yellow flag, which may be hoisted or not according to circumstances, or the telegraph flag hauled down.

Thus, Nelson used Howe's numeral flags in conjunction with Popham's Vocabulary at the battle of Trafalgar, October 21st 1805. His historic signal was made at approximately 11.56 a.m., in twelve hoists; the first eight words were to be found in the Vocabulary, each having a three-figured number, but the last word, 'duty', had not been included by Popham, and had therefore to be spelt out in full by the numerical alphabet, which was known by the numbers one to twenty-five. This alphabet had two peculiarities: (1) 'I' and 'J' were bracketed as one letter—thus only twenty-five flags were necessary; (2) 'V' preceded 'U', which accounts for the fact that many people have been puzzled at the spelling of the word 'duty'.

Nelson's famous message ran thus: ENGLAND(253) EXPECTS(269) THAT(863) EVERY(261) MAN(471) WILL(958) DO(220) HIS(370) D(4) U(21) T(19) Y(24).

Some twenty minutes after this signal was made, the general signal for close action was hoisted: it was Nelson's favourite, No. 16 —'Engage the enemy more closely' (Plate 38).

When Nelson first dictated his message to his signal officer, Lieutenant John Pasco, he used the words 'England confides that every man will do his duty'; however, the word 'confides' was not in the Vocabulary and, in order to save spelling out the word, he agreed to substituting the word 'expects'.

In regard to the 'Telegraph' flag, there has been, and still is, much controversy as to whether it was flown as shown in figure (A) or (B). We have already seen that Popham apparently intended it to be hoisted as depicted in the former version. The reason for this, it is suggested, may well have been that, at a

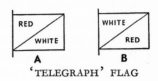

'TELEGRAPH' FLAG

great distance and/or in bad visibility, there would be little chance of its being mistaken for another flag: we refer to Howe's No. 6 flag, which, incidentally, became Zero flag when the numeral flags were transposed on November 4th 1803. The field of this flag was divided diagonally in exactly the same manner, namely, from the top of the fly to the bottom of the hoist, but coloured white and blue, the white being uppermost (Plate 38).

It should be pointed out that flags in most of the signal books of his day were illustrated in line only, the hand colouring of them being left to the recipient; also that many manuscript copies of these books were made. This naturally allowed variations and errors to creep in. It is not surprising, therefore, that flag research workers can be misled easily in such circumstances. Thus the 'Telegraph' flag has, from time to time, been illustrated and described by some authorities as being 'diagonal red and white', and by others, 'diagonal white and red'.

Up to the time of writing, there is no official document extant recording precisely which version, (A) or (B), was used in the *actual* flag flown in the *Victory* at Trafalgar.

Two official publications are in favour of version (B); they are (1) an Admiralty printed plate 'Nelson's Signal at the Battle of Trafalgar', dated January 4th 1908, and (2) 'Nelson's Signals' (N.I.D. Historical No. 1), dated October 1908 (H.M. Stationery Office).

Nelson's historic signal is flown annually in the *Victory* at Portsmouth on October 21st, and visitors will notice that the

'Telegraph' flag is hoisted in accordance with the above official publications.

At the outbreak of World War II, the British Naval Code consisted of the following pieces: twenty-six Alphabetical Flags, ten Numeral Pendants, twenty-six Special Flags, ten Numbered Pendants and fourteen Special Pendants. In addition to these, the flags of the International Code were also used, making a grand total of 126 flags, some of which had definite meanings, but all of which could have their signification changed if and when it became necessary.

It will be readily appreciated that this state of affairs did not make for speedy inter-communication between units of the Royal Navy and those of the United States during the period of hostilities when the closest co-operation was of vital importance. Certain wartime arrangements were made, and worked reasonably well. Finally it was decided to revise our Naval Code and adopt a new one which closely resembled that of the United States, but with certain additions, resulting in a total of seventy-eight flags. This was brought into general use throughout the Service on December 1st 1948.

In the light of experience, and in order to ensure efficient inter-communication between all vessels taking part in combined exercises, a further revision was made in order to bring it into line with the signal books of members of the N.A.T.O.—North Atlantic Treaty Organisation—on January 1st 1952. It should be noted that there was a change in spelling—'pendants' became 'pennants'. Thus, at the time of writing, our Naval Code contains twenty-six Alphabetical Flags, ten Numbered Pennants, ten Numeral Flags, four Substitutes and twenty Special Flags and Pennants. Details of these are given on the 1952 Signal Card, No. B.R. 232(2), which is obtainable from H.M. Stationery Office.

It is to be much regretted that one of our oldest signal flags, the well-known 'Preparative'—five horizontal stripes of equal width, three blue and two white—was superseded by the yellow over green over yellow pennant, which is extremely difficult to recognise in poor visibility.

We cannot pass without mentioning a signal which is always given a very warm welcome—namely 'B over X'—'Splice the

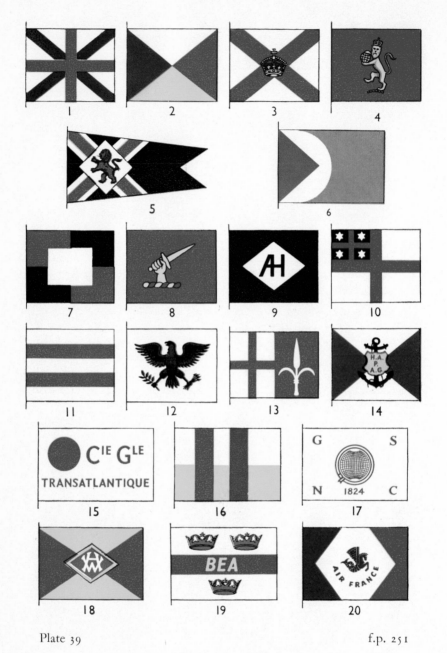

Plate 39

HOUSE FLAGS OF SHIPPING LINES,
A SHIPBUILDING COMPANY AND AIR LINES

Plate 39

HOUSE FLAGS OF SHIPPING LINES, A SHIP-BUILDING COMPANY AND AIR LINES

(See pp. 256–261)

1 Port Line

2 Peninsular and Oriental Steam Navigation Company

3 Royal Mail Line

4 Cunard Line

5 British and Commonwealth Shipping Company

6 Canadian Pacific

7 Devitt and Moore

8 Bibby Line

9 Blue Funnel Line (Alfred Holt and Company)

10 Shaw Savill and Albion Company

11 Nippon Yusen Kaisha Company (Japanese Mail)

12 United States Lines

13 Italia Line

14 Hamburg-America Line

15 Compagnie Générale Transatlantique

16 Shell-Mex and British Petroleum

17 General Steam Navigation Company

Shipbuilding Company

18 Harland and Wolff

Air Lines

19 British European Airways

20 Air France

Main Brace'. An amusing incident occurred in connection with the 'Crossing the Line' ceremony on February 10th 1947, in H.M.S. *Vanguard*, outward bound to South Africa with the Royal Family on board. When proceeding for'ard to the ceremony, His late Majesty King George VI halted to examine two ends of a twenty-eight-inch manilla rope (conveniently placed in order to arrest the Royal progress!), and was informed that it was the Main Brace. The King is reported to have said, 'Well, it's in a sorry state—you had better splice it!' Thereon the Bo'sun piped 'Splice the Main Brace' in obedience to the Royal order.

Although Popham devised a code of signals for the East India Company in 1804, it was not until 1817 that Captain Frederick Marryat drew up what has been described as the forerunner of modern commercial codes. This was used as a basis in designing the 'Commercial Code of Signals for use of all nations', which the Board of Trade issued in 1857. It consisted of eighteen alphabetical flags and a 'Code & Answering Pendant'.

In the course of time this was translated into many languages, and by about 1880 its title had become the 'International Code'. This was revised and enlarged towards the end of the century to include a separate flag for every letter and came into use on January 1st 1901, as the 'First International Code of Signals'.

This code was in existence when World War I broke out in 1914, and it was naturally subjected to a very severe test during the following four years. Speaking candidly, it failed that test. Experience showed that it was not really an International Code, for ships of different nationalities when making signals to one another often found that more messages were indecipherable than were clear.

It was thus realised that a revised code was necessary and advantage was taken of the International Radio Telegraph Conference which assembled in Washington in 1927, for Great Britain, in conjunction with France, Italy, Japan and the United States of America, to put forward revised rules for signalling, and a draft code in English, French and Italian.

The Conference then decided that Great Britain should be asked to undertake the work of revising the old code with the help of representatives from each of the Governments concerned.   The Committee accordingly assembled in London in October 1928, and completed its labours in December 1930.

The new code came into use in January 1934.   It had seven editions or copies, one each in English, French, German, Italian, Japanese, Spanish and Norwegian.   The Scandinavian countries chose Norwegian as the Scandinavian language.

It was a great improvement on former codes and was divided into two volumes, Volume I for Visual Signalling, Volume II for Radio.

The chief improvements were that whereas formerly some of the alphabetical flags were rectangular in shape and some pennant-shaped, in the 1934 code all the alphabetical flags were rectangular. Also ten pennants were added to represent the numerals 0 to 9.   In the 1901 code the alphabetical flags also represented numbers.

A further innovation was the institution of substitute flags; these were triangular in shape and made it possible to use any combination of four letters or figures (Plate 37, 7).

As a result of International collaboration the International code of 1934 has been completely revised.   It is expected that the new code will be published shortly; it can, however, be said that while the colours and patterns of the former flags remain the same, the whole publication has been changed in principle, which is best explained by the following extract from the Preface:

'The revised code is intended to cater primarily for situations related essentially to safety of navigation and persons, especially when language difficulties arise.   It is suitable for transmission by all means of communication including radiotelephony and radio-telegraphy, thus obviating the necessity for a separate radiotele-phony code and dispensing with Volume II for radiotelegraphy. The revised code embodies the principle that each signal has a complete meaning.   It thus leaves out the vocabulary method which was part of the old code.   The Geographical Section, not being considered essential, was omitted.   By these means it was possible to reduce considerably the volume of the code and achieve sim-plicity.'

It is sad to have to report that while signal flags are still used for a few specialised purposes they are becoming obsolete, superseded in this electronic age by the radiotelephone and radiotelegraph.   There were few more lovely sights than that of a squadron of warships carrying out flag drill, with the strings of colourful flags being hoisted and lowered in rapid succession.

But, although signalling by flags may be on the decline, flags are still used on important festivals to dress ship, and all must enjoy the sight of ships dressed overall, or rainbow fashion as it is called. The flags used on the 'dressing lines' to dress ship should be the signal flags, and National, House and similar flags should not be used for this purpose.   Ships should be dressed overall only while at anchor or moored in harbour; while under way only the extra masthead flags and the jacks should be flown.   Although this is the practice of warships, merchant ships frequently leave their dressing flags hoisted while moving.

Chapter Thirteen

FLAGS WORN BY
MERCHANT SHIPS

As mentioned in Chapter One, special national flags, known as ensigns, have been adopted by many nations for their ships, both warships and merchant ships, and these are described in the chapters under the headings of the individual nations.

The ensigns of Great Britain were described on page 30, where it was stated that the Red Ensign was established as the proper colours for British merchant ships by a proclamation dated 1674. The Merchant Shipping Act of 1894 brought up to date the law concerning the wearing of ensigns by British ships. Prior to this many ensigns of various designs were in use, perhaps the most interesting being those of the East India Company. There were various versions of these, one consisting of nine red and white horizontal stripes with the Union Flag in the upper canton, very similar to the Grand Union Flag of the U.S.A. (*see* page 77). Another version was similar, but consisted of thirteen red and white stripes, over which was superimposed a red St. George's Cross—again with the Union Flag in the upper canton.

The relevant portions of the Merchant Shipping Act are as follows:

Section 73

(1) The Red Ensign usually worn by merchant ships, without any defacement or modification whatsoever, is hereby declared to be the proper national colours for all ships and boats belonging to any British subject, except in the case of Her Majesty's ships or boats, or in the case of any other ship or boat for the time being allowed to wear any other national colours in pursuance of a warrant from Her Majesty or from the Admiralty.

(2) If any distinctive national colours, except such Red Ensign or except the Union Jack with a white border, or if any colours usually worn by Her Majesty's

ships or resembling those of Her Majesty, or if the pendant usually carried by Her Majesty's ships or any pendant resembling that pendant, are or is hoisted on board any ship or boat belonging to any British subject without warrant from Her Majesty or from the Admiralty, the master of the ship or boat or the owner thereof, if on board the same, and every other person hoisting the colours or pendant, shall for each offence incur a fine not exceeding £500.

(3) Any commissioned officer on full pay in the military or naval service of Her Majesty, or any officer of customs in Her Majesty's dominions, or any consular officer may board any ship or boat on which any colours or pendant are hoisted contrary to this Act, and seize and take away the colours or pendant, and the colours or pendant shall be forfeited to Her Majesty.

(4) A fine under this section may be recovered with costs in the High Court in England or Ireland, or in the Court of Session in Scotland, or in any Colonial Court of Admiralty or Vice-Admiralty Court within Her Majesty's dominions.

(5) Any offence in this section may also be prosecuted, and the fine for it recovered summarily, provided that: (a) where such offence is prosecuted summarily, the court imposing the fine shall not impose a higher fine than £100; and (b) nothing in this section shall authorize the imposition of more than one fine in respect of the same offence.

Section 74
(1) A ship belonging to a British subject shall hoist the proper national colours, (a) on a signal being made to her by one of Her Majesty's ships (including any vessel under the command of an officer of Her Majesty's navy on full pay), (b) on entering or leaving any foreign port, and (c) if of fifty tons gross tonnage or upwards, on entering or leaving any British port.

(2) If default is made on any such ship in complying with this section, the master of the ship shall for such offence be liable to a fine not exceeding £100.

(3) This section shall not apply to a fishing boat duly entered in the fishing-boat register and lettered and numbered as required by the Fourth Part of this Act.

Section 75
The provisions of this Act with respect of colours worn by merchant ships shall not affect any other power of the Admiralty in relation thereto.

Note 1. As there are now a large number of self-governing countries within the British Commonwealth of Nations, the term 'Her Majesty's dominions' has not the same significance that it bore in 1894 when the above Act came into force. The Act, therefore, no longer applies to these independent countries, unless it has specially been made to do so.

Note 2. In accordance with the Defence (Transfer of Functions)

Act of 1964, the powers formerly vested in the Admiralty to grant warrants for the wearing of special privilege ensigns are now transferred to the Secretary of State for Defence (*see* page 28).

The British Merchant Shipping Act has been quoted as an example; most other nations have similar laws covering the use of their National Flags and ensigns.

In addition to their ensigns most merchant ships wear a House Flag. This is usually flown at the main, but as so many modern ships have only one mast the flag has to be flown from the masthead.

The owners of most merchant ships are now large public companies and the House Flag is the 'marque' of the company; but this is a fairly modern innovation. The ownership of 18th-century ships was complex, and although there were exceptions, notably the East India Company and the Hudson Bay Company, the modern permanently established companies mostly appeared after 1815. The earlier ships seem often to have worn the banner of their Master (who was sometimes a part-owner), and the expeditions of the merchant adventurers and explorers, such as Columbus (*see* page 75), Magellan, Hudson and Cabot, usually sailed under the banner or flag of the leader.[1]

The modern version of the House Flag is said to have originated from the flags hoisted on Bidston Hill (overlooking the old entrance to the Mersey) to inform the owners in Liverpool of the comings and goings of their ships on Hoyle Lake, which was invisible from their office windows. At the present time there are hundreds of House Flags, and space precludes mention of more than a few; the specimens shown on Plate 39 have been taken almost at random.

As flags many are really good, being simple, effective and recognisable at a glance, especially when those of the older firms, who, of course, had a wider choice. With flags as with arms, names in natural science, and many other things the simpler forms come first, and those that have to follow must be more complicated because the ground has already been occupied. Thus, it is not easy to design a new House Flag, and a large number simply bear the initials of the firm and tend to look cheap and unsightly.

[1] See W. G. Perrin, *British Flags* (Cambridge University Press).

One of the oldest and best-known flags of the British Mercantile Marine is that of the Peninsular and Oriental—known generally as the P and O (Plate 39, 2).   The P and O Company was originally Messrs. Willcox and Anderson, who rendered great service to the Queen of Portugal in 1832–3; hence the four triangles of which the House Flag of the P and O is comprised are the blue and white taken from the Portugese Royal Standard and the red and yellow of Spain.

The old East India Company does not appear to have had a House Flag, but had its own special ensigns (*see* page 254).

Among the more interesting House Flags are those of the General Steam Navigation Company—perhaps the earliest steamship company, founded in 1824 (Plate 39, 17), and Shaw Savill and Albion (Plate 39, 10), who have the flags of the original company, said to have been originally designed as a National Flag for New Zealand.

The well-known red and white chequered flag which was the House Flag of the ships of the Canadian Pacific Railway Company for seventy years or more has been replaced by a new flag.   This has a somewhat unusual design in two shades of green and white (Plate 39, 6).   Other services of the Canadian Pacific use the same design for their flags but in their own colour variations (*see* page 75).

At the turn of the century the two principal British steamship lines operating in the North Atlantic were the Cunard Steam Ship Company and the White Star Company.   These two lines were amalgamated and became the Cunard White Star Company, and for many years the ships of the amalgamation flew the House Flags of both the Cunard and the White Star.   The Cunard flag, which used to be flown above that of the White Star, has a red field charged with a golden lion rampant guardant (Plate 39, 4).   The White Star flag is a red 'broad pennant' with two tails and charged with a white five-pointed star.   In 1968 the flying of the White Star flag was discontinued and only the Cunard flag is flown by Cunard ships, except on one day of the year, April 20th, when the two flags are flown together as formerly in commemoration that this is the birthday of the last surviving officer of the old White Star Line.

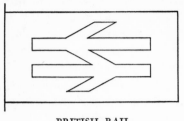

BRITISH RAIL

In 1965 the old House Flag for the ships of British Railways, introduced in 1949, was replaced by a new flag. This has a field of blue, known as 'British Rail blue', with a device which can be described as symbolic double arrows, the latter in white. This flag is now flown by all the ships, and is the only flag in use by the Shipping Division of British Rail.

There is a similarly designed House Flag for use ashore by British Rail. This differs from the maritime flag by having a flame-red field (*see* page 51).

The United States Lines fly a white flag charged with a representation of the American eagle in blue (Plate **39**, 12).

The well-known Japanese Line, Nippon Yusen Kaisha, possesses a very simple flag, the same pattern appearing on its black funnels (Plate **39**, 11).

Messageries Maritimes is easily recognised, and so is the Compagnie Générale Transatlantique (Plate **39**, 15). Quaintly enough, this is—next to the Tricolour of France—perhaps the best-known flag in the Sahara, for the company has built some thirty hotels in that territory, from each of which flies the House Flag.

The Batavier Line flag also needs no comment—the initials being those of the owners, William H. Muller & Co.

The two leading Italian Lines, Lloyd Triestino and Italia, fly flags of the same design; in the case of the former (which includes the Lloyd Triestino, Marittima Italiana and Sitmar Lines) the red cross is in the fly, while in the case of Italia, which covers the Cosulich, Lloyd Sabaudo and Navagazione Generale, the flag is reversed, and in this case the red cross appears in the hoist (Plate **39**, 13). The Hamburg-America 'Hapag' flag is easily picked out by its blue-and-white triangles and the centre-piece (Plate **39**, 14), and so is the white flag with the blue crossed key and anchor of the Norddeutscher Lloyd of Bremen.

The Nigerian National Shipping Line was established and registered in Lagos early in 1959.

2. Racing Flag of *Britannia* when owned by King Edward VII and King George V

Plate 40

YACHT FLAGS

(See pp. 262–267)

1 Royal Yacht Squadron, Burgee

2 Racing Flag of *Britannia* when owned by King Edward VII and King George V

3 Royal Cornwall Yacht Club, Burgee

4 Royal Thames Yacht Club, Burgee

5 Racing Flag *Bluebottle* (*By gracious permission of H.M. the Queen and H.R.H. the Duke of Edinburgh*)

6 Royal Fowey Yacht Club, Burgee

7 Royal Lymington Yacht Club, Burgee

8 New York Yacht Club, Burgee

9 Yacht Club Argentino, Burgee

10 Royal Cornwall Yacht Club, Ensign

11 Royal Fowey Yacht Club, Ensign

12 Royal Norwegian Yacht Club (K.N.S.), Burgee

13 Yacht Club de France, Ensign

14 Royal Cruising Club, Burgee

15 Yacht Club de France, Burgee

16 Island Sailing Club, Burgee

17 Royal Sydney Yacht Club Squadron, Burgee

18 United States of America, Yacht Ensign

19 Royal Norwegian Yacht Club (K.N.S.), Ensign

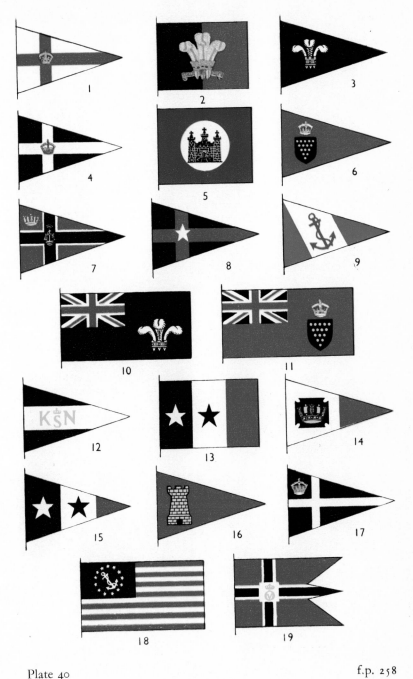

Plate 40

f.p. 258

YACHT FLAGS

For a House Flag it adopted one having an emerald-green field, three by two, bearing a large letter 'N', in white, in the centre thereof and occupying one half the depth of the hoist.

The above brief epitome is enough to indicate the nature of the House Flags of the mercantile vessels of the world, and may be taken as typical of all. However, there are various publications in which are included lists and illustrations of a very great number of these flags (for details *see* Bibliography, page 268).

It will, no doubt, come as a surprise to many to learn that there are over fifty British shipbuilding companies possessing a distinctive House Flag. Some of the designs date back to the 18th century, whilst others of many years' standing have been re-designed recently or superseded by entirely new ones. Space will not permit a detailed description of these flags; however, a coloured illustration of one of the big shipbuilding companies will be found on Plate 39, 18.

When a merchant ship is launched the shipbuilder's House Flag is generally displayed in company with that of the owners; the former is again flown during her trials. When these have been successfully completed it is replaced with that of the owners, thus indicating that she has been accepted.

The custom of displaying special flags in naval vessels during the launching and naming ceremony probably dates back some 450 years or more. It would appear, from the accounts recorded by contemporary chroniclers, that during the reign of Henry VIII this became a well-established practice in the Royal Dockyard at Deptford (*Deptford Strond* as it was called in those days), where subsequently Peter the Great studied the art of shipbuilding, on the River Thames.

At that time, launching flags comprised banners and streamers bearing the Royal Arms and the Banner of St. George. The Elizabethan striped ensigns were added towards the end of the Tudor period, and the first Union Flag in 1606. By the middle of the 18th century the Royal Standard was displayed at the main, the Lord High Admiral's or Admiralty Flag at the fore, and the Union Flag at the mizzen, also the Jack and Ensign at their respective staves. Since 1906 the Royal Standard has ceased to figure among

a vessel's launching flags.   Some two years later the Admiralty
adapted and regularised this very old custom to modern requirements, and issued an order in which it was laid down that at her
launching a vessel should wear her Ensign and Jack, and the
Admiralty Flag amidships.   However, the flags to be worn on
other masts erected temporarily in intermediate positions were not
specified.   As a consequence, various flags were used; these sometimes included the shipbuilder's House Flag.   That of John Brown
was the last to be used in this way; the occasion was at the launching
of H.M.S. *Vanguard* by Princess Elizabeth on November 30th
1944.

An addition to *King's Regulations and Admiralty Instructions* made
on October 4th 1945, restricted the number of launching flags
displayed to three, namely, the Admiralty Flag, Ensign and
Jack.

Article No. 1242 of *Queen's Regulations and Admiralty Instructions*
1956, states:

> At all launches of ships built for the Royal Navy at which there is a naming
> ceremony, the White Ensign is to be hoisted at the ensign staff, the Union Flag at
> the Jackstaff and the Admiralty Flag at the main masthead or equivalent position.
> No other flag is to be worn. Exceptionally, in the case of launches with ceremony
> of Inshore Minesweepers, Seaward Defence Boats, Fast Patrol Boats (M.T.B.s,
> M.G.B.s) and other similar and small craft, only the White Ensign need be
> hoisted, unless it is desired to conform to the general practice stated in this
> clause.
>
> 2. None of the aforesaid flags is to be hoisted again, whether or not the vessel
> is in commission, before her official acceptance from the shipbuilders, except
> dockyard-built ships temporarily commissioned for trials, which wear the
> White Ensign. Contract-built ships undergoing sea trials while still under the
> control of the contractor should wear the Red Ensign.

Although, as a result of the Defence (Transfer of Functions)
Act of 1964, the Admiralty Flag will in future be a Royal Flag, it is
understood that it will still be worn by ships built for the Royal
Navy at their launching.   At the successful conclusion of the
acceptance trial the ship is handed over to the Royal Naval crew at
sea, when the Red Ensign and the House Flag of the contractor are
replaced by the White Ensign and the Commissioning Pennant.   A

slightly different procedure is followed in the case of ships built in one of the Royal dockyards.

In recent years it has become the custom to hold a commissioning ceremony just before the ship proceeds on acceptance trials, and it is now usual to hoist the White Ensign and Commissioning Pennant during this ceremony; but at the end of the ceremony the Red Ensign and the builder's House Flag are rehoisted and worn until finally hauled down after the acceptance trials.

Chapter Fourteen

YACHT FLAGS

Yachts usually fly the following flags: their national colours or ensigns, and the burgee or flag of the Yacht Club to which the owner belongs; sailing yachts, when racing under British rules, wear a racing flag in place of the burgee, and yachts may also fly the owner's private or distinguishing flag. Owners of yachts who are flag officers of their club fly a special flag in place of the burgee. All these flags will be described later. The most important flag is the National Ensign. Quite a few countries, including Belgium, Denmark, Eire, Italy, France, Netherlands, Poland, the United States of America and Great Britain, grant certain of their yachts the privilege of wearing a special ensign. The special Yacht Ensigns are described in the sections dealing with those nations which authorise the use of them.

This wearing of special Yacht Ensigns appears to have started in Great Britain, possibly because the first yacht owner was King Charles II. In more recent years it has been due to the desire to foster the sport of yachting, as yachtsmen provide a source of reserves for the Royal Navy. (In passing it can be said that the yachtsmen of Great Britain have served their country well in two world wars.)

The rules permitting yachts to wear special or privilege ensigns differ in different countries. A number of countries have a principal or national club e.g. the Royal Norwegian Yacht Club, the Yacht Club Italia etc. These clubs are the bodies which control yachting in their countries, and only yachts owned by members of these clubs are privileged to wear the special ensign. In the U.S.A. all yachts may wear the special Yacht Ensign (Plate 40, 18); there is also another special U.S.A. ensign for the 'U.S. Power Squadron' (*see* page 88). This is flown by members of this squadron, sometimes in place of the National Ensign and sometimes in addition. It is reported that the custom of wearing the U.S. National Ensign in preference to the Yacht Ensign is growing.

The rules authorising British yachts to wear a privilege ensign are very strict and the Secretary of State for Defence is the Authority which grants the privilege (*see* page 28). There is an idea that the privilege of having a special ensign is connected with the title 'Royal', which many yacht clubs have, or that there is some difference between a yacht and a sailing club; this is not so. The prefix 'Royal' to the title is granted by the Sovereign, but in all matters concerning ensigns the Secretary of State for Defence is the sole arbiter. Briefly, the practice is that the yacht or sailing club is given a warrant permitting it to use a special or privilege ensign. This may be a plain Blue Ensign, or a Blue Ensign or Red Ensign defaced by a badge. This badge is almost invariably in the fly, but there are one or two cases where it is placed in the centre of the Union in the upper canton. The owner of a yacht, who is a member of a yacht or sailing club which holds a warrant, applies through his club to the Secretary of State for Defence for a warrant for his yacht to wear the privilege ensign; note that the warrant is granted to the yacht and not the owner. There are a number of other strict rules which it is impossible to go into in this book.

The history of our British National Flag and ensigns is a fascinating one. In the early years of the 19th century there were four British ensigns afloat, and not three, the fourth being a white one without a red cross; this one still remains with us as the flag of the Commissioners of Northern Lights, although this is defaced by a representation of a lighthouse, and uses the first Union Flag (pre-1801) in the upper canton (*see also* page 48). Even as late as February 19th 1835, an Admiralty Warrant was granted to the Royal Thames Yacht Club, authorising their vessels to carry a White Ensign without a red cross with the Union in the upper canton and bearing in the fly a crown over the letters R.T.Y.C. in red. This Ensign, without any lettering, may have been flown unofficially by members of the Yacht Club, now the Royal Yacht Squadron, when it was founded in 1815, but it was replaced in 1821 (the year after we hear of the Royal Yacht Club) by the Red

18

Ensign, which in its turn was replaced by the present White Ensign—known to many as the St. George's Ensign—granted by the Admiralty Warrant of 1829.

The Royal Yacht Club, which by King William's wish in 1833 became the Royal Yacht Squadron, is the only yacht club now flying the Ensign of the Royal Navy, but the 1829 warrant did not grant an exclusive use, for in 1832 a similar warrant was issued to the Royal Western of Ireland. In 1842, at the request of Lord Yarborough, the Admiralty decided that the privilege should be restricted to the Squadron—of which he was then the commodore —and sent out copies of a minute to that effect to the Royal Thames, the Royal Southern, the Royal Western of England, the Royal Eastern, the Holyhead, the Wharncliffe and the Gibraltar clubs, which were all under the White Ensign, with or without the cross; but owing to there being two Royal Westerns, one of England and one of Ireland, the minute was sent by mistake to one and not to both, so that the Irish Club went on with the white flag, and in 1853 actually obtained permission to continue with it. In 1858, however, the Royal St. George of Kingstown, and the Holyhead which had to haul down its White Ensign in 1842, applied for authority to enjoy the same privilege, thus bringing the matter officially before the Board, who promptly refused both applications, and at the same time ordered the Irish Royal Western to strike its white colours, so that for the future they should be distinctive of the Squadron which has always been under the special patronage of the Royal Family.

It is not known when yacht clubs first obtained official recognition. The first Yacht Club in the British Isles was the Cork Water Club which was formed in 1720. This was also the first club to have its own distinctive flags; these were the Union Jack with in the centre a golden harp on a green escutcheon, and a Red Ensign with this Union in the canton. It does not appear that it had any official permission to use these special flags, which were eventually 'inherited' by the Royal Cork Yacht Club. It appears, however, that by the year 1788 there was some form of Admiralty Warrant or licence, for in the *Public Advertiser* of June 7th of that year there is an advertisement announcing a meeting of the members of the

Cumberland Fleet (that is the Royal Thames in its early stage) at which 'the gentlemen who enter boats are to attend at the same time to draw lots for situation at starting, and are hereby informed that they are expected either to produce their licence from the Admiralty or other proofs of being owners of the vessels they intend to sail'.

It can therefore be seen that only those yachts whose owners are members of yacht clubs which hold Ministry of Defence Warrants are permitted to fly special ensigns, and all others whose owners belong to any club should wear the Red Ensign. It is interesting to note that the Island Sailing Club of Cowes, Isle of Wight, which has one of the largest memberships of any British club has no warrant and its members wear the Red Ensign.

In addition to the ensign nearly all yachts fly from their mainmast head a burgee. The burgee is the distinguishing flag of the yacht club to which the yacht belongs; it has been likened to the Commissioning Pennant flown by Her Majesty's ships. A burgee is a triangular flag, generally of dimensions three by two, and on it is the badge of the club. If the club has a warrant for a privileged ensign, the badge on the ensign is generally similar to the device on the burgee, but this is not always so; for instance, the badge on the Blue Ensign of the Royal Ocean Racing Club is a white 'Naval Crown', while the badge on the burgee is a white heraldic sea-horse, which is attractive and unusual.

Although many of the designs of the burgees are pleasant and many have some local association, they are not particularly outstanding. Many of the clubs, of both foreign and British countries, which have the appellation 'Royal', incorporate a crown in the badge on their ensign and on their burgees, and of these one with a very neat design is that of the Royal Yacht Squadron; the white burgee with a golden crown and three red stars of the Royal Danish Yacht Club is very pretty.

BURGEE OF ROYAL
DANISH YACHT CLUB

It is worth noting that there are still a few Yacht clubs in Eire that retain their old prefix 'Royal', and until quite recently they continued to use the British Blue Ensign. Now, with the exception of the Royal St. George, they all use the blue yacht ensign of Eire. This has a blue field with the club badge in the fly and in the canton the National Flag of Eire, the green, white and orange tricolour. Among the latter is the Royal Cork, mentioned on page 264, which has amalgamated with the Royal Munster Yacht Club.

A random selection of ensigns and burgees is given on Plate 40, but as in Great Britain alone there are some 1200 yacht and sailing clubs, to say nothing of those in foreign countries, it is impossible to illustrate all of them. Lloyd's Register of Shipping, however, publish a Flag Supplement to their Yacht Register, which illustrates a very large number of the yacht ensigns and burgees of all nations.

This supplement also carries an extensive selection of the private distinguishing flags of yachtsmen. Many yachtsmen fly these private flags from their yachts while they are on board, and they are loosely called House Flags.

When sailing yachts race in British waters they do so under the rules of the International Yacht Racing Union. These rules lay down no instruction, but the British National Authority, the Royal Yachting Association, prescribes that yachts when racing under British jurisdiction must carry a rectangular flag at the masthead. This 'racing' flag is generally of the same design as the private distinguishing flag mentioned above. Formerly, the racing flag was very important, as it was the only means of distinguishing one yacht from another, but practically every yacht which races nowadays has an insignia and number on her sail and the racing flag is a pleasing conceit; in fact, in the smaller classes, many yachts fly a simple rectangular flag of one colour without any device. It is sad that these racing colours are losing their importance, for with the large number of craft taking part—in the dinghy classes there are sometimes close on 200 starters, and even in the Fastnet Ocean Race of 1963 there were some 130 starters—it would be an impossible task for the race officers to recognise all of them by their racing flags alone.

Over the years a comprehensive flag etiquette for yachts has grown up. Briefly, this lays down recommendations as to what flags to fly and when and where they should be flown. The official booklet on this subject is *Flag Etiquette for Yachts*, published by Iliffe.

Finally, the Royal Yachting Association —the British National Body which watches over the interests of all British yachtsmen, racers, cruisers, power and sail—has its own flag, a white rectangular flag with a blue cross superimposed, and in the centre a badge consisting of a stylised Naval Crown.

FLAG OF ROYAL YACHT-
ING ASSOCIATION

BIBLIOGRAPHY

British Flags, W. G. Perrin.   Cambridge University Press.
An Atlas of the World, Andrew Boyd.   Methuen.
The Observer's Book of Flags, I. O. Evans.   Warne.
The Bayeux Tapestry, Norman Denny and Josephine Sankey. Collins.
Flags of the World (Chart).   The Flag Research Center, Lexington, Mass., U.S.A. and the Foundation of Vexillology and Heraldry, Holland.   De Geillustreerde, N.V., Amsterdam.
Flags, Funnels and Hull Colours, Colin Stewart.   Hart-Davis.
Lloyd's Register of Shipping—Flag Supplement to Yacht Register.
Flag Etiquette for Yachts, Captain E. M. C. Barraclough, O.B.E., R.N.   Iliffe.
Naval Flags of All the Nations in the World.   Bowles (published 1785).
Histoire Anecdotique du Drapeaux Français, Désiré Lacroix (published 1876).
La Chine Septentionale, Eduard Chavannes.   British Museum.
The Sovereign and the Navy, Admiral of the Fleet the Earl Mountbatten (privately).
Boutell's Heraldry, J. P. Brooke-Little, Richmond Herald of Arms. Warne.
Civic Heraldry, C. W. Scott-Giles, Fitzalan Pursuivant of Arms Extraordinary.   Dent.
Standards, Guidons and Colours of Commonwealth Forces, Major T. J. Edwards, M.B.E., F.R.Hist.S.   Gale & Polden.
Heraldry in War, Lieutenant-Colonel Howard C. Poole, O.B.E. Gale & Polden.
'Japanese Heraldry—A Study of Mon', Paul Martin Spiegel, LL.B. *Coat of Arms* No. 68.
Tableaux historique des drapeaux Français, C. Pasch (privately).

INDEX

19